Second Edition

Basketball

STEPS TO SUCCESS

Hal Wissel

Assistant Coach, Memphis Grizzlies
National Basketball Association

Human Kinetics

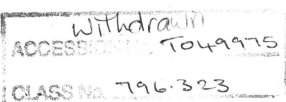

Library of Congress Cataloging-in-Publication Data

Wissel, Hal, 1939-
 Basketball : steps to success / Hal Wissel.-- 2nd ed.
  p. cm. -- (Steps to success sports series)
 ISBN 0-7360-5500-2 (softcover)
 1. Basketball--Training. 2. Basketball--Coaching. I. Title. II. Series.
 GV885.35.W55 2004
 796.323--dc22

                                                        2004009546

ISBN-10: 0-7360-5500-2
ISBN-13: 978-0-7360-5500-0

Developmental Editor: Cynthia McEntire
Assistant Editor: Scott Hawkins
Copyeditor: Barbara Field
Proofreader: Jim Burns
Graphic Designer: Nancy Rasmus
Graphic Artist: Tara Welsch
Cover Designer: Keith Blomberg
Photographer (cover): Andrew D. Bernstein/NBAE via Getty Images
Art Manager: Kareema McLendon
Illustrator: Roberto Sabas
Printer: United Graphics

Human Kinetics books are available at special discounts for bulk purchase. Special editions or book excerpts can also be created to specification. For details, contact the Special Sales Manager at Human Kinetics.

Printed in the United States of America   10 9 8 7 6 5 4 3 2

Human Kinetics
Web site: www.HumanKinetics.com

United States: Human Kinetics
P.O. Box 5076
Champaign, IL 61825-5076
800-747-4457
e-mail: humank@hkusa.com

Canada: Human Kinetics
475 Devonshire Road Unit 100
Windsor, ON N8Y 2L5
800-465-7301 (in Canada only)
e-mail: orders@hkcanada.com

Europe: Human Kinetics
107 Bradford Road
Stanningley
Leeds LS28 6AT, United Kingdom
+44 (0) 113 255 5665
e-mail: hk@hkeurope.com

Australia: Human Kinetics
57A Price Avenue
Lower Mitcham, South Australia 5062
08 8277 1555
e-mail: liaw@hkaustralia.com

New Zealand: Human Kinetics
Division of Sports Distributors NZ Ltd.
P.O. Box 300 226 Albany
North Shore City
Auckland
0064 9 448 1207
e-mail: info@humankinetics.co.nz

Dedicated to

David M. Wissel
1967 - 2000

David's gentle, caring nature touched all who came in contact with him.
David would smile, make you laugh, listen to you and say good things about you.

The David M. Wissel Youth Foundation has been founded to continue his love for
children and to provide disadvantaged youth with opportunities that will
foster their growth and development.

David M. Wissel Youth Foundation
955 Russell Avenue, Suffield CT 06078

www.highgoals.com

◧ Contents

◪ Climbing the Steps to Basketball Success

Basketball is a team game in which you can help your team by improving your individual skills. Basketball requires integration of individual talent into unselfish team play. It requires the sound execution of fundamental skills, which, once learned, can be connected to the entire game. Basketball drills instill confidence, transfer skills to game situations, and contribute to long-term enjoyment.

Despite the size, conditioning, and talent of today's professional players, basketball success is still determined by one's ability to execute fundamental skills consistently. Fundamental skills include footwork, shooting, passing and catching, dribbling, rebounding, moving with and without the ball, and defending.

Although this book is a resource for teachers, coaches, and parents, it is primarily for the player. Players who love the game continually seek ways to improve their skills. This book focuses on the development of fundamental skills and their integration into team play through individual, small-group, and team drills. Disciplined practice of the principles described in this book will improve your skills and build your confidence.

Many young players become frustrated when they cannot shoot or handle the ball. Confidence-building offensive skills should be emphasized early because they take more time to master than skills that do not involve the ball. More advanced players improve through game competition and individual practice. Strong competition helps the advanced player improve and also reveals weaknesses to be corrected. Average players practice what they do well; exceptional players practice their weaknesses, turning them into strengths. If you have trouble shooting, learn to shoot the correct way and then practice. If you have trouble dribbling with your weak hand, practice dribbling with that hand. You will not only improve your skills, but you will increase your confidence as well.

Success depends on getting players to believe in themselves. Although confidence is greatest after success, you can develop confidence through practice. It is common to think of self-confidence in relation to natural physical talent. It is a mistake, however, to consider physical talent alone. In your playing career, you will come up against players with more physical talent. To have the confidence to defeat them, you must believe that you have worked harder and are better prepared, particularly in fundamental skills.

Each of the 10 steps in this book takes you to the next level of playing skill. The first few steps provide a solid foundation of fundamental skills and concepts. As you practice each fundamental skill, your progress will allow you to connect skills. Practicing common combinations of basketball skills will give you the experience you need to make quick, intelligent decisions on the court. You will learn to make the right moves in game situations. As you near the top of the staircase, you will become more confident in your ability to play and communicate with teammates.

Follow the same sequence with each step:

1. Read the explanation of the step, why it is important, and how to perform it.
2. Follow the illustrations.
3. Review the missteps, which note common errors and corrections.
4. Perform the drills. Drills appear near the skill instructions so you can refer to the instructions easily if you have trouble with the drill.

Once you feel confident in your ability to perform the skill, have a qualified observer such as a coach, teacher, or a skilled player evaluate your technique. This subjective evaluation of your skill will help you identify any weaknesses in technique before you move on to the next step.

◨ Acknowledgments

As with any project of this magnitude, many people have contributed to its successful completion. I would like to thank Human Kinetics for the opportunity to share my basketball experiences with others. Particular thanks go to Dr. Judy Patterson Wright, the developmental editor of the first edition, and Cynthia McEntire, the developmental editor of the second edition, whose patience, suggestions, and good humor helped me persevere through the writing. Thanks to Roberto Sabas, who did the illustrations. Thanks also to the models in the photos used to create the illustrations for the first edition, Lafayette college student-athletes Keith Brazzo, Charles Dodge, Elliot Fontaine, Ross Gay, Stephanie Hayes, Jon Norton, Nuno Santo, Christine Sieling, and Leslie Yuen.

This book is based not only on my experiences as a coach, but also on my study of publications on playing and coaching basketball, attendance at numerous coaching clinics, and discussions about basketball with many coaches and players. I would like to express my sincere appreciation to Paul Ryan, my high school coach; Dr. Edward S. Steitz, my college mentor and advisor and the coach who gave me my first opportunity to coach at the college level; the inspiring coaches I have worked under, especially Hubie Brown, Mike Dunleavy, Frank Hamblen, Del Harris, Frank Layden, and Lee Rose, who gave me opportunities to work in the National Basketball Association; my loyal and dedicated assistant coaches Wes Aldrich, Ralph Arietta, P.J. Carlesimo, Tim Cohane, Seth Hicks, Kevin McGinniss, Scott Pospichal, Joe Servon, Sam Tolkoff, and Drew Tucker; Hank Slider, a master teacher who contributed greatly to my knowledge and understanding of shooting; and Stan Kellner, coach, author, and clinician, who stimulated my interest and research in sport psychology. Special thanks to the many dedicated players I have had the privilege of teaching and coaching and who continue to be a source of inspiration.

Last, thanks to my wife, Trudy, and our children, Steve, Scott, David, Paul, and Sharon, for listening to ideas, reading copy, questioning methods, serving as subjects for the photos for the illustrations, and especially for their love, understanding, and inspiration.

◨ The Sport of Basketball

Basketball was invented in December 1891 by Dr. James Naismith, a faculty member at the International YMCA Training School (now known as Springfield College) in Springfield, Massachusetts. Naismith invented basketball in response to an assignment given him by Dr. Luther Gulick, the director of the physical education department, who asked Naismith to devise a competitive game like football or lacrosse that could be played indoors during the cold winter months. Basketball immediately became popular and quickly spread nationally and internationally because of the travels of the YMCA Training School graduates.

Competition among colleges spread after the turn of the 20th century. The National Invitation Tournament (the first national collegiate tournament) was initiated in 1938, and the National Collegiate Athletic Association (NCAA) tournament was started in 1939. Professional leagues were formed as early as 1906. The National Basketball Association (NBA), the major professional basketball league, was formed in 1946. Basketball first became an Olympic sport in 1936.

Today basketball is the fastest-growing sport in the world for many reasons. First, basketball is a tremendously popular spectator sport, particularly on television. The televising of NBA games worldwide and of men's and women's college games nationally has influenced many young athletes to participate in the sport.

The nature of the sport keeps people involved. Although basketball was invented to be an indoor sport, it is now played indoors and outdoors in all seasons. Almost 40 percent of play is outside in an unorganized environment.

Basketball is for everyone. Although it is an extremely youthful sport, with teenage males participating the most, it is played by both sexes of all ages and sizes and also by the physically challenged, including people in wheelchairs. Although there are advantages to being tall, there are also many opportunities for a smaller, skilled player. Participation among older players and female players is growing. More girls play interscholastic high school basketball than any other sport, and women's support groups are building networks that will continue the expansion of female participation.

The international growth of basketball has created even more excitement and participation. The addition of NBA players into Olympic competition in 1992 had a tremendous impact on the popularity of basketball, a game that was already being played throughout the world. Currently, almost 200 countries have basketball federations.

Basketball competition is unique because, unlike other sports, it can be easily modified to accommodate smaller groups, different skill levels, and different kinds of players. Although most organized basketball competition consists of teams of five players, unorganized basketball competition can be played from full-court five-on-five down to smaller groups of half-court three-on-three, two-on-two, or one-on-one. Growth in organized three-on-three basketball tournaments has been particularly rapid. The NBA is leading the way by sponsoring NBA Hoop It Up tournaments in more than 60 countries. Individual competition in the form of free throw and other shooting contests sponsored by schools, clubs, and other organizations has also increased.

Finally, basketball can be played alone. All you need is a ball, a basket, a confined space (such as a driveway or playground), and your imagination to provide a competitive gamelike experience that other sports simply cannot match.

EQUIPMENT AND FACILITIES

Basketball shoes are necessary for traction on the court. Athletic shorts, tank tops or loose-fitting T-shirts, and white socks are recommended. You may wear soft pads to protect your knees and elbows and eyeglass protectors or goggles to protect your eyes. Wearing jewelry is prohibited.

Basketballs are spherical and an approved orange color. The circumference of the men's ball is a maximum of 30 inches and a minimum of 29 1/2 inches; the women's ball is a maximum of 29 inches and a minimum of 28 1/2 inches.

The backboard is a rectangle with a flat surface. It measures 6 feet horizontally and either 3 1/2 or 4 feet vertically. A rectangular box measuring 24 inches horizontally and 18 inches vertically is centered on the backboard behind the ring (rim), with the top edge of its baseline level with the ring.

The basket is 18 inches in inside diameter and is attached to the backboard with its upper edge 10 feet above the floor and its nearest edge 6 inches from the backboard.

The playing court is a rectangular surface 50 feet by 94 feet (usually 84 feet for high schools).

Markings designating specific areas of the court are shown in figure 1.

Court areas are referred to by specific names. The boundary lines at each side and each end of the court are called the sidelines and end lines or baselines, respectively. A team's frontcourt refers to the half of the court between its end line and the nearer edge of the division or midcourt line, including the basket. The backcourt includes the other half of the court where the opponent's basket is located.

There are three circles on the court: two free throw circles (one at each end) and a center circle. The free throw line, 15 feet from the backboard, bisects each free throw circle. Lines from the ends of the free throw line to the baseline are called lane lines. Along with the free throw line and the baseline, the lane lines mark an area called the free throw lane or key. Additional markings on each side of the lane lines are called the block and hash marks.

On college and high school courts, the three-point line is marked at 19 feet, 9 inches from the center of the basket. On NBA courts, the three-point line is at 23 feet, 9 inches.

PLAYING THE GAME

The game of basketball is played by two teams of five players on a court. The objective of each team is to score by putting the ball into its own basket and to prevent the other team from putting the ball into its basket. The ball can be advanced only by passing it with the hands or by dribbling it on the floor once or several times without touching it with both hands simultaneously. Fundamental

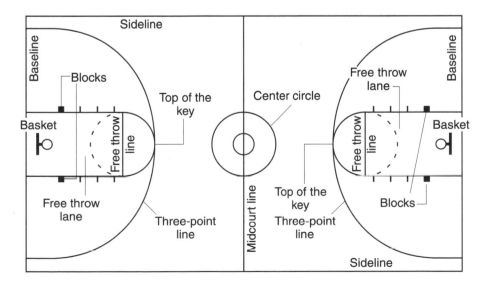

Figure 1 The basketball court.

skills include footwork, shooting, passing and catching, dribbling, rebounding, moving with and without the ball, and defending.

Although players are allowed to play in any position, the most common positions are point guard or number 1 (the best ball handler), shooting guard or number 2 (the best outside shooter), small forward or number 3 (a versatile inside and outside player), power forward or number 4 (a strong rebounder), and center or number 5 (inside scorer, rebounder, and shot blocker).

Currently, several sets of basketball rules are in use worldwide. International rules for competition between nations are established by the Federation Internationale de Basketball (FIBA). In the United States, professional players play under the National Basketball Association rules. College men and women play under separate sets of rules as established by the National Collegiate Athletic Association. High schools play by rules established by the National Federation of State High School Associations. In recent years, there has been a movement toward uniformity in rules. Differences remain, mostly in terms of length, distance, and time, rather than in substance and content. To foster children's enjoyment and development, modified rules have been devised calling for smaller basketballs, lower baskets, and scaled-down courts.

A goal from the field beyond the three-point line counts 3 points. Any other field goal counts 2 points, and a free throw counts 1 point.

Professional games consist of four quarters of 12 minutes each. College games consist of two halves of 20 minutes each. High school games consist of four quarters of 8 minutes each. Overtime periods are used for tie games. The length of youth games is adjusted according to the age of the players.

The game clock is stopped between quarters or halves, during time-outs, when the ball goes out of bounds, and when free throws are attempted. Shot clocks vary in length for professional, international, college men's, college women's, and high school competition.

Fouls

Fouls are called by officials for the purpose of not allowing a team to gain an advantage through rough play. Fouls carry penalties. In the college game, a player who commits five personal fouls is disqualified from the game. (In the NBA, players are allowed six personal fouls.)

A player who is fouled in the act of shooting is awarded free throws, two if the player was shooting inside the three-point line and three if the player was attempting a shot from beyond the three-point line. When a player is fouled in a situation other than when shooting, the fouled player's team receives the ball out of bounds. When a team commits more than a specified number of fouls in a quarter or half, the opposing team is allowed to shoot bonus free throws for nonshooting fouls. Here are some types of fouls that may be called:

- Holding, pushing, charging, tripping, or impeding an opponent's progress by extending a body part into a position other than a normal one or using any rough tactics
- Using your hands on an opponent in any way that inhibits the opponent's freedom of movement or acts as an aid in stopping or starting
- Fully or partially extending your arms, other than vertically, to hinder your opponent's freedom of movement
- Using an illegal screen by continuing to move when an opponent makes contact

Violations

Ball-handling and time violations give possession of the ball to the defense. Following are some common ball-handling violations:

- Out of bounds: causing the ball to go out of bounds
- Over and back: causing the ball to return to the backcourt after it has crossed into the frontcourt without the defense touching it
- Traveling: taking more than one step before the start of a dribble or taking two or more steps before releasing a pass or shot
- Double dribble: resuming dribbling after having stopped dribbling or dribbling with both hands simultaneously
- Charging: running into or pushing a stationary defender

Here are some common time violations:

- Five seconds to inbound: failure of a team to inbound a ball within five seconds after a made basket or after the official hands the ball to the inbounder
- Ten seconds in backcourt: taking 10 or

more seconds to get the ball across the midcourt line

- Three seconds in lane: being in the offensive free throw lane for three or more consecutive seconds without a member of your team shooting

WARMING UP AND COOLING DOWN

Preparing your body for basketball practice or a game involves two phases: a five-minute warm-up to increase heart rate, and basketball warm-up drills.

The first phase of preparing for strenuous basketball activity is to warm up with five minutes of offensive and defensive footwork. This will increase blood circulation and gradually prepare the body for the demands of basketball. Choose from warm-up activities such as trotting, changing pace and direction, short sprints, and defensive slides. Move from baseline to baseline on the court using a third of the width of the floor (lane line to lane line or lane line to sideline). Here are some offensive footwork warm-up drills to try:

- Trotting. Run easily from baseline to baseline and return. Do at least two round-trips.
- Sprinting. Run to half-court, change pace to a trot, and continue to the opposite baseline. Return in the same manner.
- Change of pace. Run from baseline to baseline with at least three quick changes of pace from sprint to trot to sprint. Return in the same manner.
- Change of direction. Run from baseline to baseline, changing direction as you go. Begin in an offensive stance with your left foot touching the intersection of the baseline and the lane line on your left. Run diagonally at a 45-degree angle to the lane line on your right. Make a sharp 90-degree change of direction from right to left and run diagonally to the imaginary lane line extended on your left. Make a sharp 90-degree change of direction from left to right. Continue in this manner to the opposite baseline. Return in the same manner.

- One-two stops. Run to the opposite baseline, making four one-two stops as you go. Alternate the foot you land on first on each one-two stop. Land on your left foot first on one stop, then land on your right foot first on the next. Return in the same manner.

Defensive footwork skills also make good warm-up drills. For each drill, start with your back to the far basket in a staggered defensive stance with one foot up, touching the baseline, and the other foot spread directly back. Here are some defense-inspired warm-up drills to try:

- Zigzag. Use defensive retreat steps to move back diagonally until your back foot touches the nearest sideline or lane line. Quickly drop step with your lead foot and use retreat steps to move back diagonally until your back foot touches the nearest imaginary lane line extended or sideline. Continue changing direction at each imaginary lane line extended or sideline as you proceed to the opposite baseline. Return in the same manner.
- Defensive attack and retreat. Use defensive attack and retreat steps until your back foot touches the half-court line. Quickly drop step, moving the other foot back, and move backward to the baseline using attack and retreat steps until your back foot touches the baseline. Vary your attack and retreat steps as you move down the floor. Return in the same manner.
- Reverse-run-and-turn. Move backward using defensive attack and retreat steps. Imagine that a dribbler beats your lead foot and you must recover by using a reverse-run-and-turn. Reverse to the side of your lead foot, keeping your eyes on the

imaginary dribbler, and run at least three steps before establishing a defensive position with your original lead foot up. From the baseline to the half-court line, make two reverse-run-and-turns starting with your left foot forward. From the half-court line to the opposite baseline, make two reverse-run-and-turns starting with your right foot forward. Return in the same manner.

The second phase of warming up includes basketball warm-up drills. The ball-handling warm-up described in step 2 (page 24) and the two-ball dribble drills described in step 3 (page 44) are excellent warm-up drills for the entire body. They also enhance ball-handling and dribbling skills and increase confidence. Step 4 describes several shooting warm-up drills. The hook shot warm-up and alternate hand hook shooting drills are excellent for loosening the shoulders while helping develop strong- and weak-hand hook shots. The shooting warm-up helps you warm up for shooting while enhancing shooting mechanics, rhythm, and confidence. The one-footed vertical jump training described in step 1 and the toss-back passing described in step 2 are also excellent basketball warm-up drills that improve skill and confidence.

At the end of basketball practice, take about five minutes to cool down. This is an excellent time to stretch because muscles are warm. Choose at least one stretch for each body part.

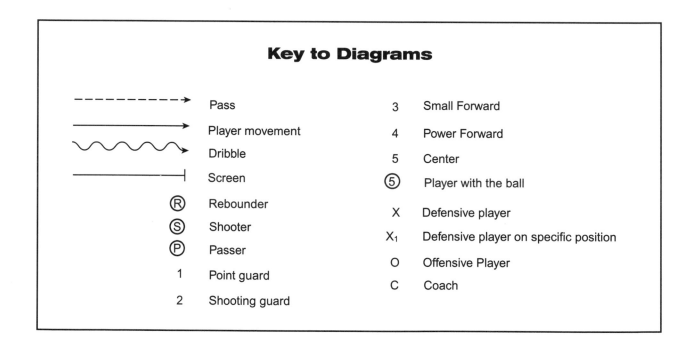

Key to Diagrams

- - - →	Pass	3	Small Forward
——→	Player movement	4	Power Forward
∿∿∿→	Dribble	5	Center
———⊣	Screen	⑤	Player with the ball
Ⓡ	Rebounder	X	Defensive player
Ⓢ	Shooter	X₁	Defensive player on specific position
Ⓟ	Passer	O	Offensive Player
1	Point guard	C	Coach
2	Shooting guard		

Balance and Quickness

Although basketball is a team game, individual execution of fundamental skills is essential for players to play well as a team. Shooting, passing, dribbling, rebounding, defending, and moving both with and without the ball are the fundamental skills to master.

The prerequisites for soundly executing each of these skills are *balance* and *quickness*. Height is commonly associated with basketball success, but balance and quickness are the most important physical attributes a player can have. And although you can't increase your height, you can improve balance and quickness through practice.

Balance means that your body is under control and in a state of readiness to make quick movements. Quickness is an asset only if you can still execute properly. Rushing or hurrying is different from being quick. If you rush, using excessive haste or performing too rapidly, you're apt to make mistakes. Rushing reflects a lack of emotional as well as physical balance or control.

Quickness refers to speed of movement when performing a skill, not just running speed. Quickness is specific to the fundamental being performed, such as quick movement of your feet on defense, quickly going for a rebound, or a quick release of a shot.

Quickness and balance are closely related to footwork, which is basic to all fundamental basketball skills. Being ready to start, stop, and move in any direction with quickness and balance requires good footwork. Developing good footwork lays the foundation; employing effective footwork lets you keep your body under control so that you can move with timing, deception, and quickness.

Good footwork is important to both offense and defense. An offensive player has the advantage over the defender of knowing what move will be made and when. Offensive footwork is used to fake the defender, get the defender off balance, move off screens, cut to the basket, prevent charging into a defender, and elude a blockout when going for an offensive rebound.

Developing good footwork is especially important when playing defense. You can try to anticipate moves, but you can never be certain what your opponent will do. Much defensive success depends on the ability to react instantly in any direction to the moves of the opponent, which requires executing defensive footwork with balance and quickness. Good footwork can force your opponent to react to you, enable you to disrupt the offensive poise of your opponent, force low-percentage shots, and force turnovers.

You may question just how much you can increase your natural quickness. Quickness is largely determined by genetics. But by thoroughly understanding the basic mechanics of footwork, you can definitely improve your quickness if you work at it.

Footwork is the foundation for executing each of the fundamental skills of basketball with balance and quickness. Have a trained observer—your coach, teacher, or a skilled player—watch your offensive and defensive footwork. The observer can use the checkpoints in figures 1.1 through 1.10 to evaluate your performance and provide constructive feedback.

Some observers have said that Michael Jordan was born with great natural ability and that young players cannot hope to develop his quickness and jumping ability. This type of thinking fails to consider that, although Jordan was naturally gifted, he also worked very hard to improve every facet of his game. Other naturally gifted NBA players capable of equally amazing feats simply lack Jordan's work ethic. Jordan derived sheer joy from playing and was so obsessed with winning that he constantly pushed himself to work harder in practice than anyone else. Jordan was not only regarded as the greatest player of all time, he was also regarded as the greatest practice player of all time. He can be a model for all of us trying to bring out the best in ourselves.

BALANCED STANCE

A well-balanced offensive stance enables you to move quickly, change direction, stop under control, and jump. In your offensive stance, your head is over your waist and your back is straight. Your hands are above your waist with your elbows flexed, and your arms are kept close to your body. Your feet are at least shoulder-width apart, and the weight is evenly distributed on the balls of your feet. Your knees are flexed so that you are ready to move (figure 1.1a).

On defense, you must be able to move quickly in any direction and change direction while maintaining balance. The prerequisite is a well-balanced stance. The defensive stance resembles the offensive stance: head over your waist, back straight, chest out, but your feet are more than shoulder-width apart and staggered, with one foot in front of the other (figure 1.1b). Having your head over your waist keeps the center of gravity over its base. Distribute weight evenly on the balls of your feet, and flex your knees so your body is low, ready to react in any direction.

In the basic defensive stance, in which the feet are staggered one in front of the other, the front foot is called the lead foot. This stance makes it easy to move back in the direction of the back foot. Moving back requires only a short step with the back foot as you start to move. Moving back in the direction of the lead foot is much more difficult, requiring a vigorous drop step (reverse) with the lead foot while pivoting on the back foot as you start to move.

Protect your lead foot as you establish your basic defensive stance. Position your lead foot outside your opponent's body and place your back foot in line with the middle of your opponent's body. This position protects the weakness of your lead foot and also gives the impression of an opening toward your back foot, strengthening your defensive stance.

There are three basic defensive hand positions. In the first, one hand is kept forward on the lead foot side to pressure the shooter while the other hand is at the opposite side to protect against passes. In the second basic hand position, both hands are at waist level, palms up, to pressure the dribbler. This position allows you to flick at the ball with the hand that is closer to the direction in which your opponent is dribbling.

In the third basic hand position, both hands are kept above the shoulders (figure 1.1b). This higher position forces lob or bounce passes that are more easily intercepted, readies the hands to block shots, prepares you to rebound with two hands, and helps prevent reaching fouls. When both hands are above the shoulders, take care that they do not spread away from your body, causing you to lose balance. Flex your elbows to keep your arms from reaching out.

When guarding an opponent who has the ball, your eyes should be directed at your opponent's midsection. If the offensive player you are defending does not have the ball, one hand should point toward the offensive player and the other should point toward the ball.

Errors in offensive and defensive stances vary with the individual. Tall players often have greater balance problems than shorter players. Typically, a tall player does not spread or flex the knees enough to keep the center of gravity low. To maintain balance in an offensive stance, spread your feet shoulder-width apart and flex your knees so you are balanced and ready to move in any direction. If you find that you do not protect your lead foot when in the defensive stance, correct this error by positioning your lead foot outside your opponent's body and aligning your back foot with the middle of your opponent's body. If you find you are susceptible to your opponent's head and ball fakes, be sure to keep your eyes focused on your opponent's midsection, not on your opponent's head or the ball.

Figure 1.1   Well-Balanced Stances

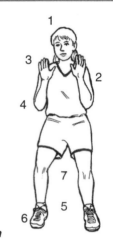

a

b

OFFENSIVE STANCE

1. Head over waist, able to see rim and ball
2. Back straight
3. Hands above waist
4. Elbows flexed, arms close to body
5. Feet staggered, shoulder-width apart
6. Weight even on balls of feet, ready to move
7. Knees flexed

DEFENSIVE STANCE

1. Head over waist
2. Back straight
3. Hands above shoulders
4. Elbows flexed
5. Wide base, weight even on balls of feet
6. Feet staggered, shoulder-width apart or wider
7. Knees flexed

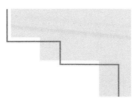

Misstep: Offensive Stance

Your balance is off in a forward direction.

Correction

Flex your knees to get low, rather than bending at the waist, so you are ready to move backward as quickly as you can move forward.

Misstep: Defensive Stance

You reach away from your body with your arm, becoming off balance in the direction of the reach.

Correction

Keep your head over your waist, your hands above waist level, and your elbows flexed, with your arms close to your body.

Footwork Drill 1. *Stance*

First assume the offensive stance, then shift your weight too far back on your heels. Next, lean too far forward, bending at the waist with your weight forward on your toes. Now correct the stance, positioning your head over your waist, moving your hands up and close to your body, distributing weight evenly on the balls of your feet, flexing your knees, and spreading your feet at least shoulder-width apart.

To Increase Difficulty

- Have a partner try to upset your balance backward by gently pushing on your shoulders.
- Have a partner try to upset your balance forward by pulling you by one of your hands.

Success Check

- Keep your head over your waist to maintain your center of gravity.
- Keep your arms close to your body.
- Stand with knees flexed, feet at least shoulder-width apart, weight on balls of feet.

Score Your Success

Give yourself 1 point for each element of the balanced stance you are able to execute, for a total of 5 points:

Head over waist ___

Hands up and close to body ___

Weight evenly distributed ___

Knees flexed ___

Feet at least shoulder-width apart ___

Your score ___

If you increase the difficulty, give yourself 1 point each time you are able to resist your partner's attempt to upset your balance. Attempt to complete three consecutive cycles of the offensive stance without your partner pushing or pulling you off balance.

Your score ___

Footwork Drill 2. *Footfire*

Have a partner give commands. On the "Stance!" command, quickly assume an offensive stance. On the "Go!" command, move your feet up and down as quickly as you can, maintaining correct stance form for 10 seconds or until you hear the command "Stop!" Do three repetitions for 10 seconds each with 10-second rest intervals.

Success Check

- Maintain correct offensive stance form.
- Move your feet quickly.
- Aim for hitting the floor with your feet 40 to 50 times in each 10-second period.

Score Your Success

Give yourself 5 points each time you are able to hit the floor 40 to 50 times in each 10-second period, 3 points each time you hit the floor 30 to 39 times in each 10-second period, and 1 point each time you hit the floor 20 to 29 times in each 10-second period. Hitting the floor fewer than 20 times doesn't earn any points.

Times feet hit the floor, first 10-second period ___; points earned ___

Times feet hit the floor, second 10-second period ___; points earned ___

Times feet hit the floor, third 10-second period ___; points earned ___

Your score ___ (number of points earned; maximum of 15)

Footwork Drill 3. *Jump Rope*

Start in a balanced stance with your knees flexed and your weight on the balls of your feet. Hold the rope handles with your hands out to your sides at waist level and your elbows close to your body. Place the rope behind your feet and swing it over your head from back to front. Jump over the rope. Add variety by skipping, jumping on one foot, crossing your arms, and jumping backward.

The best way to start a jump rope program is to jump rope for 30 seconds followed by a 30-second rest interval. Limit this program to five minutes, or a total of five sets. As you progress, you can jump for 60 seconds with a 30-second rest interval between sets. Once you have progressed to a 60-second set, see the "Score Your Success" section to determine your mastery.

To Increase Difficulty

- Perform a 60-second set of jumping rope followed by a 30-second rest interval.

To Decrease Difficulty

- Perform a 30-second set of jumping rope followed by a 30- to 90-second rest interval.

Success Check

- Maintain a proper balanced stance.
- Keep your elbows close to your body as you swing the rope.

Score Your Success

Count your maximum number of jumps in 60 seconds.

Fewer than 20 jumps in 60 seconds = 0 points

20 to 29 jumps in 60 seconds = 2 points

30 to 39 jumps in 60 seconds = 4 points

40 to 49 jumps in 60 seconds = 6 points

50 to 59 jumps in 60 seconds = 8 points

60 jumps or more in 60 seconds = 10 points

Your score ___

OFFENSIVE FOOTWORK

Moving with and without the ball is important to individual and team offense. As an offensive player, you have an advantage over your defender in knowing what move you will make and when you will make it. Moving quickly with balance is the key. Once you develop the skills, footwork and fakes should allow you to keep your balance as you attempt to elude the defender, who will have difficulty reacting instantly to your moves. Moving continually with and without the ball also demands superior physical conditioning. Successful players master the necessary skills and develop their physical conditioning to excel in this important part of the game.

You need to master eight basic offensive movements: change of pace, change of direction, the one-two stop and the jump stop, the front turn and reverse turn, and the two-footed and one-footed jumps.

Change of Pace

Change of pace is a way to alter your running speed to deceive and elude the defender. Change from a fast running speed to a slower pace and then quickly back to fast without changing your basic running form.

As you run, keep your head up so you can see the rim of the basket and the ball. Take your first step with your back foot, crossing it in front of your lead foot. Run on the balls of your feet, pointing your toes in the direction you are going. Lean your upper body slightly forward and pump your arms forward in opposition to your legs, keeping your elbows flexed. Completely extend your support leg. Get your knee up and your thigh parallel to the floor as you bring it forward.

The effectiveness of your change of pace comes from deception and quickness in changing speed. To slow your speed, shorten your stride and decrease its speed. Use less force to push off your back foot. Do not completely extend your back knee. For better deception, avoid leaning your head and shoulders back as you slow your pace. If you have trouble being deceptive when changing pace from fast to slow, try to keep your upper body from leaning forward.

To increase your speed, lengthen your stride to its maximum and increase its speed. To accelerate quickly to a faster speed, push off your back foot forcefully. You have the advantage in changing your pace because *you* decide when to change speeds. With good deception and a forceful push off your back foot, you should be at least a step quicker than your defender immediately after the change to a faster speed.

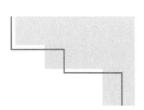

Misstep

You do not make a quick change from slow to fast.

Correction

Push forcefully off your back foot to accelerate quickly.

Change of Direction

Change of direction underlies almost every basketball fundamental, but it is particularly important for getting open to receive a pass. An effective change of direction depends on sharply cutting from one direction to another. To execute a change of direction, step first with one foot and then with the other without crossing your feet. Begin with a three-quarter step rather than a full step. On your first step, flex your knee as you plant your foot firmly to stop your momentum. Turn on the ball of your foot and push off in the direction you want to go. Shift your weight and take a long step with your other foot, pointing your toes in the new direction. After the change of direction, get your lead hand up as a target to receive a pass.

Although changing direction seems like a simple move, it takes concentrated practice to execute sharply and effectively. If you find you have trouble disguising your change of direction and you slow your speed with short steps on your approach, use normal running form and concentrate on a two-count move: when changing from right to left, concentrate on a two-count right-left; when going from left to right, concentrate on a two-count left-right (figure 1.2).

Figure 1.2 | Change of Direction

a

b

FIRST STEP

1. Three-quarter first step
2. Knee flexed

SECOND STEP

1. Turn on ball of foot and push off in new direction
2. Shift weight
3. Take long second step
4. Point toes in new direction
5. Keep lead hand up as target

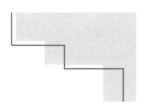

Misstep

You circle your turn rather than making a sharp cut.

Correction

Use a three-quarter first step and flex your knee so you can pivot sharply and push off in the direction you want to go. Then shift your weight and take a long second step.

Stopping

Starting quickly is important, but so is stopping quickly. Inexperienced players often lose balance when trying to stop quickly. Learning two basic stops—the one-two stop and the jump stop—will help you stop under control.

In the one-two stop, the back foot lands first, followed by the other foot. If you execute the one-two stop as you receive a pass or on your last dribble, the foot that lands first becomes the pivot foot. The one-two stop is useful when you are running too fast to use the jump stop, when on the perimeter away from the basket, and especially when on the fast break.

Use normal running form. To execute the one-two stop (figure 1.3), first hop before the stop. This allows gravity to help slow your movement. Then lean in the opposite direction. Land on your back foot first, then on your lead foot. Land with a wide base. The wider your base, the more balance you will have. Flex your back knee to lower your body to a "sitting" position on the heel of your back foot. The lower you get, the better your balance. Keep your head up.

7

Figure 1.3   One–Two Stop

HOP AND LEAN BACK

1. Hop before stop
2. Lean in opposite direction

LAND WITH ONE–TWO STEP

1. Land on back foot first
2. Land on lead foot second
3. Land on wide base
4. "Sit" on back heel
5. Keep head up

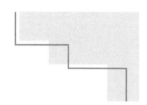

Misstep

You lose balance, going forward, causing you to drag your pivot foot.

Correction

Hop before you stop, allowing gravity to slow your forward momentum. Lean back, landing first on your back foot, then on your front foot. Keep a wide base. "Sit" on the heel of your back foot. Keep your head up.

In the jump stop, both feet land simultaneously. As you catch the ball and land with a jump stop, you can use either foot as a pivot foot. The jump stop is particularly advantageous when you are moving under control without the ball, especially when you receive a pass with your back to the basket in the low-post area (within eight feet of the basket).

When executing the jump stop (figure 1.4), hop before the stop to allow gravity to help slow your movement, similar to the one-two stop. Lean back, then stop with both feet landing simultaneously, shoulder-width apart, knees flexed. Shift your weight onto the backs of your feet to keep your body from moving forward.

Figure 1.4   Jump Stop

HOP

1. Hop before stop
2. Keep shoulders back

LAND ON BOTH FEET

1. Land on both feet with feet shoulder-width apart
2. Flex knees
3. Shift weight to back of feet
4. Keep head up

Misstep

One foot lands before the other.

Correction

Hop before you stop, lean back, and keep your feet shoulder-width apart and your knees flexed.

Offensive Footwork Drill 1. *Jump Stops*

Pretend you are a low-post player with your back to the basket. Start in a balanced offensive stance at the dotted line in the three-second lane, facing the foul line. Your feet are parallel and your hands are above your waist. Use short side steps toward the offensive right box and make a balanced jump stop outside the lane and above the box. Again using short side steps, return to the dotted line and make a jump stop there. Now move to the offensive left box and make a jump stop outside the lane and above the box. Continue making jump stops, going from box to dotted line to box.

Success Check

- Be sure to land on both feet simultaneously, coming to a complete, balanced stop.

- Maintain your balance.
- Try to execute 10 successful jump stops.

Score Your Success

6 or fewer consecutive successful jump stops = 1 point

7 consecutive successful jump stops = 2 points

8 consecutive successful jump stops = 3 points

9 consecutive successful jump stops = 4 points

10 consecutive successful jump stops = 5 points

Your score _____

Pivoting and Turning

When you possess the ball, the rules allow you to take as many steps as you need in any direction with one foot while pivoting (turning) on your other foot. The foot you pivot with, or turn on, is called the pivot foot. Once you establish your pivot foot, you cannot lift it before you release the ball from your hand to dribble. When attempting a pass or shot, you may lift your pivot foot as long as you release the ball before your pivot foot hits the floor again. Once you have established your pivot foot, you cannot change to pivot on your other foot.

Pivoting is often an essential part of another basketball skill. To pivot well, you need a balanced stance: head over waist, back straight, and knees flexed. Keep your weight on the ball of the pivot foot and do not pivot on your heel.

The two basic pivots are pivoting forward and pivoting backward. These are called the front turn, or forward pivot, and the reverse turn, or drop step. Both are important to learn. Both pivots are used to move into an advantageous position against an opponent.

For the forward pivot or front turn, your chest leads the way. Maintaining a balanced stance, keep your weight on the ball of your pivot foot and step forward with the nonpivot foot (figure 1.5a).

In the drop step or reverse turn, your back leads the way. Maintaining a balanced stance, keep your weight on the ball of your pivot foot and drop your nonpivot foot back (figure 1.5b).

Figure 1.5   Pivots and Turns

FRONT TURN

1. Balanced stance
2. Weight on ball of pivot foot
3. Chest leads
4. Pivot on ball of foot
5. Step forward with other foot

REVERSE TURN (DROP STEP)

1. Balanced stance
2. Weight on ball of pivot foot
3. Back leads
4. Pivot on ball of foot
5. Drop other foot back

Misstep

You lose balance and lift or drag your pivot foot.

Correction

Keep your weight on the ball of your pivot foot as you move your nonpivot foot and maintain a balanced stance.

Offensive Footwork Drill 2. *Half-Court and Full-Court*

These drills allow you to practice offensive footwork such as sprinting, changing pace, changing direction, and making one-two stops. You will use a third of the floor width from lane line to sideline as you run between baselines.

For the half-court sprint, start in an offensive stance with your feet touching the baseline. Sprint to half-court, change pace to a trot, and continue to the opposite baseline. Return in the same manner.

For the full-court change of pace, start in an offensive stance with your feet behind the baseline. Run to the opposite baseline, changing pace at least three times from sprint to trot to sprint. Return in the same manner.

For the full-court change of direction, start in an offensive stance with your left foot touching the intersection of the baseline and lane line on your left. Run diagonally at a 45-degree angle to the sideline on your right. Make a sharp 90-degree change of direction from right to left and run diagonally to the imaginary lane line extended on your left. Change direction, making a sharp 90-degree turn from left to right. Continue to change direction at each sideline and imaginary lane line as you proceed to the opposite baseline. Return in the same manner.

For the full-court one-two stops, start in an offensive stance with your feet behind the baseline. Run to the opposite baseline, making four one-two stops. Alternate the landing foot on each one-two stop. Land first on your left foot, then land first on your right foot for the next stop. Return in the same manner.

Success Check

- Try to complete two round-trips successfully for each drill.
- Use proper form and technique.
- Move quickly, using short, quick steps.

Score Your Success

Give yourself 5 points for completing two round-trips for each drill.

Number of round-trips for the half-court sprint ___; points earned ___

Number of round-trips for the full-court change of pace ___; points earned ___

Number of round-trips for the full-court change of direction ___; points earned ___

Number of round-trips for the full-court one-two stops ___; points earned ___

Your score ___ (out of 20)

Jumping

Everyone recognizes the importance of jumping in basketball, including the role jumping plays in rebounding, blocking shots, and shooting. Jumping is more than gaining height. How quickly and how often you jump are more important than jumping height. Timing, balance in the air, and landing are also important components of jumping.

There are two basic jumps: the two-footed jump and the one-footed jump. Use the two-footed jump when you are not on the move, when it is important to land in balance (such as in shooting a jump shot), and for jumping in succession, such as in rebounding. Start in a balanced stance—head over waist, back straight, elbows flexed, arms close to your body, and weight on the balls of your feet. Before jumping, flex your knees 60 to 90 degrees, depending on leg strength. If you can, take a short step before your takeoff. At takeoff, push quickly and forcefully off both feet, extending your ankles, knees, and hips.

The key to attaining maximum height is an explosive takeoff. The quicker and more forcefully you push against the floor, the higher you will jump. Lift both arms straight up as you jump. To increase the reach you have with one hand, at the top of your jump, extend your nonreaching arm downward. A smooth, fluid action without tension results in a higher jump. Land in the same spot on the balls of your feet with your knees flexed to jump again or move (figure 1.6).

Figure 1.6 Two-Foot Jump

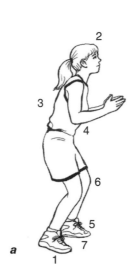

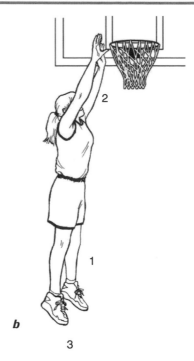

STATIONARY START

1. Short step before takeoff
2. Head over waist
3. Back straight
4. Elbows flexed, arms close to body
5. Weight on balls of feet
6. Knees flexed 60 to 90 degrees
7. Quick and forceful push off both feet

TWO-FOOT JUMP

1. Extend ankles, knees, and hips
2. Lift both arms straight up
3. Land in same spot

Misstep

You do not get an explosive takeoff, limiting the height of your jump.

Correction

Flex your knees 60 to 90 degrees, depending on leg strength. The stronger your legs, the more you can flex your knees. Through trial and error, determine the correct angle for your strength that allows you to produce a quick, forceful push against the floor.

The one-footed jump is for jumping on the move: shooting a layup off a drive, moving to block a shot, or moving for an offensive rebound. When moving, it is quicker to jump off one foot than off two feet. To jump off two feet, you have to take time to stop and prepare for the jump. One disadvantage of the one-footed jump is that it is difficult to control your body in the air and may result in a foul or even a collision with other players. It also is more difficult to land in balance after a moving one-footed jump and harder to change direction or make a quick second jump.

Start the one-footed jump (figure 1.7) from a run. To jump high, you must gain speed on the last three or four steps of the approach but also be able to control that speed. The last step before the jump should be short so you can quickly dip your takeoff knee. This will change forward momentum to upward momentum.

Your takeoff knee should flex from 60 to 90 degrees, depending on leg strength. The takeoff angle should be as vertical as possible. From a balanced stance, push quickly and forcefully off your takeoff foot, extending your ankle, knee, and hip. Remember how vital takeoff explosiveness is: The quicker and more forcefully you push against the floor, the higher you will jump. Lift your opposite knee and your arms straight up as you jump. As with the two-footed jump, to increase your reach, extend your nonreaching arm downward at the top of the jump. Use a smooth, fluid action without tension, and land in balance on the balls of your feet with your knees flexed.

Figure 1.7 One-Foot Jump

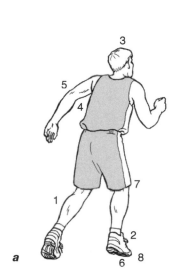

RUNNING START

1. Running approach, increasing speed last few steps
2. Short step before takeoff
3. Head over waist
4. Back straight
5. Elbows flexed, arms close to body
6. Weight on ball of takeoff foot
7. Takeoff knee flexed 60 to 90 degrees
8. Quick and forceful push off takeoff foot

ONE-FOOT JUMP

1. Lift non-takeoff knee; extend ankle, knee, and hip of takeoff foot
2. Reach high, extending nonreaching arm downward
3. Land in same spot

Misstep

You long jump rather than high jump.

Correction

Shorten your last step before takeoff so you can quickly dip your takeoff knee and change forward momentum to upward momentum. On takeoff, lift your opposite knee straight up as you lift your arms. The combination of a forceful upward lift of your knee and arms increases upward momentum.

Offensive Footwork Drill 3. *Two-Foot Vertical Jump Test*

Chalk your fingertips, face a smooth wall, and make a mark at the height of your two-handed standing reach. Stand with your shoulders to the wall. You are allowed one step before you jump. Perform a stationary two-foot jump as high as you can, touching the wall at the top of your jump with the fingertips of your near hand. Measure the distance between the two chalk marks using a yardstick and record to the nearest half inch. Do three vertical jumps, pausing for 10 seconds between each attempt.

Success Check

- Use proper form for a two-footed jump.
- Reach as high as you can.

Score Your Success

Note your inches for each trial. More than 17 inches is excellent and earns 5 points; 15 to 16 inches earns 3 points; 13 to 14 inches earns 1 point; fewer than 13 inches earns 0 points. Use your best score as your final score.

Trial 1 ___ inches; points earned ___

Trial 2 ___ inches; points earned ___

Trial 3 ___ inches; points earned ___

Your score ___ (5 points maximum)

Offensive Footwork Drill 4. *One-Foot Vertical Jump Training*

This short drill consists of a set of 3 preliminary jumps and 5 to 10 all-out running, one-footed vertical jumps. Have a partner measure the height of your jumps at a net or backboard. The preliminary one-footed vertical jumps should be progressive in effort. On the approach, use however many steps will allow for your best jumps.

For your first jump, try to touch the net or backboard about 12 inches below your best jumping height. On your second jump, touch about 6 inches above your first jump. On your third attempt, jump as high as possible. Pause 10 seconds before each jump to mentally plan for it. After the third jump, stand under the net or backboard and reach with two hands. Have your partner use a yardstick to determine the difference between your two-handed standing reach and the mark at your highest running one-footed vertical jump, recording it to the nearest half inch.

To Increase Difficulty

- Do five more jumps, trying to improve on each succeeding jump.

- If you still are improving with the fifth jump, continue until you do not touch any higher on two successive attempts.

Success Check

- Use proper technique.
- Reach as high as you can.

Score Your Success

Since this is a progressive-improvement drill, the scoring is a little different. Record your inches for each trial in the spaces provided. You want to improve with each trial, and if you do so, give yourself 5 points.

Trial 1 ___ inches

Trial 2 ___ inches

Trial 3 ___ inches

Your score ___ total inches; points earned ___

DEFENSIVE FOOTWORK

Moving your feet on defense is hard work. Success depends on desire, discipline, concentration, anticipation, and superior physical conditioning. Moving quickly with balance is the key to reacting to your opponent's moves and changing direction instantly.

To move on defense, use short, quick steps with your weight evenly distributed on the balls of your feet. Push off the foot farther from where you are going and step with the closer foot. Do not cross your feet. Make an exception only when your opponent moves near your lead foot. If that happens, execute a drop step to recover your defensive position. Your feet should not move closer than shoulder-width apart. Keep them as close to the floor as possible.

Flex your knees and keep your body low, your upper body erect, and your chest out. Keep your head steady. Avoid up-and-down body movements. Hopping or jumping movements are slow and put you in the air; you should be on the floor reacting to an opponent. Pressure the ball with quick flicks of whichever hand is closer to the direction your opponent is going, but do not reach or lean. Keeping your head over your waist, your arms close to your body, and your elbows flexed will help you maintain balance.

You should master these basic defensive steps or movements: the side step or slide, the attack step and retreat step, and the reverse or drop step. Each step starts from a defensive stance.

Side Step or Slide

Maintain a balanced, defensive stance between your opponent and the basket. If your opponent moves to the side, execute a side step or slide (figure 1.8). Quickly move your feet from a staggered stance to a parallel stance. Both feet should be aligned with the direction you are going. Use short, quick steps with your weight evenly distributed on the balls of your feet. Push off the far foot and step with the foot closer to where you are going. Never cross your feet. Concentrate on keeping your balance to make quick changes of direction.

Figure 1.8   **Side Step or Slide**

EXECUTION

1. Push off far foot, using short, quick steps
2. Step with foot closest to where you are going
3. Lead foot continues outside opponent's body
4. Align back foot with middle of opponent's body
5. Keep feet no closer than shoulder-width apart; never cross feet
6. Keep feet close to floor
7. Keep knees flexed; no hopping or up-and-down movements
8. Keep head steady and over waist
9. Keep back straight; no leaning
10. Keep hands up
11. Keep elbows flexed, arms close to body
12. Pressure ball with quick flicking motion; do not reach

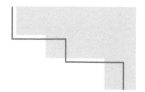

Misstep

You reach or lean, losing your balance.

Correction

Keep your head over your waist, hands up, elbows flexed, and arms close to your body.

Defensive Footwork Drill 1. Lane Defensive Slide

Start in the lane, facing the foul line, with your right foot on the lane line to your right. Use a balanced defensive stance with your feet parallel and hands up. Using short, quick defensive side steps, move quickly to the lane on your left, change direction, and move back to the lane on your right. Continue as quickly as you can between the left and right lane lines.

Success Check

• Maintain correct form for a balanced defensive stance.

• Step to the side using short, quick steps.
• Keep hands up.
• Try to touch 15 lines in 30 seconds.

Score Your Success

8 lines in 30 seconds = 1 point

9 to 10 lines in 30 seconds = 2 points

11 to 12 lines in 30 seconds = 3 points

13 to 14 lines in 30 seconds = 4 points

15 or more lines in 30 seconds = 5 points

Your score ___

Attack and Retreat

Attacking, or moving up on your opponent, is often referred to as *closing out*. This is not an easy skill. It requires good judgment and balance. You cannot close on your opponent so fast that you lose your balance and are unable to change direction backward. Use short, quick attack steps, without crossing your feet, and protect your lead foot by positioning it slightly outside your opponent's body (figure 1.9a).

If your opponent makes a move toward the basket on the side of your back foot, you should retreat, or move back, without losing balance. You cannot retreat so fast that you lose your balance and are unable to react quickly to get closer

to your opponent. As with attacking, use short, quick retreat steps and do not cross your feet (figure 1.9b).

Attacks and retreats basically require the same footwork but in different directions. They both use short, quick steps, with one foot up and the other back. Keep your weight evenly distributed on the balls of your feet. Push off your back foot and step with your lead foot to attack; push off your front foot and step with your back foot to retreat. In attacking, never cross your back foot in front of your lead foot, and in retreating, never cross your front foot in front of your back foot. For both your attack and retreat, strive for good defensive footwork.

Figure 1.9   Attack and Retreat

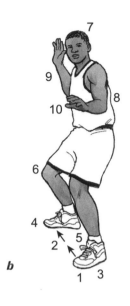

ATTACK

1. Push off back foot
2. Use short, quick steps, keeping feet close to floor
3. Lead foot continues outside opponent's body
4. Keep back foot aligned with middle of opponent's body
5. Keep feet no closer than shoulder width; never cross feet
6. Keep knees flexed; no hopping or up-and-down movements
7. Keep head steady and over waist
8. Keep back straight; no leaning
9. Keep hands up, elbows flexed, arms close to body
10. Pressure ball with quick flicking motion; do not reach

RETREAT

1. Push off front foot
2. Use short, quick steps, keeping feet close to floor
3. Lead foot continues outside opponent's body
4. Align back foot with middle of opponent's body
5. Keep feet no closer than shoulder-width apart; never cross feet
6. Keep knees flexed; no hopping or up-and-down movements
7. Keep head steady and over waist
8. Keep back straight; no leaning
9. Keep hands up, elbows flexed, arms close to body
10. Pressure ball with quick flicking motion; do not reach

Misstep: Attacking

You hop forward with both feet parallel, preventing a quick change of direction backward.

Correction

Keep your head steady, knees flexed, and use short, quick steps. Maintain a staggered stance. Do not hop—keep your feet close to the floor.

Misstep: Retreating

You cross your front foot in front of your back foot, preventing a quick change of direction.

Correction

Push off your front foot and step with your back foot. Do not cross your feet or bring them closer than shoulder-width.

Defensive Footwork Drill 2. Lane Defensive Attack and Retreat

Start by facing the foul line, with your right foot on the defensive right box and your left foot forward and in the lane. Use a staggered defensive stance with your left foot forward at a 45-degree angle from your right foot and your hands up. Take short, quick attack steps with your left foot (the lead foot) forward until it touches the middle of the foul line. Quickly drop step with your left foot. Change to retreat steps, backing up until your left foot touches the defensive left box. Immediately change direction, switching to attack steps until your right foot touches the line. Step back to the box as quickly as you can.

Success Check

- Maintain correct form for the defensive stance.
- Use short, quick steps.

- Execute drop steps and retreat steps using proper technique.
- Try to touch a total of 15 lines and boxes in 30 seconds.

Score Your Success

8 lines and boxes in 30 seconds = 1 point

9 to 10 lines and boxes in 30 seconds = 2 points

11 to 12 lines and boxes in 30 seconds = 3 points

13 to 14 lines and boxes in 30 seconds = 4 points

15 or more lines and boxes in 30 seconds = 5 points

Your score ___

Reverse or Drop Step

In the basic defensive stance, the feet are staggered one foot in front of the other. The weakness of this stance is in the lead foot: It is more difficult to move back in the direction of the lead foot than in the direction of the back foot. If an opponent dribbles toward the basket past your lead foot, quickly drop step with your lead foot while making a reverse pivot with your back foot (figure 1.10). After making the drop step, use quick side steps to reestablish defensive position with your lead foot forward. If you are not in position to do this, you must run and chase your opponent, then turn into position with your intended lead foot forward.

Take your drop step in the direction of your opponent's move. Keep your head up and over your waist and your eyes focused on your opponent. Do not turn in the opposite direction or take your eyes off your opponent. As you reverse pivot, vigorously push off your back foot in the direction of the drop step. The drop step should be straight back. The foot should move low to the floor. Do not circle or lift the lead foot high. For added momentum in the drop step, forcefully move the elbow on the side of your lead foot back close to your body.

Figure 1.10 | Reverse or Drop Step

a   b   c

REVERSE PIVOT AND DROP STEP	REESTABLISH DEFENSIVE POSITION	REESTABLISH LEAD FOOT

REVERSE PIVOT AND DROP STEP

1. Reverse pivot on back foot
2. Drop step straight back with lead foot, keeping foot low to floor
3. Move lead elbow back close to body

REESTABLISH DEFENSIVE POSITION

1. Keep eyes on opponent's midsection
2. Reestablish defensive position by using retreat steps

REESTABLISH LEAD FOOT

1. Front turn to reestablish intended lead foot
2. Be ready to change direction

Misstep

You turn away from your opponent's move, losing sight of your opponent.

Correction

Drop step in the direction of your opponent's move, keeping your eyes on your opponent.

Defensive Footwork Drill 3. *Lane Defensive Zigzag*

Start in the lane, facing the foul line, with your right foot on the defensive right *T* (the intersection of the lane and foul lines). Stand in a staggered defensive stance with your left foot back at a 45-degree angle. Use short, quick retreat steps to move back diagonally until your left foot touches the lane line on your left, just above the box. Quickly drop step with your right foot and use retreat steps until your right foot touches the intersection of the baseline and lane line to your right. Quickly change to an offensive stance and sprint diagonally to the defensive

left *T,* where you will change to a defensive stance with your left foot on the *T.* Use retreat steps until your left foot touches the lane line on your right. Drop step with your left foot and retreat until it touches the intersection of the baseline and lane line on your left. Change to an offensive stance and sprint to the defensive right *T.* Continue a defensive zigzag from *T* to lane to the intersection of baseline and lane line, then sprinting to the opposite *T,* as quickly as you can.

Success Check

- Maintain proper form for both the offensive and defensive stances.
- Use short, quick steps.
- Try to touch 15 lines in 30 seconds.

Defensive Footwork Drill 4. *The Wave*

Start in the middle of the half-court. A partner stands 20 feet in front of you, randomly giving verbal commands and hand signals. On the "Defense!" command, quickly assume a defensive stance. On the "Slide!" command, move quickly to the side signaled by your partner. Your partner should also signal you to move up and back and to the other side. Use defensive side steps for moving to the side and attack and retreat steps for moving up and back. Maintain a balanced defensive stance and execute good footwork with quick changes of direction.

To Increase Difficulty

- Have your partner randomly add the command "Rebound!" On the rebound command, quickly execute a two-footed jump and simulate grabbing a rebound with two hands.
- Have your partner randomly add the command "Loose ball!" On the loose ball command, quickly assume a position with hands and feet on the floor, simulating going for a loose ball, and get back up just as fast.
- Have your partner randomly add the command "Fast break!" Sprint forward on the fast break command.

Success Check

- Use proper technique for the defensive stance and footwork.
- Use short, quick steps.
- Try to go for 30 seconds without stopping or making a mistake.

Defensive Footwork Drill 5. *Full-Court Defensive Footwork*

This drill allows you to practice defensive footwork such as the zigzag, attack and retreat, and reverse. In each variation you will use a third of the floor width from lane line to sideline.

For the full-court defensive zigzag, start with your back to the far basket, standing in a staggered defensive stance with your left foot forward and touching the intersection of the baseline and the sideline on your left and your right foot back at a 45-degree angle. Use defensive retreat steps to move diagonally back until your right foot touches the imaginary lane line extended to your right. Quickly drop step with your right foot. Continue changing direction at each imaginary lane line extended and at each sideline as you proceed to the opposite baseline. Return in the same manner.

For the full-court defensive attack and retreat, imagine that you are guarding a dribbler. Start with your back to the far basket, standing in a balanced defensive stance with your left foot forward and touching the baseline and your right foot spread directly back. Move backward to the half-court line using defensive attack and retreat steps until your right foot touches the half-court line. Quickly drop step, moving your left foot back. With your right foot forward, move backward to the baseline using attack and retreat steps until your left foot touches the baseline. Vary your attack and retreat steps, avoiding a pattern as you move down the floor. Return in the same manner.

For the full-court defensive reverse run-and-turn, imagine that a dribbler beats your lead foot and you must recover by using a reverse run-and-turn. Start in a staggered defensive stance with your back to the far basket, with your left foot forward and touching the baseline and your right foot spread directly back. Move backward using defensive attack steps and a quick reverse run-and-turn. Reverse to the side of your lead foot, keeping your eyes on the imaginary dribbler. Run at least three steps before you turn back into position with your original foot up. From baseline to half-court line, make two reverse run-and-turns starting with your left foot forward. From half-court line to the opposite baseline, make two reverse run-and-turns starting with your right foot forward. Return in the same manner.

Success Check

- Try to complete two round-trips successfully for each drill.
- Use proper form and technique.
- Move quickly, using short, quick steps.

Score Your Success

Give yourself 5 points for completing two round-trips for each drill.

Number of round-trips for the full-court defensive zigzag ___; points earned ___

Number of round-trips for the full-court defensive attack and retreat ___; points earned ___

Number of round-trips for the full-court defensive reverse run-and-turn ___; points earned ___

Your score ___ (out of 15)

Defensive Footwork Drill 6. *Full-Court One-on-One Cutter*

Work with a partner. You will play defense against your partner, who will be an offensive cutter without the ball. Your partner will attempt to use quick starts, stops, and changes of pace and direction to get a head and shoulder by you. The offensive player must stay within a third of the floor width from lane line to sideline while moving down the floor from one baseline to the other. Once your partner gets a head and shoulder by you, both of you stop. As a defender, you must stay within touching distance of the offensive player, attempting to draw an offensive foul by beating your partner to the intended spot in a set position.

Get in a defensive stance facing your partner and touch your partner's waist to start the drill. The offensive player gets a point each time a head and shoulder gets by you, and you get a point each time you gain an offensive foul. Continue the drill from whatever spot the point was gained, again starting with a defensive touch. When you reach the opposite baseline, switch roles for the return trip.

Success Check

- Use proper defensive form.
- Score more points than your partner.

Score Your Success

Give yourself 5 points if you score more points than your partner does.

Your score ___

Your partner's score ___

RATE YOUR SUCCESS

Quickness and balance are key fundamentals to improved play on the court. The information and drills presented in this step will help you be ready to make that offensive move to the basket, create a turnover when you are on defense, or move out on a fast break.

In the next step, we will look at the fundamentals of passing and catching the ball. Before going to step 2, however, look back at how you performed the drills in this step. For each of the drills presented in this step, enter the points you earned, then add up your scores to rate your total success.

Footwork Drills

1. Stance	____ out of 5
2. Footfire	____ out of 15
3. Jump Rope	____ out of 10

Offensive Footwork Drills

1. Jump Stops	____ out of 5
2. Half-Court and Full Court	____ out of 20
3. Two-Foot Vertical Jump Test	____ out of 5
4. One-Foot Vertical Jump Training	____ out of 5

Defensive Footwork Drills

1. Lane Defensive Slide	____ out of 5
2. Lane Defensive Attack and Retreat	____ out of 5
3. Lane Defensive Zigzag	____ out of 5
4. The Wave	____ out of 5
5. Full-Court Defensive Footwork	____ out of 15
6. Full-Court One-on-One Cutter	____ out of 5
TOTAL	____ *out of 105*

If you scored 85 or more points, congratulations! You have mastered the basics of this step and are ready to move on to step 2, passing and catching. If you scored fewer than 85 points, you may want to spend more time on the fundamentals covered in this step. Practice the drills again to develop mastery of the techniques and increase your scores.

Passing and Catching

At its best, basketball is a game in which five players move the ball as a team. Good passing and catching are the essence of team play—the skills that make basketball such a beautiful team sport.

Passing is the most neglected fundamental of the game. Players tend to not want to practice passing. Perhaps because of the attention fans and media give the players who score, not enough credit is given to players who make the assists. A team of good passers is a threat to the defense because the players can get the ball to any teammate at any time. Developing your ability to pass and catch makes you a better player and helps you make your teammates better.

Two basic reasons for passing are to move the ball to create good shot opportunities and to maintain possession of the ball, thereby controlling the game. Deceptive, timely, and accurate passes create scoring opportunities for your team. To be in position for a shot, the ball must be dribbled or passed into the scoring area. A pass travels many times faster than a dribble. Once in the scoring area, quick, accurate passes from the ball side of the court to the offside open up offensive opportunities. Moving the ball keeps defenders on the go and makes them less able to give defensive help or to double-team the player with the ball.

A team that controls the ball with good passing and catching provides few opportunities for the opposition to score. Knowing when and where to pass under pressure not only provides your team a chance to score, but also keeps your team from losing the ball through interceptions, which often result in your opponent getting easy scores.

Specific uses of the pass are to

- get the ball out of a congested area, for example, after a rebound or when a player is being double-teamed;
- move the ball quickly up the court on a fast break;
- set up offensive plays;
- get the ball to an open teammate for a shot; and
- move the ball around, using the pass and cut to create an opportunity for your own shot.

Developing your ability to pass and catch makes you a better player and helps make your teammates better. Have a trained observer—your coach, teacher, or a skilled player—watch you pass and catch. The observer can use the checkpoints in figures 2.1 through 2.7 to evaluate your performance and provide constructive feedback. Also, ask your coach to evaluate your decision making in passing.

PRINCIPLES OF PASSING

Understanding the principles of passing and catching improves your judgment, anticipation, timing, faking, deceptiveness, accuracy, force, and touch, all factors that affect your ability as a playmaker. These principles will help you on different levels of play.

See the rim. When you have the rim in view, you will be able to see the entire court in front of you, including open teammates, and whether a defender is playing you for the pass, shot, or drive.

Pass before you dribble. A pass travels many times faster than a dribble. This is particularly important during a fast break and when moving the ball against a zone.

Know your teammates' strengths and weaknesses. Recognize the position to which your teammate is moving and the next move he is likely to make. Pass the ball to your teammate when and where he can do some good.

Time lead-passes. Anticipate your teammate's speed on a cut to the basket and make a well-timed lead-pass, slightly ahead of your teammate, to the open area.

Use deception. Fake before you pass, but do not telegraph the pass by looking in the direction you are passing. Use your peripheral vision to see your target without looking at your receiver. Use the element of surprise.

Draw-and-kick. Draw your defender to you with a shot fake or dribble before passing. Do not attempt to pass against a sagging defender, who will have more time and distance to react and intercept or deflect the pass.

Make passes quick and accurate. Eliminate wasted motion. Do not wind up to pass or start the pass behind the plane of your body.

Judge the force of your pass. Pass forcefully for longer distances and use touch when you're close to the receiver.

Be sure about your pass. It is better not to pass than to risk a pass that cannot be completed. A good pass is one that is caught. Do not force a pass into a crowd or before you have an open teammate.

Pass away from the defender. When your teammate is closely guarded, pass to the side away from the defender. If you receive a pass but are not in position to shoot, keep your hands above your waist, meet the pass, and catch the ball with relaxed hands, in position to make another pass.

Pass to the open shooter's far hand. When a teammate is open and in position to shoot, pass the ball to the shooter's far hand. The shooter should not have to move her hands or change body position to catch a pass that is off target. When you are open in position to shoot and receive the pass, let the ball come to you. Jump behind the ball, catching it with your hands relaxed in block-and-tuck position, ready to shoot (see page 80).

Basic passes include the chest pass, bounce pass, overhead pass, sidearm pass, baseball pass, and behind-the-back pass. Practice each type of pass to make these fundamental passes automatic. Then learn to apply the correct pass for different court situations. You can practice with a partner or by yourself to develop quickness and accuracy in passing. For practicing alone, you need a ball and a flat wall or tossback. Learn decision making in passing by practicing in competitive group drills and game situations.

Warm-Up Drill. *Ball Handling Warm-Up*

This warm-up drill consists of passing and catching the ball, moving the ball from one hand to the other. The six parts of the ball-handling drill are over your head, around your head, around your waist, around one leg, around the other leg, and figure eights through your legs.

Start in a balanced stance. Pass the ball from one hand to the other forcefully by flexing your wrists and fingers. To improve your weak hand, emphasize it through the ball. Follow through completely on each pass, pointing your fingers at your catching hand. Work for force and control, not just for quickness. On each part of the drill, pass the ball 10 times in one direction, then reverse direction and pass the ball another 10 times.

Success Check

- Attempt to go three minutes with no more than three errors.
- Maintain force and control.
- Follow through by pointing your fingers at your catching hand.

CHEST PASS

The chest pass (figure 2.1) is the most common pass in basketball. It can be used with quickness and accuracy from most positions on the floor.

Start in a balanced stance. Hold the ball with two hands in front of your chest, keeping your elbows in. Your hands should be slightly behind the ball in a relaxed position. Locate your target without looking at it. Look away or fake before passing. Step in the direction of your target, extending your legs, back, and arms. Force your wrists and fingers through the ball. Emphasize forcing your weak hand through the ball—the strong hand tends to dominate. The ball will go where your fingers direct it. Releasing it off the first and second fingers of both hands creates backspin and gives the ball direction. Follow through by pointing your fingers at the target with the palms facing down.

Figure 2.1 — Chest Pass

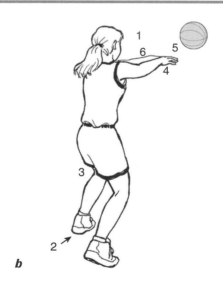

a   *b*

BALL IN FRONT OF CHEST

1. Locate target without looking
2. Maintain balanced stance
3. Keep hands slightly behind ball in a relaxed handshake position
4. Keep ball in front of chest
5. Keep elbows in

CHEST PASS

1. Look away or fake before passing
2. Step in direction of pass
3. Extend knees, back, and arms
4. Force wrist and fingers through ball; force weak hand through ball
5. Release ball off first and second fingers
6. Follow through with arms extended, palms down, and fingers pointing to the target

Misstep

Your chest pass lacks force.

Correction

Start the pass with your elbows in and force your wrists and fingers through the ball.

Passing Drill 1. *Tossback Passing on the Move*

Practicing the drill to a tossback while moving from side to side develops quickness, accuracy, and confidence. Place the tossback in the middle of the lane. Start 12 feet away from it with your outside foot touching the lane line to your left. Use the chest pass when passing and catching on the move. Starting in good passing position, pass and catch the ball as quickly and accurately as you can while moving laterally, taking short, quick side steps and not crossing your feet. Move laterally until your outside foot touches the lane line to your right. Change direction and move back to the lane line to your left, passing and catching on the move. Keep moving laterally as you pass and catch, changing direction each time you touch the line. If a tossback is unavailable, use a wall. Use tape to mark lines 12 feet apart to serve as lane lines.

To Increase Difficulty

- Run laterally instead of stepping, making a one-two stop as you catch each pass.

Success Check

- Do not cross your feet when moving laterally.
- Use short, quick steps.
- Attempt to complete 20 chest passes in 30 seconds at 12 feet while moving from lane line to lane line.

Score Your Success

Fewer than 10 chest passes in 30 seconds = 0 points

10 to 11 chest passes in 30 seconds = 1 point

12 to 14 chest passes in 30 seconds = 2 points

15 to 17 chest passes in 30 seconds = 3 points

18 to 19 chest passes in 30 seconds = 4 points

20 or more chest passes in 30 seconds = 5 points

Your score ___

Passing Drill 2. *Rapid-Fire Passing*

For the rapid-fire tossback drill, you will pass to a tossback from a distance of only five feet. A wall can be used if a tossback is unavailable. This drill is excellent for developing quickness, accuracy, and confidence in passing and catching with one hand (strong and weak hands). In this drill, you will execute sidearm and behind-the-back passes.

Start in a balanced stance, five feet in front of a tossback. Turn your body so your chest is at a right angle to the tossback. Start with the ball in your strong hand and your weak hand down at your side. Using a sidearm pass with your strong hand, pass the ball with as much force and accuracy as you can. Catch the return off the tossback with only your strong hand. Next perform the same action with your weak hand. Now perform a behind-the-back pass using your strong hand to pass and catch the ball. Then perform a behind-the-back pass and catch with your weak hand.

Success Check

- Use proper passing form for each type of pass.

Score Your Success

For the sidearm passes, give yourself 5 points for completing 30 or more passes in 30 seconds, 3 points for completing 25 to 29 passes in 30 seconds, 1 point for completing 20 to 24 passes in 30 seconds, and 0 points for completing fewer than 20 passes in 30 seconds.

Number of sidearm passes made with strong hand in 30 seconds ___; points earned ___

Number of sidearm passes made with weak hand in 30 seconds ___; points earned ___

For the behind-the-back passes, give yourself 5 points for completing 20 or more passes in 30 seconds, 3 points for completing 15 to 19 passes in 30 seconds, 1 point for completing 10 to 14 passes in 30 seconds, and 0 points for completing fewer than 10 passes in 30 seconds.

Number of behind-the-back passes made with strong hand in 30 seconds ___; points earned ___

Number of behind-the-back passes made with weak hand in 30 seconds ___; points earned ___

Your score ___ (total points earned; maximum of 20)

BOUNCE PASS

When a defender is between you and the target, one option is to use a bounce pass under the defender's arms. The bounce pass (figure 2.2) can move the ball to a wing on the end of a fast break or to a player cutting to the basket. Because the ball bounces off the floor, it is a slower pass than the chest pass.

Execute the bounce pass the same as the chest pass. Pass the ball so that it bounces off the floor at a distance, allowing it to be received at about waist level. To judge the correct distance, aim for a spot two-thirds of the distance or a few feet in front of your target. Bouncing the ball too far from your target results in a high, slow bounce that is easily intercepted. Bouncing the ball too close to the receiver makes it too low to handle. Remember, the ball will go where the fingers direct it. Follow through by pointing your fingers at the target with the palms of your hands facing down.

Figure 2.2　Bounce Pass

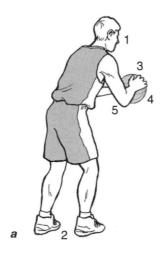

BALL AT WAIST LEVEL

1. Locate target without looking
2. Maintain balanced stance
3. Keep hands slightly behind ball in a relaxed handshake position
4. Hold ball at waist level
5. Keep elbows in

BOUNCE PASS

1. Look away or fake before passing
2. Step in direction of pass
3. Extend knees, back, and arms
4. Force wrist and fingers through ball; force weak hand through ball
5. Release ball off first and second fingers
6. Aim about two-thirds of the distance to the target
7. Follow through with arms extended, palms down, and fingers pointing to the target

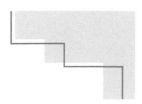

Misstep

Your bounce pass bounces too high and is too slow.

Correction

Start the pass from waist level and aim the ball's bounce closer to the receiver.

OVERHEAD PASS

Use the overhead pass (figure 2.3) when you are closely guarded and have to pass over the defender, as an outlet pass to start a fast break against pressing defenders, or as a lob to a player cutting backdoor to the basket. Like the sidearm pass discussed in the next section, the overhead pass is an option for feeding the low post.

Start in a balanced stance, holding the ball above your forehead with your elbows in and flexed about 90 degrees. Do not bring the ball behind your head; it takes longer to execute the pass if you begin with the ball behind your head and may allow the ball to be stolen. Step in the direction of the target, extending your legs and back to get maximum power. Quickly pass the ball, extending your arms and flexing your wrists and fingers. Release the ball off the first and second fingers of both hands. Follow through by pointing your fingers at the target, palms down.

Figure 2.3 | Overhead Pass

BALL ABOVE FOREHEAD

1. Locate target without looking
2. Maintain balanced stance
3. Keep hands slightly behind ball in a relaxed handshake position
4. Hold ball above forehead
5. Keep elbows in

OVERHEAD PASS

1. Look away or fake before passing
2. Step in direction of pass
3. Extend knees, back, and arms
4. Flex wrist and fingers
5. Release ball off first and second fingers
6. Follow through with arms extended, palms down, and fingers pointing to the target

Misstep

Your overhead pass lacks force and accuracy.

Correction

Make sure you are starting the pass with the ball above your forehead, not behind your head. Do not break the plane of your body with the ball. Generate force by keeping your elbows in, flexing your wrists and fingers, and extending your legs, back, and arms. Produce accuracy by pointing the first and second fingers of each hand toward the target.

SIDEARM PASS

Use the sidearm pass (figure 2.4) when you are closely guarded and have to pass around a defender. Like the overhead pass, a sidearm pass is an option for feeding the low post. Except for the position of the ball in the preparation phase, execution of the sidearm pass is similar to the overhead pass.

In the sidearm pass, start by moving the ball to one side between your shoulder and hip as you step to that side. Do not bring the ball behind your body; it will take longer to execute the pass when the ball begins behind the body, and the ball can also be stolen. Follow through by pointing your fingers toward the target, palms to the side.

You can use two hands for the sidearm pass, as in the overhead pass, or just one hand. For a one-handed sidearm pass, place your passing hand behind the ball. Keep your nonpassing hand in front of and on the ball until the point of release so you can stop and fake when needed. Practice the one-handed sidearm pass with your weak hand as well as your strong hand.

Figure 2.4   **Sidearm Pass**

BALL AT SIDE

1. Able to see target without turning to look
2. Balanced stance
3. Hands slightly behind ball in a relaxed handshake position
4. Ball between shoulder and hip
5. Elbows in

SIDEARM PASS

1. Look away or fake before passing
2. Step in direction of pass
3. Extend knees, back, and arms
4. Flex wrist and fingers
5. Release ball off first and second fingers
6. Follow through with the arms extended, palms to the side, and fingers pointing to the target

Misstep

Your sidearm pass lacks force and accuracy.

Correction

Make sure you are not starting the pass with the ball behind your body. Do not break the plane of your body with the ball. Generate force by keeping your elbows in, flexing your wrists and fingers, and extending your legs, back, and arms. Produce accuracy by pointing the first and second fingers of each hand toward the target.

BASEBALL PASS

For a long pass, often you will want to use the baseball pass (figure 2.5). The baseball pass can be used as an outlet pass to start a fast break, as a long lead pass to a teammate cutting toward the basket, or to inbound the ball.

Start in a balanced stance. Pivot on your back foot, turning your body to your passing arm side. Bring the ball up to your ear with your elbow in, your passing hand behind the ball and your balance hand in front of it, like a catcher starting to throw a baseball. As you pass the ball, shift your weight from your back foot to your front foot. Extend your legs, back, and passing arm toward the target. Flex your wrist forward as you release the ball off your fingertips. Follow through by pointing your fingers at the target with the palm of your passing hand facing down. Although this is a one-handed pass, keep your nonpassing hand on the ball until the release so you can stop and fake if necessary.

Figure 2.5 | Baseball Pass

BALL AT EAR

1. Able to see target without turning to look
2. Balanced stance
3. Body to side
4. Weight on pivot foot (back foot)
5. Hands relaxed, with passing hand behind the ball and nonpassing hand in front of it
6. Ball at ear
7. Elbow in

BASEBALL PASS

1. Look away or fake before passing
2. Step in direction of pass
3. Extend knees, back, and arms
4. Keep two hands on ball until release
5. Flex wrist and fingers
6. Release ball off first and second fingers
7. Follow through with arm extended, palm down, and fingers pointing to the target

Misstep

Your baseball pass curves.

Correction

Keep your passing hand directly behind the ball—not to the side—and point your fingers at the target. The pass will go where your fingers direct it to go.

BEHIND-THE-BACK PASS

Advanced players must be able to pass behind the back. The behind-the-back pass (figure 2.6) is especially useful when a defender comes between you and a teammate on a two-on-one fast break.

Pivot on the ball of your back foot, turning your body to your passing arm side. Using both hands, move the ball to a position behind your hip. Hold the ball with your passing hand behind it and your nonpassing hand in front. Shift your weight from your back foot to your front foot as you pass the ball behind your back and toward the target. Extend your passing arm and flex your wrist and fingers, releasing the ball off your fingertips. Follow through by pointing your fingers at the target, passing hand palm up and passing arm contacting your back. Practice the behind-the-back pass with your weak hand as well as your strong hand.

Figure 2.6   Behind-the-Back Pass

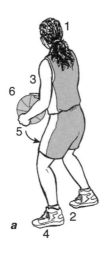

BALL BEHIND HIP

1. Able to see target without turning to look
2. Balanced stance
3. Body to side
4. Weight on pivot foot (the back foot)
5. Hands relaxed, with passing hand behind the ball and nonpassing hand in front of it
6. Ball behind hip

BEHIND-THE-BACK PASS

1. Look away or fake before passing
2. Step in direction of pass
3. Shift weight from back foot to front foot
4. Keep both hands on ball until release
5. Pass ball behind your back
6. Extend passing arm
7. Flex wrist and fingers
8. Release ball off first and second fingers
9. Follow through with the arm extended, palm up, and fingers pointing to the target

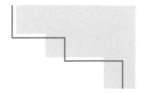

Misstep

Once you start the behind-the-back pass, you are unable to stop and fake.

Correction

Be sure to start the pass with both hands on the ball. Do not take the nonpassing hand off the ball too soon. Use both hands to move the ball behind your hip, and keep both hands on the ball until the release.

Passing Drill 3. *Ricochet Passing*

This challenging, competitive, and fun drill is performed with a partner. The objective is to develop accuracy and confidence in chest passing while also developing quickness and agility.

Stand 12 feet away from and facing a tossback or wall. Your partner stands behind you. Starting in good passing position, make a chest pass as accurately as you can to the middle of the tossback and move laterally to your right, taking short, quick side steps without crossing your feet. Your partner catches the ball as it comes off the tossback and makes a chest pass before moving laterally to the right. After your partner passes, quickly move laterally to your left and behind your partner. Catch the ball as it comes off the tossback and make a chest pass before moving laterally to the right. After you pass, your partner quickly moves laterally to the left and behind you and catches the ball as it comes off the tossback. Continue the drill in this manner, passing and moving laterally to your right and then to your left and behind the passer. You can modify this drill by moving laterally to the left after each pass.

Success Check

- Do not cross your feet as you move laterally.
- Use short, quick steps.
- Attempt to complete 20 chest passes in 30 seconds at 12 feet while moving laterally.

Score Your Success

10 or fewer chest passes completed in 30 seconds = 0 points

11 to 12 chest passes completed in 30 seconds = 1 point

13 to 14 chest passes completed in 30 seconds = 2 points

15 to 17 chest passes completed in 30 seconds = 3 points

18 to 19 chest passes completed in 30 seconds = 4 points

20 or more chest passes completed in 30 seconds = 5 points

Your score ____

Passing Drill 4. *Partner Passing*

This drill develops quickness, accuracy, and confidence in passing. Choose a partner to pass and catch the ball, executing chest, bounce, overhead, sidearm, baseball, and behind-the-back passes.

For the chest, bounce, overhead, sidearm, and behind-the-back passes, start in a balanced stance 15 feet in front of your partner with the ball in good passing position. For the baseball pass, move back to 20 feet. Pass and catch the ball as quickly and accurately as you can, using a fingertip release to impart backspin and accuracy. Point your fingers in the direction of the pass, exaggerating your follow-through by leaving your arms up until the pass is caught. When you catch, make sure you are in a balanced stance with your hands up as a target, ready to move to meet each pass.

Success Check

- Use proper technique for each type of pass.
- Use proper technique for catching passes.

Score Your Success

For the chest, overhead, sidearm, and behind-the-back passes, give yourself 5 points if you complete 30 or more passes in 30 seconds at 15 feet, 3 points if you complete 25 to 29 passes, 1 point if you complete 20 to 24 passes, and 0 points if you complete fewer than 20 passes.

Number of chest passes in 30 seconds at 15 feet ____; points earned ____

Number of overhead passes in 30 seconds at 15 feet ____; points earned ____

Number of sidearm passes in 30 seconds at 15 feet ____; points earned ____

Number of behind-the-back passes in 30 seconds at 15 feet ____; points earned ____

For the bounce pass, give yourself 5 points if you complete 20 or more passes in 30 seconds at 15 feet, 3 points if you complete 15 to 19 passes, 1 point if you complete 10 to 14 passes, and 0 points if you complete fewer than 10 passes.

Number of bounce passes in 30 seconds at 15 feet ___; points earned ___

For the baseball pass, give yourself 5 points if you complete 20 or more passes in 30 seconds at 20 feet, 3 points if you complete 15 to 19 passes, 1 point if you complete 10 to 14 passes, and 0 points if you complete fewer than 10 passes.

Number of baseball passes in 30 seconds at 20 feet ___; points earned ___

Your score ___ (points earned; maximum of 30)

Passing Drill 5. *Pass and Follow*

This challenging, competitive, and fun drill requires several teammates. Divide into two lines, 12 feet apart. The free throw circle or center circle can be used to help space the lines 12 feet apart. When practicing the baseball pass, move the lines to 20 feet apart. The first players in each line face each other; one of them has a ball. The first player in line with the ball throws a chest pass to the first player in the other line, then follows the pass by running to the right behind the receiver's line. The receiver catches the ball, passes it to the next player in the first line and follows the pass by running to the right behind the player who receives the pass and to the end of that line. The drill continues with each player catching, passing with quickness and accuracy, and following the pass. Each type of pass is practiced for 60 seconds.

Success Check

• Use proper passing form for each type of pass.

Score Your Success

For the chest, overhead, sidearm, and behind-the-back passes, give yourself 5 points if you complete 60 or more passes in 60 seconds at 12 feet, 3 points if you complete 50 to 59 passes, 1 point if you complete 40 to 49 passes, and 0 points if you complete fewer than 40 passes.

Number of chest passes in 60 seconds at 12 feet ___; points earned ___

Number of overhead passes in 60 seconds at 12 feet ___; points earned ___

Number of sidearm passes in 60 seconds at 12 feet ___; points earned ___

Number of behind-the-back passes in 60 seconds at 12 feet ___; points earned ___

For the bounce pass, give yourself 5 points if you complete 40 or more passes in 60 seconds at 12 feet, 3 points if you complete 35 to 39 passes, 1 point if you complete 30 to 34 passes, and 0 points if you complete fewer than 30 passes.

Number of bounce passes in 60 seconds at 12 feet ___; points earned ___

For the baseball pass, give yourself 5 points if you complete 40 or more passes in 60 seconds at 20 feet, 3 points if you complete 35 to 39 passes, 1 point if you complete 30 to 34 passes, and 0 points if you complete fewer than 30 passes.

Number of baseball passes in 60 seconds at 20 feet ___; points earned ___

Your score ___ (points earned; maximum of 30)

Passing Drill 6. *Star Passing*

Another challenging, competitive, and fun drill is the star passing drill. At least 10 players are needed for this drill. Set up in star formation with five lines spaced 12 feet apart around the free throw circle or center circle. When practicing the baseball pass, move the lines to 20 feet apart. The first player in one of the lines has a ball. The player with the ball passes to the first player two lines to the right, then follows the pass by running to the right behind the receiver's line. The receiver then passes the ball to the first player two lines to the right and follows the pass, running to the right behind the second receiver. The drill continues with each player catching, passing with quickness and accuracy, and following the pass. Each type of pass is practiced for 60 seconds.

Success Check

- Use proper passing form for each type of pass.

Score Your Success

For the chest, overhead, sidearm, and behind-the-back passes, give yourself 5 points if you complete 60 or more passes in 60 seconds at 12 feet, 3 points if you complete 50 to 59 passes, 1 point if you complete 40 to 49 passes, and 0 points if you complete fewer than 40 passes.

Number of chest passes in 60 seconds at 12 feet ___; points earned ___

Number of overhead passes in 60 seconds at 12 feet ___; points earned ___

Number of sidearm passes in 60 seconds at 12 feet ___; points earned ___

Number of behind-the-back passes in 60 seconds at 12 feet ___; points earned ___

For the bounce pass, give yourself 5 points if you complete 40 or more passes in 60 seconds at 12 feet, 3 points if you complete 35 to 39 passes, 1 point if you complete 30 to 34 passes, and 0 points if you complete fewer than 30 passes.

Number of bounce passes in 60 seconds at 12 feet ___; points earned ___

For the baseball pass, give yourself 5 points if you complete 40 or more passes in 60 seconds at 20 feet, 3 points if you complete 35 to 39 passes, 1 point if you complete 30 to 34 passes, and 0 points if you complete fewer than 30 passes.

Number of baseball passes in 60 seconds at 20 feet ___; points earned ___

Your score ___ (points earned; maximum of 30)

Passing Drill 7. *Bull in the Ring*

This fun passing drill is done with five players on offense and one player on defense. The offensive players spread out equidistant around the free throw circle or center circle. One offensive player has the ball. The one defender, the bull in the ring, stands in the middle of the circle. The bull tries to intercept, deflect, or touch the passes. The player with the ball may use any type of pass to any player in the circle except the closest players on either side. The passer may not hold the ball longer than two seconds. If the bull touches the ball or the passer makes a bad pass or commits a violation, the passer becomes the bull in the ring and the defender switches to offense.

Success Check

- Use proper passing form for each type of pass.

- Do not hold the ball for more than two seconds.
- Attempt to complete five consecutive passes without a deflection, bad pass, or violation.

Score Your Success

Completing fewer than three consecutive passes without error = 0 points

Completing three to four consecutive passes without error = 1 point

Completing five consecutive passes or more without error = 5 points

Your score ___

CATCHING PASSES AWAY FROM THE SCORING AREA

When you are away from your scoring area and closely guarded, give the passer a good target and go to the ball to meet the pass (figure 2.7). To catch the ball, keep your hands soft. Catch the ball with your hands in a relaxed position, forming a natural cup with your palm off the ball and your thumb and fingers relaxed but not spread. Give with the ball as you catch it, bringing your arms and hands into position in front of your chest. After receiving the pass, land with a one-two stop, look to the rim, and be ready to pass upcourt.

| Figure 2.7 | Catching a Pass Away From a Scoring Area |

a   b   c

SHOW HANDS

1. Eyes on ball
2. Balanced stance with feet shoulder-width apart
3. Knees flexed
4. Back straight
5. Hands up at ball distance with fingers relaxed

MEET THE BALL

1. Come to meet the ball
2. Make a two-handed catch
3. Keep fingers relaxed
4. Give with ball on catch
5. Land with one-two stop

FOLLOW-THROUGH

1. Front turn pivoting on inside foot
2. Bring ball to front of chest with elbows out
3. See the rim
4. Keep feet shoulder-width apart
5. Keep knees flexed
6. Keep back straight

Misstep

You fumble the ball as you receive it.

Correction

Keep your hands up. Watch the ball all the way into your hands. Keep your hands relaxed and give with the ball as you catch it.

Passing Drill 8. *Tossback Passing*

The tossback passing drill consists of passing to a tossback to develop quickness, accuracy, and confidence in passing. A wall can be used if a tossback is unavailable. In this drill, you will execute the chest pass, bounce pass, overhead pass, sidearm pass, baseball pass, and behind-the-back pass. Start in a balanced stance 12 feet in front of a tossback or wall, with the ball in good passing position. Pass and catch the ball as quickly and accurately as you can. The correct fingertip release will impart backspin and direct the ball straight back to you. Keep your arms up on your follow-through until the ball hits the tossback.

Success Check

- Begin in a balanced stance.
- Use proper passing technique for each type of pass.
- Follow through with each type of pass.

Score Your Success

For the chest, overhead, sidearm, baseball, and behind-the-back passes, give yourself 5 points if you complete 30 or more passes in 30 seconds at 12 feet, 3 points if you complete 25 to 29 passes, 1 point if you complete 20 to 24 passes, and 0 points if you complete fewer than 20 passes.

Number of chest passes in 30 seconds ___;
   points earned ___

Number of overhead passes in 30 seconds ___; points earned ___

Number of sidearm passes in 30 seconds ___;
   points earned ___

Number of baseball passes in 30 seconds ___;
   points earned ___

Number of behind-the-back passes in 30 seconds ___; points earned ___

For the bounce pass, give yourself 5 points if you complete 20 or more passes in 30 seconds at 12 feet, 3 points if you complete 15 to 19 passes, 1 point if you complete 10 to 14 passes, and 0 points if you complete fewer than 10 passes.

Number of bounce passes in 30 seconds ___;
   points earned ___

Your score ___ (points earned; maximum of 30)

RATE YOUR SUCCESS

Good passing and catching technique is vital for team players who want to help their teams perform. In this step, we have covered the proper way to make various passes and the correct form for catching the pass to be in position to shoot, pass, or drive.

In the next step, we will look at the fundamentals of dribbling the ball. Before going to step 3, however, look back at how you performed the drills in this step. For each of the drills presented in this step, enter the points you earned, then add up your scores to rate your total success.

Basketball: Steps to Success

Warm-Up Drill

1. Ball Handling Warm-Up	___ out of 5

Passing Drills

1. Tossback Passing on the Move	___ out of 5
2. Rapid-Fire Passing	___ out of 20
3. Ricochet Passing	___ out of 5
4. Partner Passing	___ out of 30
5. Pass and Follow	___ out of 30
6. Star Passing	___ out of 30
7. Bull in the Ring	___ out of 5
8. Tossback Passing	___ out of 30
TOTAL	**___ out of 160**

If you scored 140 or more points, congratulations! You have mastered the basics of this step and are ready to move on to step 3, dribbling. If you scored fewer than 140 points, you may want to spend more time on the fundamentals covered in this step. Practice the drills again to develop mastery of the techniques and increase your scores.

Dribbling

Dribbling is an integral part of basketball and vital to individual and team play. Like passing, it is a way of moving the ball. To maintain possession of the ball while you move, you have to dribble.

At the start of the dribble, the ball must leave your hand before you lift your pivot foot from the floor. While dribbling, you may not touch the ball with both hands simultaneously or allow it to come to rest in your hand.

The ability to dribble with your weak hand as well as your strong hand is a key to advancing your level of play. If you only dribble well with your strong hand, you can be overplayed to that side and be made virtually ineffective. To protect the ball while dribbling, keep your body between your defender and the ball. In other words, when you drive to your weak-hand side (to your left if you are right-handed), you dribble with the weak (left) hand to protect the ball with your body.

Dribbling allows you to move the ball by yourself. By dribbling, you can advance the ball up the court and evade pressure by defenders. Every team needs at least one skilled dribbler who can advance the ball up the court on a fast break and protect it against defensive pressure.

Some specific uses of the dribble are to

- move the ball out of a congested area when passing to a teammate is impossible, such as after a rebound or when being double-teamed;
- advance the ball up the court when no receivers are open, especially against pressure defenses;
- move the ball up the court on a fast break when teammates are not open in position to score;
- penetrate the defense for a drive to the basket;
- draw a defender to you to create an opening for a teammate;
- set up offensive plays;
- improve your position or angle before passing to a teammate; and
- create your own shot.

Dribbling is the most misused fundamental of the game. You need to understand when and when not to dribble. A pass travels many times faster than a dribble, so before you dribble, look to pass to open teammates. If you dribble too much, your teammates will tend to stop moving, making the defense's job easier. Excessive dribbling can destroy teamwork and morale.

Learn to minimize the use of the dribble. Dribbling should have a purpose—it should take you somewhere. Do not waste it.

Don't get into the bad habit of bouncing the ball automatically the moment you receive it. By dribbling unnecessarily, you may miss the opportunity to pass to an open teammate or you may stop your dribble before you have an open teammate. When you immediately dribble the ball once or twice and then pick it up, you have made it easier for your defender to apply pressure against your shot. It will also be easier for your opponent to defend against the pass, as you are no longer a threat to drive. Once you start to dribble, remember not to stop until you have an open teammate to receive your pass.

To be an effective playmaker, you must become skilled at dribbling with either hand. Strive to feel that the ball is an extension of your hand. Keep your head up to see the entire court, and make the right decision at the right time. How well you dribble—your control, timing, deceptiveness, and quickness—largely determines your progress as a playmaker.

Have a trained observer—your coach, teacher, or a skilled player—watch your dribbling skills. The observer can use the checklists in figures 3.1 through 3.10 to evaluate your performance and provide corrective feedback. Also, ask your coach to evaluate your decisions in using the dribble.

The basic dribble moves to learn include the control dribble, speed dribble, footfire dribble, change-of-pace dribble, retreat dribble, crossover dribble, inside-out dribble, reverse dribble, and behind-the-back dribble. Practice to make dribbling skills so automatic that you do not think about dribbling but devote full attention to the various situations taking place on the court. Learn how quickly you can dribble while maintaining control. In practice, strive to improve your ability, but in games, know your limitations. Dribbling is a skill that you can practice by yourself. All you need are a ball, a level spot, and an eagerness to improve.

Dribbling Drill 1. *Dribble Warm-Up*

The dribble warm-up develops ability and confidence in dribbling with either the strong or weak hand. The drill's five parts are crossover, figure eight, one knee, sitting, and lying down.

Crossover. From a balanced stance, change the ball from one hand to the other, dribbling it below knee level and no wider than your knees. Keep your nondribbling hand up to protect the ball. Also change the position of your feet and body to protect the ball. Alternating from right to left and left to right, complete 20 repetitions (10 with each hand).

Figure eight. Dribble the ball in a figure eight from back to front through your legs. Change from one hand to the other after the ball goes through your legs. After 10 repetitions, change direction and dribble the ball in a figure eight from front to back through your legs for 10 more repetitions.

One knee. Dribble the ball as you kneel on one knee. Starting in front of your knee, dribble around to one side and under your knee. Change hands and dribble behind your back leg. Again change from one hand to the other and continue to the starting point in front of your knee. Dribble in a figure eight for 10 repetitions in one direction, then reverse and dribble in a figure eight for 10 repetitions in the opposite direction.

Sitting. Continue dribbling as you sit down. Dribble for 10 repetitions on one side while sitting. Raise your legs, dribble the ball under them to the other side, and dribble on that side for 10 repetitions.

Lying down. Continue dribbling as you lie on your back. While lying down, dribble for 10 repetitions on one side. Sit up, raise your legs, dribble the ball under them to the other side, lie down, and dribble on the other side for 10 repetitions.

Success Check

- Dribble with confidence.
- Work your weak hand as much as your strong hand.
- Attempt to complete 10 repetitions without error in each direction for each part of the drill.

Score Your Success

For each drill, record how many dribbles you completed to each side without error. Give yourself 5 points for completing 10 or more repetitions without error to each side.

	Right	Left	Points
Crossover	____	____	____
Figure eight	____	____	____
One knee	____	____	____
Sitting	____	____	____
Lying down	____	____	____
Your score ___			

CONTROL DRIBBLE

Use the control dribble (figure 3.1) when you are closely guarded and must keep the ball protected and under control. A well-balanced stance, basic to the control dribble, makes you a triple threat to shoot, pass, or drive. It allows you to move quickly, change direction, change pace, and stop under control while protecting the ball. Keep your head up and the rim of the basket in view. This will allow you to see the entire court, open teammates, and defenders.

Learn to dribble without looking at the ball. Keep your head over your waist and your back straight. Your feet should be at least shoulder-width apart, your weight evenly distributed on the balls of your feet, and your knees flexed. Be prepared to move. Keep the elbow of your dribbling hand close to your body. Your dribbling hand should be in a relaxed position with the thumb relaxed and the fingers spread comfortably. Dribble the ball off your finger pads with fingertip control, flexing your wrist and fingers to impart force to the ball. Do not pump your arm. Dribble the ball no higher than knee level and keep it close to your body. Keep your nondribbling hand in a protective position close to the ball. Position your body between your defender and the ball.

Figure 3.1 Control Dribble

CONTROL DRIBBLE

1. Keep head up, see the rim
2. Dribble ball close to body at knee level or lower
3. Make sure ball leaves hand before pivot foot leaves floor
4. Dribble ball off finger pads using strong wrist and finger flexion
5. Use body, nondribbling hand to protect ball

Misstep

You look at the ball when dribbling.

Correction

Keep your head up and the rim in view.

Dribbling Drill 2. *Knock the Ball Out of the Circle*

This drill develops the ability to dribble with the head up and protect the ball against pressure. Select another player as an opponent. You each have a basketball. Dribble within either the free throw circle or center circle. Each of you tries to deflect the other's basketball outside the circle.

To Increase Difficulty

- You and your opponent dribble with your weak hands only.
- Allow more contact than normal to work on dribbling under severe defensive pressure.

Success Check

- Keep your head up.
- Protect the ball with your body and your non-dribbling hand.
- Be aware of your partner's movements.

Score Your Success

Score 1 point each time you knock your opponent's ball out of the circle. Play until someone scores 5 points.

Your score ____

SPEED DRIBBLE

The speed dribble (figure 3.2) is useful when you are not closely guarded, when you must move the ball quickly on the open floor, and when you have a quick drive to the basket. For speed dribbling, use a high dribble at waist level, keep your head up, and keep the rim of the basket in view. This will allow you to see the entire court, open teammates, and defenders.

Start by throwing the ball out several feet and running after it. Remember, the ball must leave your hand before you lift your pivot foot. Push the successive dribbles out at waist level, flexing your wrist and fingers to put force on the ball. Dribble the ball off your finger pads with fingertip control.

Figure 3.2   **Speed Dribble**

SPEED DRIBBLE

1. Keep head up, see the rim
2. Throw the ball out several feet and run after it
3. Push the dribble forward at waist level
4. Make sure ball leaves hand before pivot foot leaves floor
5. Dribble ball off finger pads using strong wrist and finger flexion
6. Use body, nondribbling hand to protect ball

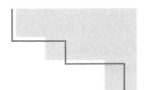

Misstep

You take too many dribbles.

Correction

Push each dribble out at waist level and run after it, keeping the number of dribbles to a minimum.

Speed dribbling is important, but so is stopping quickly with balance. After dribbling at full speed, inexperienced players often lose balance and control as they try to stop quickly. The one-two stop (figure 3.3) can prevent you from dragging your pivot foot and traveling when you stop after speed dribbling. This is especially important on a fast break.

In the one-two stop, your back foot lands first, followed by your other foot. When the one-two stop is executed on your last dribble, the foot that lands first becomes your pivot foot.

Hopping before executing the one-two stop allows gravity to help slow your momentum. Lean in the opposite direction and land with a wide base. The wider your base, the more stable you will become. Flex your back knee to lower your body to a "sitting" position on the heel of your back foot. The lower you get, the more you will be in balance. Keep your head up.

Figure 3.3   One-Two Stop After the Speed Dribble

HOP AND LEAN BACK

1. Hop before stop
2. Lean back
3. Catch ball off last dribble

ONE-TWO STOP

1. Land first on back foot
2. Land second on lead foot
3. Land with a wide base
4. Keep head up, see the rim

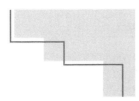

Misstep

You lose balance forward, causing you to drag your pivot foot.

Correction

Hop before you stop to allow gravity to slow your momentum. Lean back, landing first on your back foot, then on your front foot. Maintain a wide base for stability. "Sit" on the heel of your back foot. Keep your head up.

Dribbling Drill 3. *Two-Ball Dribble*

Dribbling two balls is fun and will develop dribbling ability and confidence with both hands. This drill has six parts: dribble together, alternate one up and one down, crossover, dribble inside out, dribble through the legs, and side-pull forward and back dribble. Each part includes dribbling two balls simultaneously. If a ball gets away, keep dribbling with the other while you recover the stray ball.

Together. Dribble two basketballs below knee level simultaneously.

Alternate one up and one down. Dribble two basketballs simultaneously so that one ball is up while the other is down.

Crossover. Switch the balls from one hand to the other by crossing them back and forth in front of you, keeping them low and close to your body. Mix how you make the changes rather than executing each crossover with the same hand going in front.

Inside out. An inside-out dribble is a fake change of direction. Start the ball inside, but then rotate your hand over the ball to dribble it outside your base on the same side. Perform the inside-out dribble alternating hands and then with both hands simultaneously.

Through the legs. Dribble first one ball, then the other, and then both balls through the legs.

Side pull forward and back. Start by dribbling a ball on each side of your body. Then dribble them backward and forward by flexing your wrist and fingers in an action that is similar to pushing the balls back and forth.

Success Check

• Work both hands.
• Attempt to complete 20 dribbles without error for each part of the drill.

Dribbling Drill 4. *Moving Two-Ball Dribble*

After dribbling two balls in a stationary position, a greater challenge is to dribble two balls while moving. The moving two-ball dribble will improve weak- and strong-hand dribbling ability and thus confidence. This drill also has six parts: zigzag, attack and retreat, stop and go, change of pace, reverse, and fake reverse.

Zigzag. Dribble two balls up the court in a zigzag manner; that is, dribbling diagonally to one side and then the other. Change direction by crossing both balls in front.

Attack and retreat. Dribble two balls up the court using an attack and retreat; that is, dribbling forward and then back without crossing your feet. Alternate the lead foot each time you attack and retreat.

Stop and go. Dribble two balls up the court using a stop-and-go dribble. Speed dribble by pushing both balls forward. Stop sharply, with your body under full control, and keep dribbling as you stop.

Change of pace. Dribble two balls up the court while changing pace (speed to control and control to speed). Use imagination to add deception, accelerating at various speeds.

Reverse. Dribble two balls while zigzagging up the court, changing direction by using a reverse pivot. Dribble both balls back to one side, then reverse pivot on your lead foot while pulling both balls close to where your body was before your reverse pivot.

Fake reverse. Dribble two balls while zigzagging up the court. Use a fake reverse before changing direction by dribbling both balls back to one side and turning your head and shoulders back. Then quickly turn your head and shoulders forward as you dribble both balls forward again.

Success Check

- Dribble with confidence.
- Work both weak and strong hands.

- For the zigzag and attack-and-retreat drills, attempt to complete two full-court trips with no more than one error on each trip.
- For the stop-and-go, change-of-pace, reverse, and fake reverse drills, attempt to complete two full-court trips with no more than three errors on each trip.

Score Your Success

For the zigzag and attack and retreat drills, give yourself 5 points if you complete two full-court trips with no more than one error on each trip. For the stop-and-go, change-of-pace, reverse, and fake reverse drills, give yourself 5 points if you complete two full-court trips with no more than three errors on each trip.

	Number of full-court trips	Number of errors	Points
Zigzag	___	___	___
Attack and retreat	___	___	___
Stop and go	___	___	___
Change of pace	___	___	___
Reverse	___	___	___
Fake reverse	___	___	___
Your score ___			

FOOTFIRE DRIBBLE

As you approach a defender in the open court, use the footfire dribble (figure 3.4) to stop moving forward while keeping the dribble alive. The footfire dribble enables you to gain balance and see or read the defender's positioning, especially at the end of a fast break. You will be a triple threat to shoot, pass, or drive as you dribble.

To execute the footfire dribble, quickly change from a speed dribble to a control dribble, coming to a stop while keeping the dribble alive. Dribble in place, facing the basket with feet shoulder-width apart. Move your feet up and down as rapidly and as close to the floor as you can, as if they are on a hot surface. This rapid footfire movement helps you gain complete balance while also temporarily freezing your defender. The effectiveness of the footfire dribble comes from gaining complete balance and control, reading the defender's position, and faking before you make your next move to shoot, pass, or drive.

| Figure 3.4 | Executing Footfire Dribble |

a

b

SPEED DRIBBLE

1. Keep head up, see the rim
2. Speed dribble, ball at waist level

FOOTFIRE DRIBBLE

1. Change from speed dribble to control dribble and continue dribbling
2. Move feet up and down rapidly (footfire)
3. Keep head up, rim in view
4. Become a triple threat to shoot, pass, or drive
5. Head fake before the next move

Misstep

You are unstable during the footfire dribble.

Correction

Emphasize complete balance and control with your feet shoulder-width apart and knees flexed.

CHANGE-OF-PACE DRIBBLE

The change-of-pace dribble (figure 3.5) is useful for deceiving and eluding a defender. To execute the change-of-pace dribble, change your dribble method from speed to control and quickly back to speed. The effectiveness of your change of pace depends on your deceptiveness and quickness. Push the dribble out to change quickly from a slower to a faster speed. In changing your pace, you have the advantage because *you* decide when to change speeds. With good deception and a forceful push of the dribble to quickly increase speed, you should be at least a step ahead of your defender just after changing pace from control dribble to speed dribble.

Figure 3.5   Change-of-Pace Dribble

a   b

CONTROL TO SPEED DRIBBLE

1. Keep head up, see the rim
2. Change to speed dribble at waist level
3. Push dribble out and run after it

SPEED TO CONTROL DRIBBLE

1. Keep head up, see the rim
2. Change to control dribble at knee level
3. Protect ball with body and nondribbling hand

Misstep

You do not control the dribble when changing from speed dribble to control dribble.

Correction

Widen your base and flex your knees to gain balance. Dribble the ball at knee level or lower.

RETREAT DRIBBLE

The retreat dribble is used to avoid trouble caused by defensive pressure. The retreat dribble is often combined with a front change-of-direction and speed dribble to elude a trap set by two defenders. Retreating with the dribble allows you to gain space for a front change-of-direction and speed dribble, creating room for you to get by the trap.

To execute the retreat dribble (figure 3.6), use short, quick retreat steps while dribbling backward. As you retreat, protect the ball and maintain a balanced stance. Make a controlled change-of-direction dribble and explode past the defenders with a speed dribble. Keep your head up with the rim in view so you can see and pass to open teammates.

Figure 3.6 | **Retreat Dribble**

a

b

RETREAT

1. Keep head up, see the rim
2. Change to retreat dribble with ball at knee level
3. Use short, quick retreat steps
4. Protect ball with body and nondribbling hand

SPEED DRIBBLE

1. Keep head up, see the rim
2. Change to speed dribble with ball at waist level
3. Push dribble out and run after it

Misstep

You have trouble retreating quickly.

Correction

Do not lean forward; maintain your balance, and use short, quick retreat steps.

CROSSOVER DRIBBLE

The crossover dribble is important when in the open court on a fast break, when you need to get open on a drive to the basket, or when you need to create an opening for your shot. Effectiveness in the crossover dribble is based on how sharply you change your dribble from one direction to another.

To execute a crossover dribble (figure 3.7), cross the ball in front of you at a backward angle, switching the dribble from one hand to the other. Dribble the ball close to you at knee level or lower with a control dribble and at waist level with a speed dribble. When you make the change of direction, get your nondribbling hand up and change your lead foot and body position for protection.

Figure 3.7   Crossover Dribble

a

b

CONTROL DRIBBLE

1. Keep head up, rim in view
2. Control dribble at knee level
3. Protect ball with body and nondribbling hand

CROSSOVER DRIBBLE

1. Cross ball in front at a backward angle, switching hands
2. Dribble close to body
3. Protect ball with body and nondribbling hand

Misstep

You dribble the ball too high or too wide when changing direction.

Correction

Dribble at knee level and close to your body.

Dribbling Drill 5. *One-Knee Crossover Dribble*

In addition to being a valuable offensive maneuver, the crossover dribble is an exciting move. To improve confidence and skill when making a crossover dribble with either the strong or weak hand, many players, including some in the NBA, now use the one-knee crossover dribble drill.

Kneel on one knee. Crossover dribble under the raised knee, dribbling back and forth between hands. On each crossover dribble, use as much force and quickness as possible. Flex your wrist and fingers for power, and point your fingers at your receiving hand to improve accuracy. Because you are dribbling the ball with as much force as possible, use a relaxed hand position to control the ball as it is received. Crossover dribble for 30 seconds, kneeling on your left knee and dribbling under your right. Switch legs and crossover dribble for 30 seconds while kneeling on your right knee and dribbling under your left. You may want to use a towel to cushion the knee you kneel on, especially if you plan to use the drill for more than one minute.

Success Check

- Flex your wrist and fingers.
- Relax your receiving hand.
- For each knee, attempt to complete 30 crossover dribbles with three or fewer errors in 30 seconds.

Score Your Success

Count the number of dribbles you complete under each knee in 30 seconds.

10 or fewer dribbles in 30 seconds = 0 points

11 to 14 dribbles in 30 seconds = 2 points

15 to 19 dribbles in 30 seconds = 4 points

20 to 24 dribbles in 30 seconds = 6 points

25 to 29 dribbles in 30 seconds = 8 points

30 or more dribbles in 30 seconds = 10 points

Your score ___

INSIDE-OUT DRIBBLE

The inside-out dribble is a fake change-of-direction dribble off a control or footfire dribble. This deceptive dribble can be used to get open on a drive to the basket or for a shot. Set up the deception by using a head fake to the opposite side to fake a change of direction.

When executing the inside-out dribble (figure 3.8), start by crossing the ball in front of you. Instead of releasing the ball and changing the dribble to your other hand, however, rotate your hand over the ball and dribble it outside your base back to the side from which you started. Dribble close to your body at knee level. Protect the ball with your body and nondribbling hand.

Figure 3.8   Inside–Out Dribble (Fake Crossover Drill)

a

b

FAKE CROSSOVER DRIBBLE

1. Keep head up, see the rim
2. Fake crossing ball in front
3. Quickly rotate hand over ball, then push ball back to same side with inside-out motion

DRIBBLE BALL BACK

1. Dribble ball back to same side outside base
2. Control dribble at knee level
3. Protect ball with body and nondribbling hand

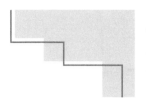

Misstep

Your inside-out dribble is not deceptive.

Correction

Make a head fake in the opposite direction.

REVERSE DRIBBLE

The reverse dribble keeps your body between the ball and the defender for protection as you change direction. The disadvantage, however, is that you temporarily take your eyes off other defenders who may attempt a blind-sided steal of the ball. The reverse dribble is best used as an offensive move to counter a strong defensive overplay to your dribbling side. It enables you to create your own shot in the opposite direction.

The reverse dribble (figure 3.9) is a two-dribble move. Start by dribbling backward, then pivot backward on your opposite foot while turning your shoulders back toward your dribbling-hand side. Bring your back foot forward as you pull a second dribble forward, close to your body, using the same hand. After completing the reverse-dribble move, change hands for your next dribble.

Figure 3.9　Reverse Dribble

a　　　　　　　　*b*　　　　　　　　*c*

DRIBBLE BALL BACK

1. Keep head up, see the rim
2. Dribble ball back behind body
3. Protect ball with body and nondribbling hand

REVERSE PIVOT

1. Reverse pivot on front foot
2. Step through with back foot
3. Pull second dribble forward

CHANGE HANDS

1. Change hands
2. Control dribble at knee level
3. Protect ball with body and nondribbling hand

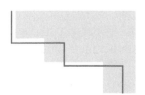

Misstep

You change hands on your dribble as you reverse, causing you to dribble too wide.

Correction

First dribble backward. As you reverse pivot, emphasize pulling the ball forward and close to your body using your same hand.

Dribbling Drill 6. *Dribble Tag*

The game of dribble tag develops the ability to dribble with the head up while quickly changing direction. Dribble tag requires five or more players. Each player has a basketball. Dribble within the half-court. One player is designated "it." The other players try to avoid being tagged by the designated player. If tagged, the tagged player becomes the new "it." The time limit for each set is two minutes.

To Increase Difficulty

- Have each player dribble with the weak hand only.

Score Your Success

Each player who avoids being tagged within the two-minute time limit scores 1 point. Play two-minute sets until one player scores 3 points and wins the game.

Your score ___

BEHIND-THE-BACK DRIBBLE

The behind-the-back dribble keeps your body between the ball and the defender for protection as you change direction. It is best used on the open floor when a defensive player in front is overplaying you to your dribbling side. Although developing the behind-the-back dribble takes more practice than other dribble moves, it is well worth the effort. Compared to the front change-of-direction dribble, the behind-the-back dribble allows you to keep your body between the ball and a defender. Compared to the reverse dribble, it allows you to change direction without taking your eyes off the rim or other defenders. The behind-the-back dribble is much quicker than the reverse dribble and almost as quick as the front change-of-direction dribble.

Like the reverse dribble, the behind-the-back dribble (figure 3.10) is a two-dribble move. Again, dribble backward. Move your pelvis forward as you pull a second dribble behind your back, close to your body, in a forward direction to your other hand. After your second dribble, change hands. Use your body and nondribbling hand for protection.

Figure 3.10	Behind-the-Back Dribble

a

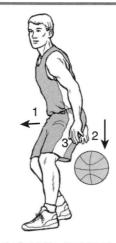

b

FIRST DRIBBLE BEHIND BODY

1. Keep head up, rim in view
2. Dribble ball behind body
3. Protect ball with body and nondribbling hand

PULL SECOND BEHIND BACK

1. Move pelvis forward
2. Pull second dribble behind back and then forward
3. Switch hands, controlling the dribble at knee level

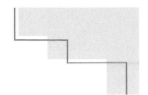

Misstep

You dribble too wide.

Correction

Emphasize pulling the ball forward and close to your body on the second dribble, using the same hand.

Dribbling Drill 7. *Dribble Cones*

Set up five cones: one at the baseline, one halfway between the baseline and half-court, one at half-court, one halfway between half-court and the opposite baseline, and one at the opposite baseline. The drill has three parts: crossover, behind-the-back dribble, and retreat dribble and crossover. Dribble at full speed during each part of the drill.

Crossover dribble. Start at the baseline cone. Dribble at full speed with your strong hand. After passing the second cone, make a crossover dribble and switch the ball to your weak hand. Speed dribble with your weak hand until you pass the next cone. Make a crossover dribble back to your strong hand. Continue in this manner to the opposite baseline. Turn and dribble back to the original cone, making a crossover dribble and switching hands as you pass each cone.

Behind-the-back dribble. This part of the drill is executed the same way except that you make a full-speed behind-the-back dribble after you pass each cone.

Retreat dribble and crossover. Speed dribble to the first cone. Execute a retreat dribble, making at least three retreat dribbles back. Perform a crossover dribble, then resume the speed dribble to the next cone.

Success Check

- Dribble with speed and confidence.
- For the crossover dribble, attempt to pass 10 cones in 30 seconds.
- For the behind-the-back dribble, attempt to pass 8 cones in 30 seconds.
- For the retreat dribble and crossover, attempt to pass 6 cones in 30 seconds.

Score Your Success

For the crossover dribble, give yourself 5 points for passing 10 cones in 30 seconds, 3 points if you pass 8 or 9 cones, 1 point if you pass 6 or 7 cones, and 0 points if you pass fewer than 6 cones. For the behind-the-back dribble, give yourself 5 points if you pass 8 cones in 30 seconds, 3 points if you pass 7 cones, 1 point if you pass 6 cones, and 0 points if you pass fewer than 6 cones. For the retreat dribble and crossover, give yourself 5 points if you pass 6 cones in 30 seconds, 3 points if you pass 5 cones, 1 point if you pass 4 cones, and 0 points if you pass fewer than 4 cones.

Number of cones passed using crossover dribble ___; points earned ___

Number of cones passed using behind-the-back dribble ___; points earned ___

Number of cones passed using retreat dribble and crossover ___; points earned ___

Your score ___ (points earned; maximum of 15)

RATE YOUR SUCCESS

If you can dribble the ball with confidence and control, you will have many options as you move the ball around the court. You will be able to move to create better passing lanes, outmaneuver the defense, and control the pace of play.

In the next step, we will look at the fundamentals of shooting the ball. Before going to step 4, however, look back at how you performed the drills in this step. For each of the drills presented in this step, enter the points you earned, then add up your scores to rate your total success.

Dribbling Drills

1. Dribble Warm-Up	____ out of 25
2. Knock the Ball Out of the Circle	____ out of 5
3. Two-Ball Dribbles	____ out of 50
4. Moving Two-Ball Dribble	____ out of 30
5. One-Knee Crossover Dribble	____ out of 10
6. Dribble Tag	____ out of 3
7. Dribble Cones	____ out of 15
TOTAL	____ *out of 138*

If you scored 80 or more points, congratulations! You have mastered the basics of this step and are ready to move on to step 4, shooting. If you scored fewer than 80 points, you may want to spend more time on the fundamentals covered in this step. Practice the drills again to develop mastery of the techniques and increase your scores.

Shooting

Shooting is the most important skill in basketball. The fundamental skills of passing, dribbling, defense, and rebounding may enable you to get a high-percentage shot, but you must still be able to make the shot. A large part of shooting is mental attitude. In addition to shooting skill, you must have confidence in yourself to shoot well. The integration of the mental and mechanical aspects of shooting fosters shooting success.

Development of an accurate shot forces your defender to play you tight and become vulnerable to a fake, allowing you to pass and drive as well as shoot. If you lack an accurate shot, a defender can play back in anticipation of a drive or a pass and be less susceptible to your fake. When you do not have the ball, your defender can play farther off you and be in better position to give defensive help to a teammate guarding another player. To be successful, a team must have players who can make the outside shot.

A great shooter is often called a *pure shooter* because of having a smooth, free-flowing shot or a soft touch. Some players think a pure shooter is naturally gifted—born that way. This is a misconception. Great shooters are made, not born.

A pure shooter such as former Boston Celtics great and Hall of Fame member Larry Bird driving hard around an opponent and then effortlessly pulling up for a soft jump shot appears to have been born a shooter. His thoughts are not on the mechanics of the shot, but rather on the position and movement of teammates and defenders. A pure shooter considers faking the shot, delivering a pass, driving for the basket, or reversing direction to pull the ball out and reset the offense. For Bird and other great shooters, the skill is automatic. Like other talented people, pure shooters perform their skills to maximum level without conscious thought. Each was a beginner at one time, however, and each developed into a pure shooter through dedicated practice.

Shooting is a skill you can practice by yourself. Once you understand correct mechanics, all you need is a ball, a basket, and an eagerness to improve. But it is also helpful to practice shooting under game conditions, including the pressure situations that occur late in a game. Practice with a partner providing the defensive pressure of an opponent. Remember that through practice you will develop shooting skill and confidence. You also can benefit from having a trained observer such as a coach, teacher, or a skilled player watch you shoot and provide corrective feedback. However, most of your shooting practice will occur when a coach or teacher is not present, so learn to analyze your shot's reaction on the rim to reinforce successful execution or reveal shooting errors and their possible causes.

SHOOTING CONFIDENCE

Believe in yourself. You want to have confidence in your ability to make the shot every time you shoot. Confident shooters control their thoughts, feelings, and shooting skill. Basketball is a mental as well as a physical game. Developing the mental aspect is a key to enhancing shooting, as well as performance in all fundamentals.

One way to improve your confidence is to realize that the basket is big. It is so large that three and a half balls can fit in the rim. This surprises most players. You can get on a ladder and fit three balls side by side over the rim and still have enough space to fit and turn your hand between each ball. Realizing that the basket is that big should give you a psychological boost.

Another way to boost your confidence is to keep your follow-through straight until the ball reaches the rim. Not only is this mechanically correct, but more important, you will look and act like a shooter.

Feel positive that each time you shoot, the ball will go in. Good shooters stay confident even when they hit a cold streak and miss a few shots. After a missed shot, mentally correct the miss and visualize a good shot. Repeating positive affirmation statements such as "I'm a shooter," "All net," or "Count it!" to yourself can promote confident thoughts about you and your ability to shoot. You can also boost your confidence by reminding yourself of past successes.

Being able to shoot under pressure distinguishes great shooters from good shooters. You want to take the shot not only when your team is ahead, but when the pressure is on. The direct correlation between shooting confidence and shooting success is the most consistent factor in great shooters.

POSITIVE SELF-TALK

As important as confidence is, accurate shooting requires more than positive thinking; it also requires shooting skill. Neither mental confidence nor mechanics alone is enough. Success results from integration of the mental and mechanical aspects of shooting.

When you think, you are in a sense talking to yourself. That talk can be either positive or negative. A technique called *positive self-talk* can help you integrate the mental and mechanical aspects of shooting, speeding the improvement of your shot. Positive self-talk uses key words to enhance performance.

Select words that reinforce correct mechanics, establish rhythm, and build confidence. The key words should be positive, concise (preferably one syllable), and personalized. A positive word that you associate with a successful shot is called an *anchor* word. Select your own personal anchor word that allows you to visualize your shot going in, such as *yes, net, whoosh, swish, in,* or *through.*

Words that key the correct mechanics of your shot are called *trigger* words. Some examples of trigger words are

- *high:* to start your shot high and prevent lowering the ball;
- *straight:* to make your shooting hand go straight to the basket;
- *front:* to key the position of the shooting hand facing the rim;
- *point:* to key the correct release of the ball off your index finger;
- *up:* to key a high arc;
- *through:* to key any part of your follow-through, including shoulders, arm, wrist, and fingers;
- *head in:* to key the follow-through of your head and shoulders toward the basket and eliminate leaning back or stepping back;
- *legs:* to key the use of your legs; and
- *down and up:* to key the down-and-up action of your legs that provides rhythm and force for your shot.

Identify two words that trigger the correct mechanics and one anchor word to reinforce shooting success. Sometimes a word can be both a trigger and an anchor word. For example, *through* as a trigger word can key the follow-through of your shoulders, arm, wrist, and fingers and can also be an anchor word for the ball going through the basket.

Say your words in rhythm, from the time your shooting motion starts with your legs until you release the ball off your index finger. For example, if *legs* and *through* are your trigger words and *yes* is your anchor word, you would say in rhythm with your shot: "Legs-through-yes!" It works better if you say your words aloud rather than to yourself.

Saying your personalized key words in an even rhythm establishes the rhythm of your shot and enhances your mechanics and confidence. Devote time to mental as well as physical practice. Relax and mentally practice saying your key words in the rhythm of your shot as you visualize shooting and seeing the ball go in the basket.

Your goal is to reduce conscious thought and promote automatic execution of your shot. Trigger words help make the mechanics of your shot automatic, and an anchor word, which reinforces a successful shot, helps build your confidence. As your shooting improves, one trigger word may suffice. Eventually, an anchor word may be all you need to trigger the automatic action of your shot.

SHOOTING RHYTHM

Skills should be smooth, free flowing, and rhythmical, and this is especially true in shooting. Mechanics are important, but you want to have good mechanics without being mechanical. Your shot should be smooth and rhythmical rather than mechanical. All parts of your shot should flow together in a sequential rhythm.

The initial force and rhythm for your shot comes from a down-and-up motion of your legs. Start with your knees slightly flexed. Bend your knees and then fully extend them in a down-and-up motion. Saying the key words *down and up* from

the start of your shot until the release of the ball will trigger the down-and-up action of your legs that provides rhythm and force for your shot. Your legs and shooting arm work together. As your legs go up, your arm goes up. As your legs reach full extension, your back, shoulders, and shooting arm extend in a smooth, continuous upward direction. Be sure to keep the ball high with your shooting hand facing the rim. Keeping the ball high fosters a quick release and also provides less chance for error. Use the down-and-up motion of your legs for rhythm rather than lowering the ball for rhythm.

EVALUATING YOUR SHOT

Learn to shoot correctly and then practice intelligently each day. Develop an understanding of your own shot. You can always benefit from having an instructor or coach watch you shoot. Most of your practice, however, occurs when a coach is not present. Personal feedback (information about your performance) can help you determine what adjustments to make. Three basic sources of performance feedback are observing the reaction of your shot on the rim, internally feeling your shot, and video analysis of your shooting form.

Analyzing a shot's reaction on the rim can reinforce successful execution or reveal most shooting errors and their possible causes. For example, the ball goes where your shooting arm, hand, and

finger direct it. If you miss to the right (or left), your shooting arm, hand, and finger are pointing in that direction. Perhaps your body faces in the direction of the miss rather than being square to the basket, or your elbow is out, causing your follow-through to go to the right.

If you see that the ball hits the right of the rim and rolls off to the left, you know you shot the ball with sidespin. In general, sidespin is caused by your shooting hand starting on the side of the ball and then rotating behind it. If you overrotate your shooting hand, the ball will hit the right rim with sidespin and roll left. If you underrotate, the ball will hit the left side of the rim and roll right. Sidespin is also caused by the ball sliding off your ring finger rather than your shooting finger.

Your sense of feel also yields clues. You might feel your shooting hand rotate to the right or the ball come off your ring finger instead of your shooting finger. Both mistakes will give the ball sidespin. An excellent method for developing feel is to shoot free throws with your eyes closed. Have a partner rebound and tell you whether the shot was successful. After a miss, your partner should tell you the specific direction of the miss and the reaction of the ball on the rim. By analyzing your shot, you can detect and correct errors before they become bad habits.

SHOOTING MECHANICS

Most players shoot seven basic shots: the one-hand set shot, the free throw, the jump shot, the three-point shot, the hook shot, the layup, and the runner. These shots all share certain basic mechanics, including sighting, balance, hand position, elbow-in alignment, shooting rhythm, and follow-through. The best way to develop your shot is to concentrate on only one or two mechanics at a time.

Sight

Focus your eyes on the basket, aiming just over the front of the rim for all except bank shots. Use a bank shot when you are at a 45-degree angle to the backboard. A 45-degree angle falls within the distance between the box and the middle hash mark on the lane line. The distance for the bank angle—called the *45-degree funnel*—widens as you move out. For shooting a bank shot, aim for the top near corner of the box on the backboard.

Sight your target as soon as possible and keep your eyes focused on the target until the ball reaches the goal. Your eyes should never follow the flight of the ball or your defender's hand. Concentrating on the target helps eliminate distractions such as shouting, towel waving, an opponent's hand, or even a hard foul.

Balance

Being in balance leads to power and rhythmic control in your shot. Your base, or foot position, is the foundation of your balance, and keeping your head over your feet (base) controls your balance.

Spread your feet comfortably to shoulder width and point your toes straight ahead. Pointing your toes straight aligns your knees, hips, and shoulders with the basket. The foot on the side of your shooting hand (right foot for a right-handed shot) is forward. The toe of your back foot is aligned with the heel of the foot on your shooting side (toe-to-heel relationship).

Flex your legs at the knees. This gives crucial power to your shot. Beginning and fatigued players often fail to flex their knees. To compensate for the lack of power from not using their legs, they tend to throw the ball from behind the head or shove the ball from the hip. Both actions produce errors.

Your head should be over your waist and feet. Your head controls your balance and should be slightly forward, with your shoulders and upper body inclining forward toward the basket. Your shoulders should be relaxed.

Hand Position

Hand position is the most misunderstood part of shooting. It is vital to start and finish your shot with your shooting hand facing the basket (behind the ball). Placing the nonshooting hand under the ball for balance is also important. This position, with the shooting hand facing the basket (behind the ball) and the nonshooting hand under the ball, is called the *block-and-tuck*. It leaves your shooting hand free to shoot the ball, rather than having to balance *and* shoot the ball.

Place your hands fairly close together. Relax both hands and spread the fingers comfortably. Keep the thumb of your shooting hand relaxed and not spread apart to avoid tension in your hand and forearm. A relaxed hand position (like a handshake) forms a natural cup, enabling the ball to contact the pads of your fingers and not your palm.

Place your nonshooting (balance) hand slightly under the ball. The weight of the ball balances on at least two fingers: the ring finger and the little finger. The arm of your balance hand should be in a comfortable position, with the elbow pointing slightly back and to the side.

Your shooting hand is turned toward the basket behind the ball, your index finger directly at the ball's midpoint. The ball is released off your index finger. On a free throw, you have time to align your index finger with the valve or other marking at the midpoint of the ball. Developing fingertip control and touch leads to a soft, accurate shot.

Elbow-In Alignment

Hold the ball comfortably in front of and above your shooting-side shoulder between your ear and shoulder. Keep your shooting elbow in. When your shooting elbow is in, the ball is aligned with the basket. Some players do not have the flexibility to turn the shooting hand toward the basket behind the ball while keeping the elbow in. In this case, first turn your shooting hand toward the basket behind the ball, then move the elbow in as far as your flexibility allows.

Shooting Motion

Shooting involves synchronizing the extension of your legs, back, shoulders, and shooting elbow and the flexion of your wrist and fingers. Shoot the ball with a smooth, evenly paced, rhythmical lifting motion.

The initial force and rhythm for your shot come from a down-and-up motion of your legs. Start with your knees slightly flexed. Bend your knees and then fully extend them in a down-and-up motion. Saying the key words *down and up* from the start of your shot until the release of the ball will trigger the down-and-up action of your legs, providing rhythm and force for your shot. Your legs and shooting arm work together. As your legs go up, your arm goes up. As your legs reach full extension, your back, shoulders, and shooting arm extend in a smooth, continuous upward direction. It is vital to keep the ball high with your shooting hand toward the basket. Use the down-and-up motion of your legs for rhythm rather than lowering the ball for rhythm. Keeping the ball high fosters a quick release and also provides less chance for error.

As your arm goes up, the ball is tipped back from your balance hand to your shooting hand. A good guide is to tip the ball back only until there is a wrinkle in the skin between your wrist and forearm. This angle provides a quick release and consistent follow-through. Direct your arm, wrist, and fingers straight toward the basket at a 45- to 60-degree angle, extending your shooting arm completely at the elbow. The final force and control of your shot comes from flexing your wrist and fingers forward and down. Release the ball off your index finger with soft fingertip touch to impart backspin on the ball and soften the shot. Keep your balance hand on the ball until the point of release.

The amount of force you should impart to the ball depends on the range of the shot. For short distances, the arm, wrist, and fingers provide most of the force. Long-range outside shots require more force from your legs, back, and shoulders. Smooth rhythm and a complete follow-through will also improve long-range shooting.

Follow-Through

After releasing the ball off the index finger, keep your arm up and fully extended with your index finger pointing straight to the target. The palm of your shooting hand should be turned down and the palm of your balance hand should be turned up. Keep your eyes on your target. Exaggerate your follow-through. Hold your arm up in a complete follow-through position until the ball reaches the basket, then react to the rebound or get into defensive position. Holding your follow-through until the ball reaches the basket is not only good mechanics, but it also makes you look and act like a shooter and increases confidence.

Shooting Drill 1. *Shooting Warm-Up*

Shooting close to the basket as a warm-up helps develop confidence and correct form and rhythm. Start in a balanced stance about eight feet in front of the basket and nine feet in front of the backboard with the ball in good shooting position in front of your shooting shoulder. Shoot, leaving your arm up on the follow-through until the ball hits the floor. Correct hand position—the shooting hand behind the ball—and release off the index finger will impart backspin, causing the ball to bounce back to you.

Say your personalized key words in rhythm with the shot from its start to the release of the ball. If you miss, visualize a successful shot with good form, again saying your key words. Get feedback from the feel of your shot and the reaction of the ball on the rim. Emphasize the key word you feel will produce a successful shot. For example, if your shot was short and you felt that the miss came from not using your legs, emphasize the word *legs.* If the shot was short due to an incomplete follow-through, emphasize the word *through.* If the shot was short due to a slow rhythm, quicken the down-and-up movement of your legs as you say the key words *down and up* with a quicker rhythm. If your shot was long, shoot with a higher arc using the word

up. If your shot missed to the side, correct the shot using the key word *straight.*

To Increase Difficulty

- After making five consecutive shots from 9 feet, increase the distance to 12 feet.
- After making five consecutive shots from 12 feet, move back to the foul line (15 feet from the backboard).

Success Check

- Use your key words in rhythm.
- Feel your shot.
- Use correct shooting mechanics.
- Successfully complete five consecutive shots from each distance.

Score Your Success

Give yourself 1 point for each shot made. Attempt to make five consecutive shots from each distance.

Consecutive shots made from 9 feet ___

Consecutive shots made from 12 feet ___

Consecutive shots made from 15 feet ___

Your score ___ (15 points maximum)

Shooting Drill 2. *One-Hand Shooting*

One-hand shooting, using either the strong hand or the weak hand, is an excellent way to develop your ability to start and complete a shot with your shooting hand facing forward. This helps eliminate side rotation. It also fosters lifting the ball to the basket rather than throwing the ball. This drill is particularly beneficial if your nonshooting hand tends to interfere with your shot (for example, if you thumb the ball with your nonshooting hand). The one-hand shooting drill allows you to focus on having your shooting hand in the correct position behind the ball with good elbow-in alignment and lifting the ball to the basket with a short stroke.

Start about nine feet from the basket with your shooting hand facing the rim. Your hand is above your shoulder between your ear and shoulder. Use your nonshooting hand to place the ball in your shooting hand. Do not reach for the ball with your shooting hand. Now lower your nonshooting hand

to your side. Balance the ball in your shooting hand with your index finger at the ball's midpoint. Check that your forearm is at a right angle to the floor and that it forms an *L* with your upper arm. This position helps you lift the ball to the basket rather than throw it. Check for elbow-in alignment to keep the ball in front of and above your shooting shoulder. Use your personalized key words in rhythm with your shot or when you are correcting your shot. If you tend to bring the ball back and throw it rather than lift it to the basket, consider using *front* or *lift* as a key word. If your shot misses because your elbow is out, consider saying *in* as a key word.

You may have a tendency to shove the ball and miss toward the opposite side of the rim when using your weak hand. Emphasize using the down-and-up movement of your legs and lift the ball to the basket. Consider using *down and up* as key words.

Success Check

- Repeat your key words in rhythm with your shot.
- Use correct shooting mechanics.
- Attempt to make five consecutive shots with both your strong and weak hands.

Give yourself 1 point for each shot made. Attempt to make five consecutive shots with each hand.

Consecutive shots made with strong hand ___

Consecutive shots made with weak hand ___

Your score ___ (10 points maximum)

Shooting Drill 3. On-Your-Back Shooting

This drill focuses on correct technique, such as shooting hand behind the ball, elbow-in alignment, correct release off the index finger, follow-through, and catching the ball in position to shoot.

Lie on your back with the ball above your shooting shoulder. Place your shooting hand behind the ball with your index finger at the midpoint of the ball. Check for elbow-in alignment. Shoot the ball up into the air with complete follow-through (full elbow extension). You want the ball to return straight back to you so that you do not have to move your hands to catch it. Say your key words in rhythm with your shot. If the ball does not return to you, visualize a successful shot and good form, again saying your key words, and use feedback from the feel of your shot and the direction of the ball. Emphasize the key word you feel will produce a successful shot. For example, if your shot is off to the side, concentrate on making your arm go straight and say "Straight." If the ball goes off the wrong finger, producing sidespin, you might say

"Point." If you catch the ball with your hand on its side, consider using the key words *hand* or *catch.*

To Increase Difficulty

- After making five consecutive shots, increase the height of each shot.
- Close your eyes.

Success Check

- Use correct shooting technique.
- Visualize a successful shot and say your key words.

Give yourself 1 point for each shot with complete follow-through (full elbow extension) that returns straight back to you. Try to produce five consecutive shots that return straight back to you.

Your score ___ (5 points maximum)

Shooting Drill 4. Shooting From a Chair

Shooting from a chair fosters consistency in lifting the ball to the basket and extending the elbow completely on the follow-through. This drill develops shooting range and helps a player who has the tendency to throw the ball. Shooting while sitting in a chair requires you to use your back, shoulders, and full arm extension to generate force for the shot.

Set the chair nine feet in front of the basket. Practice centering yourself, balancing yourself mentally and physically. When you are centered, you are in a state of readiness; your muscles relax and you breathe a little deeper and more slowly than usual. Being centered also involves balancing your weight evenly for the skill you will be performing, which is particularly helpful for gaining power. Center yourself with confident thoughts and con-

trolled breathing, and evenly balance your weight. Centering allows you to raise your center of gravity and transfer your force from back to shoulders to generate full power for the shot.

Place your shooting hand behind the ball with your index finger at the ball's midpoint. Check for elbow-in alignment. Work for the sequential buildup of force from your back, shoulders, arm, wrist, and fingers as you shoot. Say your personalized key words in the rhythm of your shot from its start to the release of the ball. Visualize a successful shot with good form. Use feedback from the feel of the shot and its distance, direction, and reaction on the rim. If the shot was short, *through* is a good key word. To increase distance, try using *back-shoulder-through* for the sequential buildup of force.

To Increase Difficulty

- After making five consecutive shots from 9 feet, move the chair back until you are 12 feet from the basket.
- After making five consecutive shots from 12 feet, move the chair back until you are 15 feet from the basket (free throw distance).
- After making five consecutive shots from 15 feet, move the chair back until you are 18 feet from the basket.
- After making five consecutive shots from 18 feet, move the chair back until you are 21 feet from the basket (top of circle).

Success Check

- Pay attention to proper alignment and form.
- Say your key words in rhythm with the shot.

- Attempt to make five consecutive shots at each distance.

Score Your Success

Try to make five consecutive shots at each distance. You earn 1 point each time you make five consecutive shots.

Consecutive shots made at 9 feet ___; points earned ___

Consecutive shots made at 12 feet ___; points earned ___

Consecutive shots made at 15 feet ___; points earned ___

Consecutive shots made at 18 feet ___; points earned ___

Consecutive shots made at 21 feet ___; points earned ___

Your score ___ (5 points maximum)

ONE-HAND SET SHOT

An inside jump shot involves jumping and then shooting the ball at the top of your jump. The arm, wrist, and fingers apply most of the force. On a one-hand set shot (figure 4.1), lift the ball simultaneously with the upward extension of your legs, back, and shoulder.

If your shot is short, usually it is because you are not using your legs, not following through, or are using a slow or uneven rhythm. Use neural feedback—feeling—to determine whether you need more force from your legs, a more consistent follow-through (keeping your arm up until the ball reaches the basket), or a quicker or more evenly paced rhythm.

If your shot is long, usually it is because your shooting arm extends on too flat a trajectory (less than 45 degrees), your shoulders lean back, or your hands are too far apart on the ball, preventing you from lifting it. Move your shoulders to a relaxed forward position, move your hands closer together, or raise your shooting arm higher to put a higher arc on your shot.

If you lean your shoulders back, step back, or use incomplete and inconsistent elbow extension, your shot likely will be inconsistently short or long. Follow through with your head in to prevent leaning back or stepping back. Extend your arm completely for every shot.

If your right-handed shot hits the left side of the rim, you are not squaring up to face the basket or you are starting with the ball on your right hip or too far to your right, shoving the ball from right to left as you shoot. Shoving the ball results from not using your legs for power. Square your body to the basket, setting the ball on the shooting side of your head between your ear and shoulder with your elbow in. Make your shooting arm, wrist, and finger go straight through to the basket.

If your shot lacks range, control, and consistency, or you miss short, long, or to either side, you probably lower the ball, bring it behind your head or shoulder, or throw the ball to the basket with an inconsistent follow-through. These errors result from not using your legs for power. Start your shot with the ball high in front of your ear and shoulder. Emphasize force from your legs, and complete the follow-through by keeping your arm up until the ball reaches the basket.

When a shot hits the rim and circles out or skims from front to back and out, rather than hitting the rim and dropping in, it means you are starting your shot with your shooting hand on the side of the ball and rotating the hand behind the ball as you shoot or are releasing the ball off your ring finger instead of your shooting finger. Another possible cause is thumbing the ball—pushing the ball with the thumb of your nonshooting hand. These mistakes give the ball sidespin instead of backspin. Start your shot with your hands in block-and-tuck position—your shooting hand behind the ball and your balance hand under the ball. Release the ball off your index finger.

If your mechanics appear to be correct but the shot lacks control and the ball hits hard on the rim, you probably rest the ball on your palm. Relax the thumb of your shooting hand and set the ball on your finger pads with your palm off the ball. Then you can release the ball off your index finger with backspin, control, and a soft touch.

Figure 4.1   One-Hand Set Shot

SHOOTING HAND HIGH AND FRONT

1. Eyes on target
2. Feet shoulder-width apart and toes straight
3. Knees flexed
4. Shoulders relaxed
5. Nonshooting hand under ball and shooting hand facing front of rim with the thumb relaxed
6. Elbow in
7. Ball high between ear and shoulder

SHOOT ONE HAND SET SHOT

1. Look at target
2. Extend legs, back, shoulders
3. Extend elbow
4. Flex wrist and fingers forward
5. Release off index finger
6. Keep balance hand on ball until release
7. Follow through with arm extended, index finger pointing to the target, shooting hand palm down, and nonshooting hand palm up

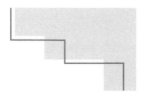

Misstep

Your mechanics appear to be correct, but you still miss the basket.

Correction

Have someone watch your eyes as you shoot. You probably do not concentrate your eyes on the target. Concentrate on the target, not on the ball's flight, until the ball reaches the basket.

FREE THROW

Successful free throw shooting requires sound mechanics, a routine, relaxation, rhythm, concentration, and confidence. Routine, relaxation, and rhythm contribute to concentration and confidence.

Think positively. You always shoot from the same place on the line. No one is guarding you. The basket is big. Three and a half balls can fit in the rim. With confidence—and sound mechanics—you cannot miss. Act like a shooter. Exaggerate your follow-through by keeping your eyes on the target and your shooting arm up until the ball reaches the basket.

Develop a sound routine for the free throw to check preshot mechanics. A routine also helps you relax, focus, and shoot with rhythm. Most important, using a routine will enhance your confidence. The routine can include dribbling a set number of times, checking mechanics, using visualization to practice your free throw mentally just before shooting it, and taking a deep breath to relax. Adopt a sound routine and stay with it; it is a mistake to copy fads or repeatedly change your routine.

Most players use the one-hand shot for a free throw (figure 4.2), taking the time to control each of the basic mechanics: sighting, balance, hand position, elbow-in alignment, shooting rhythm, and follow-through. Here is a sample routine that you can adjust to fit you. Stand a few feet behind the free throw line until the official hands you the ball. You will stay more relaxed there. If you hear negative remarks from the crowd or recognize your own negative thoughts, interrupt them with the word *stop*. Take a deep breath and let go of the negative thoughts as you exhale. Replace them with a positive statement of affirmation such as "I'm a shooter," "Nothing but net," or "Count it!"

Once you receive the ball, position your feet, making certain to line up the ball (not your head) with the middle of the basket. Use the small indentation mark in the floor at the exact middle of the free throw line that marks the free throw circle. Set your shooting foot slightly outside this mark, lining up the ball with the middle of the basket.

Set up in a balanced stance. Some players bounce the ball a certain number of times to help them relax. When you bounce the ball, keep your shooting hand on top. This helps you to have your shooting hand facing the basket when you set the ball high in position to shoot. Use a relaxed hand position, and line up your index finger with the valve on the ball. Next, check your elbow-in alignment. Take a deep breath to relax. Before shooting, visualize a successful shot. Visualization just before you shoot can produce a more free-flowing, smooth rhythm and increase confidence.

Just before shooting, concentrate on your target just over the front of the rim. Keep your focus on the target as you shoot. Start your shot high and use the down-and-up motion of your legs for rhythm rather than lowering the ball for rhythm. The down-and-up motion of your legs provides momentum for your shot and is particularly helpful when shooting late in the game when your legs are tired. By starting the ball high and using your legs for rhythm, you will lessen the chance for error that can come with lowering the ball. Exaggerate your follow-through, keeping your eyes on the target and your shooting arm up until the ball reaches the basket.

Learn to relax when shooting free throws. You have more time to think with free throws than with other shots. Trying too hard may cause undue physical or emotional tension. Use deep breathing to relax your mind and body. For a free throw, you should particularly relax your shoulders; take a deep breath and let your shoulders drop and loosen. Do the same for your arms, hands, and fingers. Learn to relax other parts of your body. Controlling your breathing and relaxing your muscles are especially useful in a free throw routine.

Shoot the free throw with a smooth, free-flowing rhythm. Use personalized key words to help establish a smooth, sequential rhythm for free throw shooting. Say your words in the rhythm of your shot. For example, if your trigger words are *legs* and *through* and your anchor word is *yes*, put them together—*legs-through-yes!*—in rhythm with your shot, from the start of your shot until the ball is released. Using personalized key words this way establishes your rhythm, enhances your mechanics, and builds confidence.

Confidence and concentration go together. Using affirmation statements can promote confident thoughts about yourself and your ability to shoot. For example, you can state to yourself, "I am a shooter," or remind yourself of past successes.

The last thing to do before shooting is to concentrate on your target just over the front of the rim. The most important step before initiating the free throw motion, however, is to eliminate all distractions from your mind, focusing on the basket. Concentrate on shooting a successful shot, and let go of the shot that missed or what you might do wrong. Stay in the present. Visualize shooting a successful free throw while you emphasize your anchor word: *Yes! Net! In! Through!* Most of all, enjoy the moment. Keep your focus on the target as you shoot. See it, shoot it, count it!

If you find you use a more uneven or slower rhythm to shoot free throws than when shooting from the field, train yourself to say your key words in the even rhythm of your shot, timing them from the start of your shot until the ball is released.

Don't be distracted by the crowd or your own negative thoughts. Concentrate. When you hear a negative statement or recognize your own negative thoughts, eliminate the negatives with the word *stop* and use positive affirmations. Visualize a successful free throw while saying your anchor word. Focus on the target.

If your free throw is short because you step off the line to get back on defense, exaggerate the follow-through by keeping your arm up and staying on the line until the ball reaches the basket.

Figure 4.2 | Free Throw

a

b

FREE THROW ROUTINE

1. Shooting foot slightly outside mark
2. Balanced stance
3. Nonshooting hand under ball, shooting hand facing basket with the thumb relaxed
4. Elbow in
5. Ball between ear and shoulder
6. Shoulders relaxed
7. Concentrate on target just over front of rim

SHOOT WITH CONFIDENCE AND RHYTHM

1. Say key words in rhythm
2. Extend legs, back, and shoulders
3. Extend elbow
4. Flex wrist and fingers forward
5. Release ball off index finger
6. Keep balance hand on ball until release
7. Shoot with confidence and rhythm
8. Follow through with arm extended, index finger pointing to the target, and arm up until the ball goes through the net

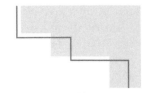

Misstep

You feel tense before and during your free throw.

Correction

Use deep breathing to relax your mind and body. Breathe in deeply and exhale fully. Relax your shoulders, letting them drop and loosen. Do the same for your arms, hands, and fingers. Learn to relax other parts of your body as necessary.

Free Throw Drill 1. *Daily Practice*

Shoot a set number of free throws each day. Practice sets of 10 free throws after other drills. Because a player rarely shoots more than two free throws in a row during a game, when doing this drill, never take more than two successive free throws without moving off the line.

Practice under pressure. Use imagination, and compete against yourself. For example, imagine that time is out and that making the free throw will win the game. Record the number of free throws you make out of every 100 attempts, and constantly challenge your own record. Do the same with consecutive free throws.

Be confident. Use positive affirmation statements before you go to the line, and visualize a successful shot just before shooting. Having a routine helps build confidence for free throws. Use deep breathing and muscle relaxation techniques. The final step before shooting is to eliminate all distractions and focus on the basket. Say your personalized key words in rhythm from the start of your free throw to the release of the ball. If you miss, visualize a successful free throw with good form, again saying your key words.

Success Check

- Use your routine and say your key words before shooting a free throw.
- Be confident in your ability to make each free throw.
- Visualize a successful shot before shooting the ball.

Score Your Success

Shoot 100 free throws. Score yourself based on the total number of free throws made. Record your score. Also record the highest number of consecutive free throws. Challenge your record every time you perform the drill.

59 or fewer = 0 points

60 to 69 = 1 point

70 to 79 = 2 points

80 to 89 = 3 points

90 to 99 = 4 points

100 = 5 points

Your score ___

Consecutive free throws made ___

Free Throw Drill 2. *Eyes Closed*

Research has shown that combining free throw practice with eyes closed and free throw practice with eyes open improves shooting more than free throw practice with eyes open alone. Shooting with eyes closed removes vision as your dominant sense, heightening your other senses, particularly the kinesthetic sense (feel of body movement) and touch.

Visualize a successful shot and focus on the basket immediately before closing your eyes. Shoot a free throw with your eyes closed. Have a partner rebound the ball and give you feedback on each shot, including the reaction of the ball on the rim. Use this feedback and your kinesthetic and tactile senses to adjust your shot as necessary. Complete 20 free throw attempts. Your partner should help you keep track of how many shots you make out of 20 and how many consecutive shots you make.

Success Check

- Use correct free throw shooting form.
- Rely on your kinesthetic and tactile senses rather than on your eyes.
- Use your key words and visualization to help you make the shot.

Score Your Success

Shoot 20 free throw attempts. Score yourself based on the total number of free throws made. Record your score. Also record the highest number of consecutive free throws. Challenge your record every time you perform the drill.

7 or fewer = 0 points

8 to 10 = 1 point

11 to 13 = 2 points

14 to 16 = 3 points

17 to 19 = 4 points

20 = 5 points

Your score ___

Consecutive free throws made ___

JUMP SHOT

A jump shot (figure 4.3) is similar to a one-hand set shot except for two basic adjustments. In a jump shot, you align the ball higher and shoot after jumping, rather than shooting with the simultaneous extension of your legs. Because you jump first and then shoot, your upper body, arm, wrist, and fingers must generate more force.

Align the ball between your ear and shoulder but raise the ball, sighting the target below rather than above the ball, as you would in a one-hand set shot. Place your forearm at a right angle to the floor and your upper arm parallel to the floor or higher. Jump straight up off both feet, fully extending your ankles, knees, back, and shoulders. Do not float forward, backward, or to the side.

How high you jump depends on the range of the shot. On an inside jump shot, when you are closely guarded, your legs should generate enough

force to jump higher than the defender. You shoot at the top of your jump; therefore, your arm, wrist, and fingers provide most of the force. You may feel as though you are hanging in the air as you release the ball.

On most long-range outside jump shots, you have more time; therefore, you don't need to jump higher than your defender. You will be able to use more force from your legs for shooting the ball rather than for gaining height on the jump. You will feel that you are shooting the ball *as* you jump rather than at the top of your jump. Strive for a balanced jump that enables you to shoot without straining. Balance and control are more important than gaining maximum height on your jump. Smooth rhythm and complete follow-through also are important components of long-range jump shooting. Land in balance in the same spot as your takeoff.

Figure 4.3 Jump Shot

a

b

SHOOTING HAND HIGH AND FRONT

1. Feet shoulder-width apart, toes straight
2. Knees flexed
3. Shoulders relaxed
4. Elbow in
5. Ball high between ear and shoulder
6. Nonshooting hand under ball, shooting hand facing front of rim

SHOOT JUMP SHOT

1. Jump, then shoot; jump height depends on range of shot
2. Extend legs, back, shoulders
3. Extend elbow
4. Flex wrist and fingers forward
5. Release ball off index finger
6. Keep balance hand on ball until release
7. Execute follow-through

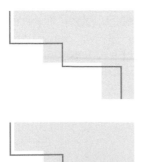

Misstep

You lower the ball for rhythm, which lengthens the shooting stroke, creating more room for error. This makes the shot easier to block.

Correction

Keep the ball high and use the down-and-up action of your legs for rhythm rather than lowering the ball.

Misstep

You float in, back, or to the side, which causes you to miss long, short, or to the side.

Correction

Jump and land in the same spot.

Jump Shot Drill 1. *Jump Shot Warm-Up*

The objectives of this drill are to develop confidence, form, rhythm, and range for making jump shots. Start in a balanced stance about nine feet in front of the basket. Perform jump shots from that distance, using correct form for each shot. For a jump shot, the ball is held higher than for a one-hand set shot. The height of your jump depends on the range. When close to the basket, you should release the ball at the top of your jump, with your arm, wrist, and fingers providing most of the force. On long-range outside jump shots, you don't need to jump as high, allowing you to use more force from your legs for the shot. Strive for a balanced jump so you can follow through until the ball hits the floor. Say your three personalized words in rhythm from the start of your shot to the release of the ball.

To Increase Difficulty

- After making five consecutive shots from 9 feet, move back to 12 feet.
- After making five consecutive shots from 12 feet, move back to the foul line (15 feet from the backboard).
- After making five consecutive shots from 15 feet, move back again. Continue to move back until you are unable to make five consecutive jump shots.

Success Check

- Say your key words in rhythm with your shot.
- Jump the correct height for the shot, depending on your range.
- Use proper mechanics for the jump shot.
- Attempt to make five consecutive jump shots at each distance.

Score Your Success

Record the number of shots made at each distance. Give yourself 1 point each time you successfully complete five consecutive jump shots.

Consecutive jump shots made at 9 feet ___; points earned ___

Consecutive jump shots made at 12 feet ___; points earned ___

Consecutive jump shots made at 15 feet (free throw distance) ___; points earned ___

Consecutive jump shots made at 18 feet ___; points earned ___

Consecutive jump shots made at 21 feet (college three-point line) ___; points earned ___

Consecutive jump shots made at 24 feet (NBA three-point line) ___; points earned ___

Your score ___ (6 points maximum)

Jump Shot Drill 2. *Bank Jump Shot Warm-Up*

The bank jump shot warm-up drill is the same as the regular jump shot warm-up drill except that you shoot from a 45-degree angle on each side of the basket. Start in a balanced stance at a 45-degree angle to the backboard, within the distance between the box and the middle hash mark on the lane. The distance of the bank angle, which widens as you move out, is called the *45-degree funnel.* For bank shots, aim for the top near corner of the box on the backboard, saying your key words in rhythm from the start of your shot to the release of the ball. Shoot from both the right and left sides of the basket.

To Increase Difficulty

- After making five consecutive bank jump shots from 9 feet on both the right and left sides of the basket, move back to 12 feet.
- After making five consecutive bank jump shots from 12 feet on both the right and left sides of the basket, move back to 15 feet.
- After making five consecutive bank jump shots from 15 feet on both the right and left sides of the basket, move back to 18 feet.

Success Check

- Say your key words in rhythm with the shot.
- Use correct mechanics for the bank jump shot.
- Successfully complete five bank jump shots from each side and each distance.

Score Your Success

Record the number of bank jump shots you make on each side and at each distance. Give yourself 1 point each time you successfully complete five consecutive bank jump shots.

Consecutive bank jump shots, 9 feet, right side ___; points earned ___

Consecutive bank jump shots, 9 feet, left side ___; points earned ___

Consecutive bank jump shots, 12 feet, right side ___; points earned ___

Consecutive bank jump shots, 12 feet, left side ___; points earned ___

Consecutive bank jump shots, 15 feet, right side ___; points earned ___

Consecutive bank jump shots, 15 feet, left side ___; points earned ___

Consecutive bank jump shots, 18 feet, right side ___; points earned ___

Consecutive bank jump shots, 18 feet, left side ___; points earned ___

Your score ___ (8 points maximum)

THREE-POINT SHOT

For a three-point shot (figure 4.4), set up far enough behind the line to avoid concern about stepping on the line and to focus your sight on the basket. Do not look down at the line and lose sight of your target. Use a balanced jump shot, shooting the ball without straining as you jump.

The longer the shot, the more important are correct mechanics, sequence, and rhythm. On three-point shots, you usually have time and do not need much height on your jump. You can use more force from your legs and can generate additional force by stepping into the shot. You can also benefit from the sequential buildup of force from your back and shoulders. It feels as if you are shooting the ball as you jump, rather than at the top of your jump (as with outjumping your defender on a closely guarded inside shot).

Strive for a balanced jump that enables you to shoot without straining. Balance and control are more important than maximum height. Smooth rhythm and a complete follow-through enhance long-range jump shooting, and as with all jump shots, on three-point shots, you should land in balance in the same spot as your takeoff.

Successful three-point shooters excel in having smooth, even rhythm; the sequential use of legs, back, and shoulders; correct mechanics, such as hand position and elbow-in alignment; and complete follow-through.

Figure 4.4 | Three-Point Shot

a

b

HANDS AND FEET READY

1. Positioned behind three-point line
2. Feet shoulder-width apart, toes straight
3. Knees flexed
4. Elbow in
5. Ball high between ear and shoulder
6. Shoulders relaxed
7. Nonshooting hand under ball, shooting hand facing basket with thumb relaxed
8. Step into shot, if necessary

SHOOT WITH CONFIDENCE AND RHYTHM

1. Jump without straining, shooting on the way up
2. Shoot with confidence and rhythm
3. Generate sequential power from legs, back, shoulders
4. Extend elbow
5. Flex wrist and fingers forward
6. Release ball off index finger
7. Keep balance hand on ball until release
8. Execute follow-through

Misstep

Your shot is short.

Correction

When a three-point shot is short, usually it is because (1) you do not use your legs, back, and shoulders; (2) you do not follow through; or (3) you have a slow or uneven rhythm. Determine through feel which element is the problem. Emphasize generating force from your legs, back, and shoulders. Complete the follow-through by keeping your arm up until the ball reaches the basket. Increase the speed of your rhythm or pace it more evenly.

HOOK SHOT

The advantage of the hook shot (figure 4.5) is that it is difficult to block, even for taller opponents. The hook shot is generally limited to an area close to the basket, a range of 10 to 12 feet. Learn to shoot the hook shot with either hand to greatly increase your effectiveness in the lane. When well executed, the hook forces an opponent to overplay you, and a fake hook can create an opening in the opposite direction for a power move, drive, or pass. Contrary to popular belief, the hook shot is not difficult to learn. With practice, you will be able to use your weak as well as your strong hand for shooting the hook shot.

Start in a balanced stance with your back to the basket, feet spread shoulder-width apart, and knees flexed. Sight your target by looking over your shoulder in the direction you will turn to shoot. Within a 45-degree angle of the backboard (above the box and below the middle hash mark on the lane line), accuracy is aided by using the backboard to soften the shot. When banking the shot, aim for the top near corner of the backboard. If you aren't at a 45-degree angle, aim just over the rim.

In most instances, you will make a ball fake in the opposite direction of your intended shot. After your fake, move your shooting hand under and your nonshooting hand behind and slightly on top of the ball. This is called the *hook shot position*. Flex the elbow of your shooting arm and position it at your hip, keeping the ball in direct alignment with your shooting shoulder.

Using the foot opposite your shooting side, step away from the defender. As you step, hold the ball back and protect it with your head and shoulders, rather than leading with the ball. As you step, pivot in, turning your body toward the basket. Lift the knee on your shooting side and jump off your pivot foot.

Shoot by lifting the ball to the basket with a hook motion as you extend your shooting arm in an ear-to-ear direction. Flex your wrist and fingers toward the target and release the ball off your index finger, keeping the balance hand on the ball until the release. Land in balance, ready to rebound any missed shot with two hands and score using a power move. A missed hook shot should be thought of as a pass to yourself. A defender attempting to block your hook shot will not be in position to box out and prevent you from getting the rebound.

If you put side rotation on the ball, the shot will hit the rim and, rather than pulling in, will circle out or skim from front to back and out. If you start with your hands on the sides of the ball and rotate them to the side as you shoot, or release the ball off your ring finger instead of your index finger, you will put side rotation on the ball. Both mistakes produce sidespin instead of backspin. Start in hook shot position, your shooting elbow aligned with your hip. Place your shooting hand under the ball and your balance hand slightly behind and on top of the ball. Release the ball off your index finger to get backspin, and the ball will pull in if it hits the rim.

If your right-handed shot hits the right side of the rim, you are bringing your arm in front of your head on the follow-through. If your right-handed shot hits the left side of the rim, you are bringing your arm behind your head on the follow-through. To correct either problem, start by holding the ball in hook shot position, your shooting elbow aligned with your hip, allowing you to extend your arm with an ear-to-ear motion straight to the basket.

If your shot is inconsistently short or long, you probably have incomplete and inconsistent elbow extension. Extend your arm completely on every shot.

Figure 4.5 **Hook Shot**

SHOOTING HAND UNDER BALL

1. Back to basket
2. Feet shoulder-width apart
3. Knees flexed
4. Shoulders relaxed
5. Shooting hand under ball, nonshooting hand behind ball
6. Elbow at hip
7. Ball back, protected by head and shoulders

STEP AND SHOOT HOOK SHOT

1. Step and pivot in
2. Lift ball in ear-to-ear direction
3. Extend elbow
4. Flex wrist and fingers
5. Release ball off index finger
6. Keep balance hand on ball until release
7. Land in balance, ready to rebound

Misstep

You lose protection and control of the ball as you shoot.

Correction

You are taking your balance hand off the ball too soon. Keep your balance hand on the ball until you release it.

Hook Shot Drill 1. *Hook Shot Warm-Up*

In this drill, you will shoot hook shots with both your strong and weak hands. Start with your head under the front of the rim, facing the sideline in a balanced stance. Hold the ball in hook shot position with your shooting elbow at your side, your shooting hand under the ball, and your balance hand slightly behind and on top of the ball. Shoot the hook by lifting the ball to the basket in an ear-to-ear motion, keeping your balance hand on the ball until the release. Use two hands to catch the ball as it comes through the basket or to rebound on a missed shot. Treat a missed shot as a pass to yourself.

Success Check

- Shoot with confidence.
- Use correct mechanics.
- Attempt to make five consecutive hook shots with each hand.

Score Your Success

Record the number of hook shots made with each hand. Give yourself 5 points each time you make five consecutive hook shots.

Hook shots made with strong hand ___; points earned ___

Hook shots made with weak hand ___; points earned ___

Your score ___ (10 points maximum)

Hook Shot Drill 2. *Hook Shot Warm-Up With Crossover Step*

After you can make five consecutive warm-up hook shots with each hand, move to the hook shot with a crossover step. Start with your head under the front of the rim. Face the sideline while holding the ball in hook shot position. Make a crossover step toward the foul line with your inside foot, the one that is closer to the basket, and shoot a hook shot. Pivot toward the basket on the crossover step and lift your shooting-side knee as you shoot.

Success Check

- Use your key words as you make the shot.
- Use correct hook shot mechanics.
- Try to make five consecutive hook shots with each hand.

Score Your Success

Record the number of hook shots made with each hand. Give yourself 5 points each time you make five consecutive hook shots.

Hook shots made with strong hand ___; points earned ___

Hook shots made with weak hand ___; points earned ___

Your score ___ (10 points maximum)

Hook Shot Drill 3. *Alternate Hand Hook Shooting (Mikan Drill)*

In this drill, you will alternate shooting right-handed and left-handed bank hook shots using a crossover step. For the first shot, use your right hand. Start under the rim, facing the right sideline. Hold the ball in hook shot position with your right hand under the ball. Execute a crossover step with your inside foot at a 45-degree angle, pivoting toward the basket on the step and lifting your right knee as you shoot. Shoot a right-handed bank hook shot, aiming for the high near corner of the box on the backboard. Catch the ball with two hands after either a made shot or a rebound. Place the ball in hook shot position with your left hand under the ball. Face the left sideline and make a crossover step with your right foot at a 45-degree angle. Pivot and shoot a left-handed bank shot, catching the ball with two hands. Continue the drill, alternating between right- and left-handed hook shots.

Success Check

• Use both hands to catch the ball after a made shot or to rebound a missed shot.

• Try to make 10 consecutive hook shots with each hand while using the crossover step.

Score Your Success

Record the number of hook shots made with each hand. Give yourself 5 points each time you make 10 consecutive hook shots.

Hook shots made with right hand ___; points earned ___

Hook shots made with left hand ___; points earned ___

Your score ___ (10 points maximum)

LAYUP

The layup shot (figure 4.6) is used near the basket after a cut or drive. To jump high on a layup, you must have speed on the last three or four steps of your cut or drive, but you also must control your speed. Step with your opposite foot. The step before your layup should be short so you can quickly dip your takeoff knee to change forward momentum to upward momentum. Lift your shooting knee and the ball straight up as you jump, bringing the ball between your ear and shoulder. Direct your arm, wrist, and fingers straight to the basket at an angle between 45 and 60 degrees and release the ball off your index finger with a soft touch. Keep your balance hand on the ball until the release.

Follow through by keeping your arm up and fully extended at the elbow, your index finger pointing straight at the target, and the palm of your shooting hand facing down. Be ready to get back on defense or rebound the ball on a miss.

The runner or extended layup shot is used away from the basket when a quick shot is needed off a cut or drive. The runner is shot the same way as the layup except the takeoff position is farther from the basket. When shooting the runner, emphasize smooth rhythm and a complete follow-through.

When you shoot the layup or runner, do not swivel the ball to the side, allowing it to be blocked or stolen. Lift the ball straight up as you shoot.

Keep your balance hand on the ball until the release. Otherwise you will lose protection and control of the ball as you shoot.

If your shooting hand rotates from the side, it will put sidespin on the ball so it rolls off the rim. Shoot with your hand directly behind the ball to give it backspin, causing it to pull into the basket.

Shoot the ball high above the backboard box so it will drop into the basket instead of going up. Even if you are fouled on the layup, the ball will still have a chance of going in.

Figure 4.6   Layup and Runner (Extended Layup)

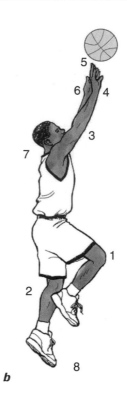

DIP KNEE, HAND ON TOP

1. Short step
2. Knee dipped on takeoff
3. Shoulders relaxed
4. Nonshooting hand under ball, shooting hand on top of ball
5. Elbow in
6. Raise ball between ear and shoulder

SHOOT LAYUP OR RUNNER

1. Lift shooting knee
2. Jump straight up, extending leg, back, and shoulders
3. Extend elbow
4. Flex wrist and fingers forward
5. Release ball off index finger
6. Keep balance hand on ball until release
7. Execute follow-through
8. Land in balance at spot of takeoff

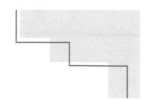

Misstep

On the takeoff, you use a long jump (floating forward or to the side) rather than a high jump.

Correction

Keep your head up and focus on your target. Make the step before your takeoff short so you can quickly dip your takeoff knee and create upward momentum. On your takeoff, lift your opposite knee straight up and lift the ball to the basket simultaneously. The combination of this forceful upward lift of your opposite knee and arms transfers the momentum to lift your entire body higher.

Layup Drill 1. *One-Dribble Layup*

This drill leads up to shooting layups off the dribble using both the strong and weak hands. First, practice with your strong hand. Start in a balanced stance at the middle hash mark on the lane off your strong side. Use your strong-side foot as a pivot foot; it should be back and your weak-side foot should be forward. Dribble with your strong hand and then take a short step with your weak-side foot. Pick up the ball at your strong-side knee with your balance hand under the ball and your shooting hand behind it in block-and-tuck position. Jump straight up and shoot a strong-hand layup high above the box on the backboard. Land in balance and catch the ball with two hands whether you make the shot or have to get a rebound.

Next, practice the same way with your weak hand. Your weak-side foot should be back and your strong-side foot should be forward. Dribble with your weak hand. Take a short step with your strong-side foot, pick up the ball at your weak-side knee, and shoot a weak-hand layup.

Success Check

- Pick up the ball in block-and-tuck position.
- Use correct layup technique.
- Try to make five consecutive one-dribble layups with each hand.

Score Your Success

Record the number of one-dribble layups you make with each hand. Give yourself 5 points each time you make five consecutive one-dribble layups.

Consecutive one-dribble layups made with strong hand ___; points earned ___

Consecutive one-dribble layups made with weak hand ___; points earned ___

Your score ___ (10 points maximum)

Layup Drill 2. *One-Dribble Runner (Extended Layup)*

This drill leads up to shooting runners off the dribble with both the strong and weak hands. Start with your strong hand. Stand in a balanced stance nine feet in front of the basket. Your strong-side foot (the pivot foot) should be back and your weak-side foot should be forward. The drill action is like the one-dribble layup. Dribble with your strong hand. Take a short step with your weak-side foot and pick up the ball at your strong-side knee with your balance hand under the ball and your shooting hand behind it in block-and-tuck position. Jump straight up and shoot a strong-hand runner. Land in balance, ready to rebound or get back on defense.

Practice the same way with your weak hand. Your weak-side foot should be back and your strong-side foot should be forward. Dribble with your weak hand. Set up with your strong-side foot and pick up the ball at your weak-side knee. Jump straight up and shoot a weak-hand runner. Land in balance, ready to rebound or get back on defense.

To Increase Difficulty

- After making five consecutive one-dribble runners from 9 feet, move back to a spot 12 feet in front of the basket.
- After making five consecutive one-dribble runners from 12 feet, move back to a spot 15 feet in front of the basket.

Success Check

- Pick up the ball in block-and-tuck position.
- Use correct layup technique.
- Try to make five consecutive one-dribble runners with each hand at each distance.

Score Your Success

Record the number of consecutive one-dribble runners you make at each distance and to each side. Give yourself 1 point each time you are able to complete five consecutive one-dribble runners.

Consecutive one-dribble runners from 9 feet, strong hand ___; points earned ___

Consecutive one-dribble runners from 9 feet, weak hand ___; points earned ___

Consecutive one-dribble runners from 12 feet, strong hand ___; points earned ___

Consecutive one-dribble runners from 12 feet, weak hand ___; points earned ___

Consecutive one-dribble runners from 15 feet, strong hand ___; points earned ___

Consecutive one-dribble runners from 15 feet, weak hand ___; points earned ___

Your score ___ (6 points maximum)

Layup Drill 3. *Speed Dribble Layup*

This challenging layup drill in which you will alternate hands combines the use of strong- and weak-hand speed and reverse dribbles. The drill consists of alternately driving from each elbow (the intersection of the foul line and lane line) and shooting layups with your right hand when dribbling right and your left hand when dribbling left.

Start at the right elbow in a balanced stance with your left foot forward and right foot back. Drive to the basket using a speed dribble with your right hand and shoot a right-handed layup. Catch the ball with two hands and speed dribble out to the left elbow, pulling the ball back toward the basket with your right hand.

Drive to the basket using a speed dribble with your left hand and shoot a left-hand layup. Catch the ball with two hands and speed dribble to the right elbow, using your left hand. Place your right foot on the elbow and reverse dribble, pulling the ball back toward the basket with your left hand. Continue the drill for 30 seconds, alternately driving and shooting layups on each side of the basket.

Success Check

- Use good layup technique.
- Catch the ball with both hands.

Score Your Success

Record the number of layups you make in 30 seconds. Give yourself 5 points for making eight or more layups in 30 seconds, 1 point for making six to seven layups, and 0 points for making fewer than six layups.

Layups made in 30 seconds ___

Your score ___

Layup Drill 4. *Give-and-Go Speed Layup*

The give-and-go speed layup drill is a challenging combination of passing and shooting layups that you perform with two partners. It consists of alternately passing and cutting from each elbow or *T* and shooting layups with your right hand when cutting right or with your left hand when cutting left.

One partner stands 12 feet to the right side of the lane, halfway between the elbow and basket. The other partner stands 12 feet to the left side of the lane, halfway between the elbow and basket. You start in a balanced stance with your left foot forward and your right foot back on the elbow. Pass to your partner on your right and cut to the basket (give-and-go). Receive a return pass and shoot a right-handed layup. Catch the ball as it comes through the net or rebound it.

Pass to your partner on the left side of the lane and cut to the left elbow. Receive a return pass and place your left foot on the left elbow. Change direction, pass to your partner on the left side of the lane, and cut to the basket. Receive a return

pass and shoot a left-handed layup, catching the ball as it comes through the net or rebounding it. Continue the drill for 30 seconds, alternately passing, cutting, and shooting layups on each side of the basket. Switch places with your partner after 30 seconds.

Success Check

- Catch, dribble, and shoot using smooth, fluid movements.
- Use proper layup technique.

Score Your Success

Record the number of layups you make in 30 seconds. Give yourself 5 points if you make eight or more layups in 30 seconds, 1 point if you make six to seven layups, and 0 points if you make fewer than six layups.

Layups made in 30 seconds ___

Your score ___

Layup Drill 5. *Speed Dribble Layup Versus Chaser*

This drill develops your ability to speed dribble and make a driving layup while protecting the ball against a pursuing defensive player. Select another player as your opponent. Start at half-court on your strong-hand side, facing the sideline. Your opponent, who will be the defensive chaser, will start one step behind you. Your opponent's lead foot will be touching your back foot.

The drill starts when you initiate a drive to the basket using a speed dribble. The chaser should provide as much defensive pressure as possible, trying to detect your dribble or pressure your shot. Use the dribble to evade the defender and shoot the layup. Switch offensive and defensive roles with your partner after each shot attempt. Each player makes five shot attempts.

To Increase Difficulty

- Start on your weak-hand side and dribble only with your weak hand.

Success Check

- Use proper layup technique.
- Use good footwork and dribble technique to move around the defender.
- Protect the ball with your nonshooting hand and arm.

Score Your Success

Each successful shot counts as 1 point. Try to score more points than your partner. Give yourself 5 points if you score more than your partner.

Your score ___

SHOOTING OFF THE CATCH

Most shots in basketball are open shots (end of fast break, draw-and-kick out, ball passed out of trap, ball rotated versus zone or help defense, cutting off screen, pick-and-pop, long rebound, etc.). On open shots, face the basket and catch and shoot in one motion. The best pass is one that enables you to catch the ball within your shooting range and in position to shoot. Your shooting range is the distance within which you can consistently make the outside shot. If you are open to shoot the ball within your shooting range, give the passer a good target with your hands up and in shooting position. As the pass is thrown, jump behind the ball, facing the basket in position to shoot. Let the ball come to your hands; do not reach for the ball.

To shoot with a quick release, have your hands and feet ready. Give the passer a good target with your hands up above your shoulders in shooting position and your knees slightly flexed. Good passes make good shots. A good pass is one that hits the target and enables the target to catch the ball in position to shoot with a quick release.

Lower your knees just before the catch and extend upward on the catch in a quick rhythmical down-and-up motion. It is vital to keep the ball high, with the shooting hand facing the basket. Create rhythm by using the down-and-up motion of your legs rather than by lowering the ball. Keeping the ball high fosters a quick release and also decreases the chance for error.

Jump behind the ball on passes that are slightly off. When you are not able to catch the ball with hands and feet ready to shoot in rhythm, use a shot fake before your shot. The shot fake gives you time to adjust your hands and feet and establish a shooting rhythm. Only use a step and turn when closely guarded.

Catch the ball with your hands in a relaxed position, giving with the ball as it is caught. Use the block-and-tuck method to catch the ball. Be in shooting position with your shooting hand facing the basket (behind the ball) and your nonshooting hand under the ball. Do not catch the ball with your hands on the sides of the ball, rotating them into position, because when rushed you'll put sidespin on the ball. The passer should aim for your far hand, which will block the pass.

Use key words to help you learn correct mechanics, establish rhythm, and build confidence. Use one to three one-syllable words in rhythm. Key words should be positive, concise, and personal. Say the words aloud in rhythm from the start of your shot until the release of the ball. Emphasize the last word for confidence. Words that key the correct mechanics of your shot are called trigger words or cue words. Examples of trigger words for a quick release and rhythmical leg action are *down and up* (to key the down-and-up action of your legs for rhythm and range) or *up and in* (to start your shot high and prevent lowering the ball).

When you receive a pass from in front (inside out), block the ball with your shooting (far) hand, tucking your nonshooting hand under the ball (figure 4.7). When you receive a pass from your strong-hand side, block the ball with your nonshooting (far) hand, placing your shooting hand behind and resetting your nonshooting hand under the ball (figure 4.8). If a pass comes from your weak-hand side, block the ball with your shooting (far) hand, tuck your nonshooting hand under the ball, then adjust your shooting hand behind the ball (figure 4.9).

Figure 4.7 Shooting off the Catch on a Pass From in Front

SHOOTING HAND IN FRONT

1. Facing basket so you can see the passer and the basket
2. Feet shoulder-width apart and toes straight
3. Knees slightly flexed
4. Shoulders relaxed
5. Elbows in
6. Hands high between ear and shoulder
7. Nonshooting hand turned up, shooting hand turned to the basket

CATCH AND SHOOT IN RHYTHM

1. Jump behind ball in position to shoot
2. Keep arms in; do not reach
3. Block ball with shooting hand
4. Tuck nonshooting hand under ball
5. Lower knees just before catch and extend knees on the catch as you shoot in a quick, rhythmical down-and-up motion

Misstep

You receive a pass but have a slow release due to lowering the ball before shooting it.

Correction

Catch the ball in position to shoot, keeping the ball high. Catch and shoot the ball in one smooth motion. Lower your knees just before the catch and extend upward on the catch in a quick, rhythmical down-and-up motion.

| **Figure 4.8** | **Shooting off the Catch on a Pass From the Strong-Hand Side** |

a   *b*

SHOOTING HAND IN FRONT

1. Facing basket so you can see the passer and the basket
2. Feet shoulder-width apart and toes straight
3. Knees flexed
4. Shoulders relaxed
5. Elbows in
6. Hands high between ear and shoulder
7. Nonshooting hand turned to passer, shooting hand turned to basket

BLOCK BALL WITH NON-SHOOTING HAND

1. Jump behind ball in position to shoot
2. Lower knees before catch
3. Keep arms in; do not reach
4. Block ball with nonshooting hand
5. Place shooting hand behind ball
6. Reset nonshooting hand under ball

Misstep

When you receive a pass from the side, you face the passer and reach for the ball, slowing your release.

Correction

Face the basket, turn your head to see the pass, and let the ball come to you. Jump behind the ball and catch and shoot in one motion.

Figure 4.9 Shooting off the Catch on a Pass From the Weak-Hand Side

SHOOTING HAND FACES PASSER

1. Facing basket so you can see the passer and the basket
2. Feet shoulder-width apart and toes straight
3. Knees flexed
4. Shoulders relaxed
5. Elbows in
6. Hands high between ear and shoulder
7. Nonshooting hand turned up, shooting hand turned to passer

RESET SHOOTING HAND

1. Jump behind ball in position to shoot
2. Lower knees before catch
3. Keep arms in; do not reach
4. Block ball with shooting hand
5. Tuck nonshooting hand under ball
6. Take shooting hand off ball and reset it behind ball

Misstep

You catch the ball with your hands on the sides and rotate the ball into position, causing sidespin.

Correction

Your shooting hand should always be behind the ball before you shoot. When you receive a pass from your weak-hand side, your shooting hand is your far hand. After catching the ball, adjust by taking your shooting hand off the ball and placing it behind the ball for the shot.

Shooting off the Catch Drill 1. Catch and Shoot off Pass From in Front (Inside Out)

In this drill, you will shoot from five outside spots—the wings and corners on each side and the top. Start at the top directly in front of the basket. Face the basket in position to catch and shoot within your shooting range. A partner stands at the inside low-post area with a ball. Your partner begins the drill by making a chest pass to your far (shooting) hand. Catch and shoot in one motion. After each shot attempt, your partner goes for a two-handed rebound and passes the ball back out to you. Take 10 shots and then switch positions with your partner. After you both shoot from the top, you and your partner move to one of the other positions. Each of you takes 10 shots at each position.

To work on three-point shooting, repeat the drill from behind the three-point line.

Success Check

- Use your key words and correct form.
- Catch and shoot in one smooth motion.

Score Your Success

Record the number of successful shots you make from each position on the court. Give yourself 1 point each time you make at least 7 out of 10 attempts.

Made shots from top ___; points earned ___

Made shots from right wing ___; points earned ___

Made shots from left wing ___; points earned ___

Made shots from right corner ___; points earned ___

Made shots from left corner ___; points earned ___

Your score ___ (5 points maximum)

Shooting off the Catch Drill 2. Front-of-Board Shooting

The front-of-board shooting drill focuses on the fundamentals: shooting hand behind the ball, elbow-in alignment, release off the index finger, follow-through, and catching the ball in position to shoot.

Face the backboard. Pick a spot near the top corner of the front of the board to serve as your target. A spot on the front of the backboard is excellent for fostering a straight shot. Begin with the ball in shooting position above your shooting shoulder. Place your shooting hand behind the ball with your index finger at the ball's midpoint. Check for elbow-in alignment. Using a complete follow-through (full elbow extension), shoot the ball to your target on the front of the board, making it return to your shooting position so you don't have to move your hands on the catch. Say your personalized key words in rhythm from the start of your shot to the release of the ball. If the ball does not return to your starting position, jump behind the ball and catch it in position to shoot. After a missed shot, visualize a successful shot in good form, again saying your key words. Use feedback from the feel and direction of the ball. For example, if the miss was caused by your arm going to the side, add the key word *straight*. Use *point* if the ball went off the wrong finger, creating sidespin. Use *hands* if you caught the ball with your hands on the side.

Success Check

- Use proper shooting technique.
- Catch the rebound in position to shoot.
- Your goal is to have 8 out of 10 shots hit the spot on the front of the board, then catch the ball in shooting position without having to move your hands.

Score Your Success

4 or fewer shots = 0 points

5 to 7 shots = 1 point

8 to 10 shots = 5 points

Your score ___

Shooting off the Catch Drill 3. *Side-of-Board Shooting*

The side-of-board shooting drill is the same as the front-of-board drill except you use the side of the board. This drill puts more emphasis on a straight shot and good catch. On a shot that is slightly off, the rebound will go to the side. This enables you to practice jumping behind the ball to catch it in position to shoot.

Face the side of the backboard. Pick a spot near the top of the side of the board to serve as your target. A spot on the side of the backboard is excellent for fostering a straight shot. Using a complete follow-through (full elbow extension), shoot the ball to your target on the side of the board, making it return to your shooting position so you don't have to move your hands on the catch. Catch the ball in position to shoot. Jump behind the ball on shots that rebound to your left or right side.

Success Check

• Use proper shooting technique.

• Catch the rebound in position to shoot.

• Your goal is to have 7 out of 10 shots hit the spot on the side of the board, then catch the ball in shooting position without having to move your hands.

Score Your Success

2 or fewer shots = 0 points

3 to 6 shots = 1 point

7 to 10 shots = 5 points

Your score ___

Shooting off the Catch Drill 4. *Point-of-Board Shooting*

The point-of-board shooting drill is the same as the front-of-board and side-of-board drills except your target is the point of the board between the front and side of the board. This drill is obviously more difficult than the side-of-board shooting drill. It puts more emphasis on focusing and releasing the ball off your index finger. It also provides a greater challenge for jumping behind the ball in position to shoot. On shots that are off, the rebound may go farther to the side than in the side-of-board shooting drill. This enables you to practice jumping behind the ball to catch it in position to shoot.

Face the point of the backboard. Pick a spot near the top of the point of the board to serve as your target. Focus on your target on the point of the board and shoot the ball, emphasizing the release of the ball off your index finger. Catch the ball in position to shoot. Jump behind the ball on shots that rebound to your left or right side.

Success Check

• Use proper shooting technique.

• Catch the rebound in position to shoot.

• Your goal is to have 5 out of 10 shots hit the spot on the point of the board, then catch the ball in shooting position without having to move your hands.

Score Your Success

0 to 2 shots = 0 points

3 to 4 shots = 1 point

5 to 10 shots = 5 points

Your score ___

Shooting off the Catch Drill 5. *Catch and Shoot off Pass From the Side*

Work with a partner. The pass will come from your strong-hand side. Shoot from three spots on the court—the elbow or *T* (the intersection of the foul and lane lines), the wing, and the corner position on your weak-hand side. Start at a spot above the elbow on your weak-hand side within your shooting range. Face the basket, ready to catch and shoot in one motion. From the elbow at your strong-hand side, your partner executes a chest pass to your far (nonshooting) hand. When you receive the pass, block the ball with your nonshooting hand, place your shooting hand behind the ball, then reset your nonshooting hand under the ball. After you shoot, your partner goes for a two-handed rebound and dribbles out to the elbow before passing to you for the next shot. Take 10 shots and then switch positions with your partner. After you have both taken 10 shots from the elbow, move to the wing. Each of you should attempt 10 shots from each of the three positions.

To Increase Difficulty

- Switch to your weak-hand side. Take 10 shots each from the elbow, wing, and corner positions on your weak-hand side. The pass from your partner comes from the elbow on your strong-hand side.
- Move farther away from the basket.

Success Check

- To receive the pass, use your nonshooting hand to block the ball, put your shooting hand behind the ball, then move your nonshooting hand under the ball.
- Use correct shooting form and your key words.

Score Your Success

Record the number of shots you make from each position on the court. Give yourself 1 point each time you make at least 7 out of 10 attempts.

Made shots from strong-hand side elbow ___; points earned ___

Made shots from strong-hand side wing ___; points earned ___

Made shots from strong-hand side corner ___; points earned ___

Made shots from weak-hand side elbow ___; points earned ___

Made shots from weak-hand side wing ___; points earned ___

Made shots from weak-hand side corner ___; points earned ___

Your score ___ (6 points maximum)

Shooting off the Catch Drill 6. *Catch and Shoot off Toss to Elbow*

One objective of this drill is to develop your ability to catch and shoot in one motion with a quick release. Another objective is to develop your ability to start a jump shot in a balanced stance while facing the basket and land in balance after the shot.

Start with the ball at the left box outside the lane, your back to the basket. Pass to yourself by tossing the ball high so it bounces high at the left elbow of the court. Run outside the lane to the left elbow and quickly jump behind the ball, turning your body in to face the basket. Land in balance with a jump stop. Have your hands and feet ready with your hands above your shoulders and your knees slightly flexed. Catch the ball with your shooting hand high and turned toward the front of the rim. Catch and shoot in one motion. Your knees should lower just before the catch and extend upward on the catch in a quick rhythmical down-and-up motion. Perform the same drill starting at the right box and tossing the ball to the right elbow. Shoot 10 shots from the left elbow, then shoot 10 more from the right elbow.

Success Check

- Have your hands and feet ready to shoot when you catch the ball.
- Catch and shoot in one quick down-and-up motion.

Give yourself 1 point for each made shot from both the right and left elbows.

4 or fewer = 0 points (need improvement)

5 to 7 = 1 point (good)

8 to 10 = 5 points (excellent)

Your score from right elbow ___; from left elbow ___ (10 total points maximum)

Shooting off the Catch Drill 7. *Shoot-Out*

The shoot-out drill helps you develop the ability to catch and shoot in one motion with a quick release. Select two players to work with you. One player keeps time. The timer blows a whistle to begin the drill, whistles again after 20 seconds at the first spot, whistles after 20 seconds at the second spot, and whistles at the one-minute mark. The other player keeps score and rebounds the ball and passes it back to you as you shoot.

You will shoot from three spots—9 feet in front of the basket, 15 feet in front of the basket, and behind the three-point line in front of the basket. Start in a balanced stance 9 feet in front of the basket with the ball in good shooting position in front of your shooting shoulder. On the first whistle, begin shooting and continue to shoot from the same spot until the second whistle. At the second whistle, move back until you are 15 feet in front of the basket and continue to shoot from that spot until the third whistle. On the third whistle, move back until you are behind the three-point line in front of the basket. Continue to shoot from that spot until the final whistle.

After you shoot for one minute, change positions. The shooter becomes the rebounder and passer,

the rebounder and passer becomes the timer, and the timer becomes the shooter.

Success Check

- A good rebounder and passer will help you get a good score because good passes help you make good shots.
- Catch and shoot in one smooth motion.

Record the number of shots made from each position on the court. Give yourself 5 points for making 25 or more shots, 3 points for making 20 to 24 shots, 1 point for making 15 to 19 shots, and 0 points for making fewer than 15 shots.

Successful shots from 9 feet ___; points earned ___

Successful shots from 15 feet ___; points earned ___

Successful shots from behind the three-point line ___; points earned ___

Your score ___ (15 points maximum)

Shooting Off the Catch Drill 8. *Three Players, Two Balls*

As the name implies, this drill uses three players and two balls. There are three shooting areas with two shooting spots in each: right corner to the right elbow *(T)*, right *T* to left *T*, and left *T* to left corner.

The shooter (S) starts in the right corner with a ball. The rebounder (R) is positioned at the oppo-

site side of the basket, and the passer (P) is at the opposite *T* or corner with a ball. The shooter shoots and moves to the right *T* in the same shooting area to receive the next ball. The shooter faces the basket to shoot, catches the ball, and shoots in one motion. If the pass is off target, the shooter must jump behind the ball. The shooter should follow through until the ball reaches the basket before moving to the next spot.

After the shooter moves to the next shooting spot, the passer passes to the shooter from the opposite *T*. The passer should be in triple-threat position to pass, facing the basket, and should fake before passing to the shooter's far hand without telegraphing the pass.

The rebounder rebounds the ball and passes it to the passer. The rebounder should use two hands to secure the rebound without letting the ball hit the floor. The rebounder should land in balance, keeping the ball high above the forehead, and should fake before making a two-handed overhead outlet pass. Continue for 25 seconds. After 25 seconds, take 5 seconds to rotate: The shooter becomes the rebounder, the rebounder becomes the passer, and the passer becomes the shooter. Perform the drill for another 25 seconds.

After the 25 seconds are up, take 5 seconds to move to the second shooting area. Perform the drill for 25 seconds in the new shooting area, take 5 seconds to rotate, and perform the drill for another 25 seconds. After the 25 seconds are up, move to the third shooting area. The drill takes 4 1/2 minutes total, with each player getting at least 30 shots, 30 rebounds, and 30 passes.

To Increase Difficulty

- Have one or more additional players or coaches put a hand up on the shooter.
- Have one or more additional players or coaches apply pressure to the passer.

- Have one or more additional players or coaches knock the ball out of the rebounder's hand if the rebounder lowers the ball below forehead level.

Success Check

- Use proper rebounding, passing, and shooting technique.
- Rotate smoothly from one role to the next.
- When you are the shooter, catch and shoot in one smooth motion.

Score Your Success

For the shooter:

Fewer than 15 shots = 0 points

15 to 19 shots = 1 point

20 to 30 shots = 5 points

Your score ___

For the passer:

Fewer than 20 accurate passes = 0 points

20 to 23 accurate passes = 1 point

24 to 30 accurate passes = 5 points

Your score ___

For the rebounder:

Fewer than 20 two-handed rebounds = 0 points

20 to 23 two-handed rebounds = 1 point

24 to 30 two-handed rebounds = 5 points

Your score ___

Shooting off the Catch Drill 9. *Pressure the Shooter*

This drill requires two players: an offensive player and a defensive player. Start as the offensive player. Be in position to catch and shoot at the three-point line or within your shooting range. The defender starts under the basket and begins the drill by making a chest pass to your shooting hand. The defender then runs at you, attempting to pressure your shot without blocking it. You score a point each time you make a shot. After each attempt, switch roles with your partner. Each player takes 10 shots.

Success Check

- Catch and shoot in a smooth, fluid motion.
- Use proper shooting technique.

Score Your Success

This is a competitive drill in which you are trying to score more points than your partner. If you score more than your partner, give yourself 5 points.

Your score ___

SHOOTING OFF THE DRIBBLE

When open, dribble to the front of your shooting knee and pick up the ball, facing the basket in position to shoot. Do not reach for the ball. Pick up the ball in front of your shooting knee with your knees flexed to gain balance for your shot and prevent you from floating forward, backward, or to the side.

Pick up the ball with your shooting hand on top and your nonshooting hand under it. As you bring the ball up to shoot, your shooting hand will face the basket (be behind the ball), enabling you to put backspin on the ball. Never pick up the ball with your hands on the sides and rotate them into position because when rushed you'll put sidespin on the ball when you shoot.

When dribbling to your strong-hand side (figure 4.10), jump behind your last dribble and pick up the ball in front of your shooting knee. When dribbling to your weak-hand side (figure 4.11), use a crossover dribble on your last dribble to pick up the ball in front of your shooting knee.

Figure 4.10   Shooting off the Dribble, Strong-Hand Side

a

DRIBBLE TO SHOOTING KNEE

1. Dribble with strong hand
2. Control dribble to front of shooting knee

b

SHOOTING HAND ON TOP

1. Jump behind ball, facing basket
2. Pick up ball with shooting hand on top
3. Place nonshooting hand under ball

c

SHOOT

1. Shoot jump shot

Misstep

The ball misses to either the right or left side of the basket.

Correction

Missing to the right or left of the basket is caused by reaching to the side for the ball and starting the shot from the side of your body. When open, dribble to the front of your shooting knee and pick up the ball while facing the basket in position to shoot. Do not reach for the ball.

Figure 4.11   Shooting off the Dribble, Weak-Hand Side

CROSSOVER TO SHOOTING KNEE

1. Dribble with weak hand
2. Crossover dribble in front of shooting knee

a

SHOOTING HAND ON TOP

1. Jump behind ball, facing basket
2. Pick up ball with shooting hand on top
3. Place nonshooting hand under ball

b

SHOOT

1. Shoot jump shot

c

Misstep

When shooting off the dribble, you float forward, back, or to the side.

Correction

Pick up the ball in front of your shooting knee with your knees flexed to gain balance for your shot and prevent floating.

Shooting off the Dribble Drill 1. *Straight Drive One-Dribble Jump Shot*

This drill leads up to shooting jump shots off the dribble going to your strong- and weak-hand sides. Start with the ball at the left box outside the lane, your back to the basket. Pass to yourself by tossing the ball high so it bounces high at the left elbow of the court. Run to the left elbow and catch the ball, your back to the basket, using a one-two stop, landing on your inside (left) foot first. Pivot on your

90

left foot, using a front turn toward the middle. Face the basket and make a jab step with your right foot, showing the ball high. Be in triple-threat stance and in position to shoot first. Dribble once with your right hand toward the middle of the free throw line. Jump behind the ball. Pick up the ball in front of your shooting knee with your shooting hand on top and your balance hand under the ball. Jump straight up and shoot a jump shot. Land in balance. Perform the drill again, starting from the right box and tossing the ball to the right elbow. Shoot 10 one-dribble jump shots from the left elbow and 10 one-dribble jump shots from the right elbow.

Note: A left-handed player will have farther to jump when going to the right in order to pick up the ball in front of the shooting knee. A right-handed player will have farther to jump when going to the left.

Success Check

- Pick up the ball at your shooting knee with your shooting hand on top.
- Jump and land in the same spot.

Score Your Success

Record the number of one-dribble jump shots you make out of 10 attempts, driving to the right from the left elbow. Record the number of one-dribble jump shots you make out of 10 attempts, driving to the left from the right elbow. Give yourself 1 point for each jump shot made.

4 or fewer = need improvement

5 to 7 = good

8 to 10 = excellent

Your score dribbling to the right ___; dribbling to the left ___ (20 total points maximum)

Shooting off the Dribble Drill 2. *Crossover One-Dribble Jump Shot*

This drill develops the ability to shoot jump shots off a crossover dribble while going to either the strong- or weak-hand side. The drill begins the same way as the previous drill. Begin with the ball at the right box outside the lane. Toss the ball to the right elbow. Catch the ball with your back to the basket using a one-two stop, landing on your inside (right) foot and pivoting toward the middle. Face the basket, making a jab step with your left foot, showing the ball high. Be in triple-threat stance, a threat to shoot first. Make a crossover step with your left foot to the outside and dribble once with your outside (right) hand at a 45-degree angle with the backboard. Jump behind the ball. Pick up the ball in front of your shooting knee with your shooting hand on top and your balance hand under the ball. Jump straight up and shoot a jump shot. Land in balance. Shoot 10 crossover one-dribble jump shots, driving right at a 45-degree angle with the backboard. Perform the same drill from the left box, tossing the ball to the left elbow. Shoot 10 crossover one-dribble jump shots, driving left from the left elbow at a 45-degree angle to the backboard. When dribbling to the weak-hand side, practice using a

crossover dribble on the last dribble to pick up the ball in front of the shooting knee.

Note: A left-handed player will have farther to jump when going to the right in order to pick up the ball in front of the shooting knee. A right-handed player will have farther to jump when going to the left.

To Increase Difficulty

- After making 8 out of 10 crossover one-dribble jump shots to the strong-hand side, try to make 8 out of 10 going to the weak-hand side.

Success Check

- Pick up the ball at your shooting knee with your shooting hand on top.
- Use a crossover dribble as the last dribble before picking up the ball in front of your shooting knee when going to the weak-hand side.
- Jump and land in the same spot.

Score Your Success

Record the number of crossover one-dribble jump shots you make out of 10 attempts going to the right and then going to the left. Give yourself 1 point for each jump shot you make.

4 or fewer = need improvement

5 to 7 = good

8 to 10 = excellent

Your score dribbling to the right ___; dribbling to the left ___ (20 total points maximum)

RATE YOUR SUCCESS

The only way to score is by putting the ball in the basket. Developing different shooting skills will help make you an offensive threat from every area on the floor.

In the next step, we will look at rebounding the ball, or what you should do if a shot is off the

mark. Before going to step 5, however, look back at how you performed the drills in this step. For each of the drills presented in this step, enter the points you earned, then add up your scores to rate your total success.

Shooting Drills

1. Shooting Warm-Up ____ out of 15

2. One-Hand Shooting ____ out of 10

3. On-Your-Back Shooting ____ out of 5

4. Shooting From a Chair ____ out of 5

Free Throw Drills

1. Daily Practice ____ out of 5

2. Eyes Closed ____ out of 5

Jump Shot Drills

1. Jump Shot Warm-Up ____ out of 6

2. Bank Jump Shot Warm-Up ____ out of 8

Hook Shot Drills

1. Hook Shot Warm-Up ____ out of 10

2. Hook Shot Warm Up With Crossover Step ____ out of 10

3. Alternate Hand Hook Shooting (Mikan Drill) ____ out of 10

Layup Drills

1. One-Dribble Layup ____ out of 10

2. One-Dribble Runner (Extended Layup) ____ out of 6

3. Speed Dribble Layup	____ out of 5
4. Give-and-Go Speed Layup	____ out of 5
5. Speed Dribble Layup Versus Chaser	____ out of 5

Shooting off the Catch Drills

1. Catch and Shoot off Pass From in Front (Inside Out)	____ out of 5
2. Front-of-Board Shooting	____ out of 5
3. Side-of-Board Shooting	____ out of 5
4. Point-of-Board Shooting	____ out of 5
5. Catch and Shoot off Pass From the Side	____ out of 6
6. Catch and Shoot off Toss to Elbow	____ out of 10
7. Shoot-Out	____ out of 15
8. Three Players, Two Balls	____ out of 15
9. Pressure the Shooter	____ out of 5

Shooting off the Dribble Drills

1. Straight Drive One-Dribble Jump Shot	____ out of 20
2. Crossover One-Dribble Jump Shot	____ out of 20
TOTAL	____ **out of 231**

If you scored 170 or more points, congratulations! You have mastered the basics of this step and are ready to move on to step 5, rebounding. If you scored fewer than 170 points, you may want to spend more time on the fundamentals covered in this step. Practice the drills again to develop mastery of the techniques and increase your scores.

Rebounding

Rebounding is the one fundamental that you cannot overdo. You can shoot too often, dribble too much, pass too much, and try to steal the ball or block shots too much, but you can never rebound too much. The team that controls the backboards usually controls the game.

Possession of the ball comes from missed shots more often than any other way. Offensive rebounding adds to your team's scoring opportunities, and defensive rebounding limits your opponent's scoring opportunities.

Attacking the offensive glass for rebounds enables your team to create second-chance scoring opportunities. More often than not, these second shots are high-percentage inside shots, and many result in three-point plays. Offensive rebounding takes desire and effort. Gaining possession of the ball by getting an offensive rebound often inspires a team.

Gaining possession of the ball through defensive rebounding, however, is even more valuable. If you control the defensive backboard, your opponent will have fewer opportunities to gain second shots that often result in easy scores and three-point plays. Defensive rebounding not only limits your opponent's second-chance scoring opportunities, but it also creates the most opportunities for starting a fast break.

REBOUNDING ESSENTIALS

The essential factors that determine a good rebounder are emotional, mental, and physical in nature in addition to skill.

Wanting the ball is the most important factor in rebounding. This is **desire.** Assume that every shot will be missed, then add to this the attitude that you will go after every rebound. Since many rebounds are not obtained by the first player to touch the ball, second effort is truly needed. The difference between good rebounders and great rebounders is that the great ones go after more rebounds. The physical contact of rebounding demands **courage.** To be a great rebounder, you must be eager to get into the battle of the boards. Often there is no glory in rebounding, just victory.

Develop rebounding intelligence. **Anticipate missed shots.** Check the rims, backboards, and bracing to determine how hard the ball will rebound. Know your teammates' shooting techniques and study your opponents' shooting to anticipate where shots will rebound. Observe the angle and distance of shots. Most shots rebound to the opposite side, and three-point shot attempts tend to have longer rebounds. **Learn about your opponent.** Get to know the strength, jumping ability, quickness, aggressiveness, blockout technique, and second-effort characteristics for each player on the opposing team.

Physically, you need to move! **Develop quickness.** On offense, move quickly around your opponent and go for the ball. On defense, move quickly to block out your opponent and then go for the ball. Work continually to improve your **jump**—not only the height, but also the quickness and explosiveness. A quick second jump is a great asset for a rebounder. Improve **muscular endurance** in your legs. This will improve not only the height of your jumps, but also your ability to jump several times in succession. Also increase your **total body strength** so you can withstand the body contact under the boards.

Use **peripheral vision** to see the total picture, including the ball and your opponent. When on defense, watch your opponent after the shot, block out, and go for the ball. On offense, determine how your opponent blocks out after the shot, use the correct method to get past the blockout, and go for the ball.

Maintain a **balanced stance** to counter physical play such as bumping, shoving, and pushing. Be on the balls of your feet, with your feet shoulder-width apart, knees flexed, back straight, head up, and hands above your shoulders. Anticipate your opponent's move and work to establish **inside position.**

Get your **hands up.** Move both hands above your forehead, spaced ball-width apart. **Time your jump** so you will reach the ball at the maximum height of your jump. In rebounding, it is not how high but **how often** you can jump that is crucial for success.

Catch the ball with two hands and aggressively protect it in front of your forehead and away from your opponent. After gaining possession and while still in the air, **spread your legs** and keep your elbows out to protect the ball.

Come down in a balanced stance. When on offense, be ready to score with a power move or to pass to a teammate. When on defense, be ready to pivot and use a quick outlet pass to start a fast break.

Have a trained observer such as a coach, teacher, or a skilled player watch your rebounding and provide corrective feedback. Also, ask your coach to evaluate your rebounding in competition, paying particular attention to your desire to go after every rebound.

Rebounding Drill 1. *Backboard Rebounding*

Start in a balanced stance eight feet in front of the backboard and to the side of the rim. Make a two-handed chest pass, aiming high on the backboard. Rebound the ball with two hands and land in balance. Protect the ball above your forehead with elbows out, and do not lower the ball. Repeat 10 times.

Success Check

- Use two hands to rebound the ball.
- Protect the ball on the rebound.
- Land in balance.

Score Your Success

3 or fewer successful rebounds = 0 points

4 to 5 successful rebounds = 1 point

6 to 7 successful rebounds = 3 points

8 to 10 successful rebounds = 5 points

Your score ___

Rebounding Drill 2. *Superman or Wonder Woman Rebounding*

Start in a balanced stance with one foot outside the lane line and above the box. Make a strong two-handed chest pass, aiming high on the opposite corner of the backboard. Pass the ball so that it rebounds above the box to the opposite side of the lane. Rebound the ball with two hands and land in balance, at least one foot outside the lane and above the box. Protect the ball above your forehead with elbows out. Perform for 30 seconds.

Success Check

- Use two hands to rebound the ball.
- Protect the ball on the rebound.
- Land in balance.

Score Your Success

5 or fewer successful rebounds in 30 seconds = 0 points

6 to 7 successful rebounds in 30 seconds = 1 point

8 to 9 successful rebounds in 30 seconds = 3 points

10 or more successful rebounds in 30 seconds = 5 points

Your score ___

DEFENSIVE REBOUNDING

The key to defensive rebounding is getting inside position on your opponent and going for the ball. When playing defense, you usually have the inside position between your opponent and the basket, giving you the early advantage in the ensuing battle for the rebound.

There are two coaching strategies for defensive rebounding. The most commonly used philosophy is to *block out* (often called *box out*) the opponent. Blocking out involves first blocking your opponent's path to the ball by putting your back to your opponent's chest and then going for the ball. The other philosophy, espoused by John Wooden (the great UCLA coach of 10 NCAA championship teams), is simply to step in your opponent's path and go for the ball. Wooden's method, called the *check-and-go*, might be best when your quickness and leaping ability are much superior to your opponent's. Blocking out is recommended for most players.

There are two methods of blocking out: the front turn and the reverse turn. Putting your back on your opponent's chest and going for the ball are more important than which blockout method you use.

The *front turn* method (figure 5.1) is best for blocking out the shooter. After the shot, you simply step into the shooter. The *reverse turn* (figure 5.2) is best when you are defending a player without the ball. After the shot, you first observe your opponent's cut and then reverse turn, dropping your foot backward and away from your opponent's cut. When guarding the player without the ball, take a defensive stance that allows you to see the ball and your opponent.

To guard a player on the ball side of the basket (also called the strong side), take a denial stance with one hand up and one foot in the passing lane. To guard a player on the opposite side of the basket (called the help side or weak side), take a defensive stance several steps away that allows you to see the ball and the player you are guarding. When you defend a player off the ball and a shot is taken, first observe your opponent's cut and then reverse turn, dropping your foot back away from your opponent's cut. Block out and get the rebound.

Develop the attitude that you are going to go after every ball. Always try to catch the ball with two hands, but if you cannot make a two-handed catch, use one hand to try to keep it alive until you or a teammate can grab it.

Figure 5.1 Defensive Rebounding: Front Turn

a

b

c

FRONT TURN

1. Defensive stance with hand up in passing lane
2. Front pivot on back foot
3. Step toward opponent

BLOCK OUT

1. Back on opponent's chest
2. Wide base
3. Hands up

GO FOR THE BALL

1. Go for the ball and catch it with two hands
2. Protect ball in front of forehead
3. Land in balance

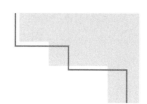

Misstep

You watch the ball, and your opponent cuts by you.

Correction

Locate your opponent first, get inside position, block out or check, and then go for the ball.

Figure 5.2	Defensive Rebounding: Reverse Turn

a	b	c

PIVOT REVERSE

1. Defensive stance with hand up in passing lane
2. Reverse pivot on foot closest to opponent's cut
3. Drop other foot back

BLOCK OUT

1. Back on opponent's chest
2. Wide base
3. Hands up

GET THE REBOUND

1. Go for the ball and catch it with two hands
2. Protect ball in front of forehead
3. Land in balance

Misstep

You lose balance when your opponent fakes.

Correction

Use a wide base and keep moving on the balls of your feet.

Defensive Rebounding Drill 1. *Block Out the Shooter*

This drill requires two players. Begin as the defensive player and have your partner start as the shooter. The shooter starts outside the free throw line with the ball, and you take a defensive stance facing your partner. Allow the shot and then use a front turn to block out the shooter and get the rebound if the shot misses. Meanwhile, the shooter tries to get an offensive rebound. If the offensive player secures the rebound, he can shoot again from the spot of the rebound. Continue until you get the rebound. Once you get the rebound, take a 10-second rest interval. After the rest interval, the offensive player starts outside the free throw line again, and the drill is repeated four more times. Rotate from defense to offense.

Success Check

- On defense, block out the shooter using good technique.
- On offense, try to get past the defender's blockout using good offensive rebounding technique.

Score Your Success

Record the number of defensive rebounds you get. Give yourself 5 points if you get five or more defensive rebounds, 1 point if you get three or four defensive rebounds, and 0 points if you get fewer than three defensive rebounds. On offense, record the number of offensive rebounds you get. Give yourself 5 points if you get at least two offensive rebounds.

Your score for defensive rebounds ___;
for offensive rebounds ___

Defensive Rebounding Drill 2. *Block Out the Player Without the Ball*

This drill requires three players: a defensive player, an offensive player, and a shooter. Assume the role of the defensive player first; you will be rebounding against an offensive player without the ball. The third player acts as the shooter only. Shooting on one side of the floor from at least 15 feet, the shooter intentionally tries to miss. On the opposite side of the basket, take a defensive stance that allows you to see the ball and the player without the ball, whom you are guarding.

On the shot, first observe your opponent's cut and then reverse turn, dropping your foot away from your opponent's cut in a backward direction. Block out and get the rebound. The offensive player will try to get an offensive rebound of a missed shot. If successful, the offensive player can shoot again from the spot of the rebound. Continue until you get the rebound. Once you get the rebound, take a 10-second rest interval. After the rest interval, the ball is returned to the shooter and the drill is repeated four more times. After five total repetitions, players rotate: The defender becomes the offensive player without the ball, the offensive player without the ball becomes the shooter, and the shooter becomes the defender.

Success Check

- On defense, watch the player you are defending and the ball.
- Block out the shooter using good technique.

Score Your Success

Record the number of defensive rebounds you get. Give yourself 5 points if you get five or more defensive rebounds, 1 point if you get three or four defensive rebounds, and 0 points if you get fewer than three defensive rebounds. On offense, record the number of offensive rebounds you get. Give yourself 5 points if you get at least two offensive rebounds.

Your score for defensive rebounds ___;
for offensive rebounds ___

OFFENSIVE REBOUNDING

The key to offensive rebounding is to move. Develop the attitude and will to move and go after every ball. Move to outmaneuver the defender, who is usually between you and the basket. Make a quick, aggressive move to get past the defender and jump to get the ball, always trying to catch it with two hands. If you cannot catch the ball with two hands, use one hand to try to tip the ball into the basket or keep it alive until you or a teammate can grab it. To avoid being blocked out, keep moving.

If you are blocked out, use every effort to get around the blockout. Even great rebounders get blocked out, but they keep moving to outmaneuver the opponent. It is not a mistake to be blocked out, but it is a mistake to stay blocked out.

Four methods of moving past the blockout are the straight cut, fake-and-go, spin, and step back. Use the straight cut (figure 5.3) when your opponent blocks you out with a front turn. Quickly cut by before the blockout can be set. Use the fake-and-go (figure 5.4) when your opponent blocks you out with a reverse turn. Fake in the direction of your opponent's reverse step and cut by the other side. Use the spin (figure 5.5) when your opponent blocks you out and holds your body. Placc your forearm on your opponent's back, reverse pivot on your lead foot, hook your arm over your opponent's arm for leverage, and cut by. Use the step back (figure 5.6) when your opponent leans back on you while blocking out. Simply step back so your opponent loses balance, then cut by and go for the ball.

Figure 5.3 | **Offensive Rebounding: Straight Cut**

a   b   c

HANDS UP	**STRAIGHT CUT**	**REBOUND**
1. View of ball and opponent	1. Opponent uses front turn	1. Catch ball with two hands
2. Offensive stance	2. Cut straight by opponent	2. Protect ball in front of forehead
3. Hands up	3. Hands up	3. Land in balance
	4. Go for ball	

Misstep

You have trouble holding onto rebounds.

Correction

Catch the ball with two hands.

Figure 5.4	Offensive Rebounding: Fake-and-Go

FAKE

1. Offensive stance with hands up
2. Opponent uses reverse turn
3. Fake in direction of opponent's reverse step

CUT OPPOSITE

1. Cut to opposite side
2. Keep hands up
3. Go for ball

REBOUND

1. Catch ball with two hands
2. Protect ball in front of forehead
3. Land in balance

Figure 5.5	Offensive Rebounding: Spin

FOREARM ON BACK

1. Offensive stance with hands up
2. Opponent holds you
3. Place forearm on opponent's back

REVERSE PIVOT

1. Reverse pivot
2. Hook arm over opponent's arm
3. Go for ball

REBOUND

1. Catch ball with two hands
2. Protect ball in front of forehead
3. Land in balance

Misstep

You hold your opponent, and your opponent hooks an arm over yours for leverage.

Correction

Keep your hands up.

Figure 5.6 Offensive Rebounding: Step Back

a *b* *c*

OPPONENT LEANS ON YOU

1. View of ball and opponent
2. Offensive stance
3. Hands up
4. Opponent leans on you

STEP BACK

1. Step back
2. Opponent falls back
3. Go for the ball

REBOUND

1. Catch ball with two hands
2. Protect ball in front of forehead
3. Land in balance

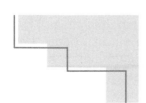

Misstep

After gaining the rebound, you have it stripped by an opponent.

Correction

Keep the ball protected above your forehead, with your elbows out and away from your opponent.

Offensive Rebounding Drill 1. *One-Versus-Two Offensive Rebound and Score*

Start in a balanced stance eight feet in front of the backboard and to the side of the rim. Two players take positions on either side of you. Make a two-handed chest pass, aiming high on the backboard. Rebound the ball with two hands and land in balance. Instead of lowering the ball below your forehead and keeping your elbows out, try to score with a power move such as a strong two-handed shot. The other players will give you some resistance by slightly bumping your arms, trying to knock the ball out of your hands after your rebound and during your scoring attempt. Perform 10 repetitions.

Success Check

- Focus on getting the rebound and making the shot.
- Use both hands to rebound the ball.

Score Your Success

0 to 1 successful rebounds and scores = 0 points

2 to 3 successful rebounds and scores = 1 point

4 to 5 successful rebounds and scores = 3 points

6 to 10 successful rebounds and scores = 5 points

Your score ___

Offensive Rebounding Drill 2. *Tipping*

Stand in front of the backboard to the side of the rim in a balanced stance. Using only one hand, shoot the ball high and softly on the backboard. Time the shot so that you tip the ball with one hand at the top of your jump. Using your strong hand, tip the ball high on the board five times in succession and then score into the basket. Use your weak hand next, tipping the ball five times in succession and then into the basket.

For variety and to add difficulty to the drill, try alternating hands on each tip. Stand in a balanced stance in front of the backboard to the side of the rim. Use your weak hand to shoot the ball high and softly on the backboard so it rebounds to the opposite side. Move quickly to the other side of the basket, jump, and tip the ball using your strong hand so it rebounds to the opposite side. Move quickly back to the first side of the basket, jump, and tip the ball using your weak hand. Continue tipping the ball high across the board, alternating hands as you tip. After three successive alternate hand tips, score on your last tip.

Success Check

- Perform the drill with both your strong hand and your weak hand.
- Tip the ball at the top of your jump.

Score Your Success

For the tipping drill, attempt five sets (five consecutive tips, then score) with each hand. Give yourself 1 point each time you successfully complete five consecutive tips and put the ball in the basket.

Your score ___

For the alternate hand tipping drill, attempt five sets (three consecutive alternate hand tips, then score). Give yourself 1 point each time you successfully complete three consecutive tips and put the ball in the basket.

Your score ___

Offensive and Defensive Rebounding Drill. *Circle Rebounding*

Three players are needed for this drill. Begin with a ball placed inside the free throw or center circle. Start as a defensive player. Assume a rebounding stance outside the circle, facing the ball. An offensive player gets in a balanced stance behind you. The third player gives commands. On the "Go!" command, the offensive player will use offensive rebounding methods to try to get to the ball while you block out. Try to keep the offensive player from getting the ball for 3 seconds. The "Stop!" command stops the drill after 3 seconds. Take a 10-second rest interval and then perform the drill for another 3 seconds. Complete five repetitions of 3 seconds each with 10-second rest intervals in between. Players then rotate: The defensive player becomes the offensive player, the offensive player moves into position to give commands, and the player who gave commands becomes the defensive player.

To add variety to the drill, add a front turn to the circle rebounding drill. Begin as the defender in a defensive stance facing the offensive player, who is assumed to be the shooter. On the "Go!" command, block out the offensive player using a front turn. The offensive player uses an offensive rebounding method to try to get the ball while you block out. Try to keep the offensive player from getting the ball for 3 seconds. The "Stop!" command stops the drill after 3 seconds. After a 10-second rest interval, perform the drill for another 3 seconds. Complete five repetitions of 3 seconds each with 10-second rest intervals in between. Players then rotate: The defensive player becomes the offensive player, the offensive player moves into position to give commands, and the player who gave commands becomes the defensive player.

Success Check

- On defense, use good blocking-out technique.
- On offense, use good offensive rebounding strategies to get past the blockout.
- Go for the ball.

Score Your Success

On defense, keep track of the number of times you are able to block out the offensive player. Give yourself 5 points if you complete at least three blockouts in five attempts. On offense, keep track of the number of times you are able to get past the blockout set by the defensive player. Give yourself 5 points if you are able to get past at least three times in five attempts.

Your score on defense ___; on offense ___

RATE YOUR SUCCESS

No matter how good a shooter you are, not every shot is going to go in the basket. Strong rebounding skills are essential to maintaining possession of the ball (offensive rebounds) or taking possession of the ball (defensive rebounds).

In the next step, we will look at offensive moves with the ball, or ways you can help your team when you are in possession of the ball. Before going to step 6, however, look back at how you performed the drills in this step. For each of the drills presented in this step, enter the points you earned, then add up your scores to rate your total success.

Rebounding Drills

  1. Backboard Rebounding   ____ out of 5

  2. Superman or Wonder Woman Rebounding   ____ out of 5

Defensive Rebounding Drills

  1. Block Out the Shooter   ____ out of 10

  2. Block Out the Player Without the Ball   ____ out of 10

Offensive Rebounding Drills

  1. One-Versus-Two Offensive Rebound and Score   ____ out of 5

  2. Tipping   ____ out of 10

Offensive and Defensive Rebounding Drill

  1. Circle Rebounding   ____ out of 10

TOTAL   ____ *out of 55*

If you scored 40 or more points, congratulations! You have mastered the basics of this step and are ready to move on to step 6, offensive moves with the ball. If you scored fewer than 40 points, you may want to spend more time on the fundamentals covered in this step. Practice the drills again to develop mastery of the techniques and increase your scores.

Offensive Moves With the Ball

Some players can score only when they get open shots. The best players develop offensive moves and become triple threats to shoot, pass, or drive. To be a triple threat, you must be able to make the outside shot, pass to an open teammate in better scoring position, and drive to the basket to finish the play with a shot or a pass to an open teammate for the score.

Every time you receive the ball, you have the opportunity to use offensive moves with the ball against your defender in a one-on-one confrontation. You can help or hurt your team, depending on what you do in the situation. A selfish one-on-one player guns the ball or drives into trouble. Team defense, in which defenders off the ball give help to the player defending the ball, prevent the selfish player from succeeding.

As a team one-on-one player, you can gain an advantage over your defender with a solid fake or penetrating drive that forces defensive help from another defender and creates an opening

that enables you to pass to your teammate for a score. This concept of one-on-one basketball, called *draw-and-kick*, is an integral part of team play. There is no greater offensive play than drawing another defensive player to react to stop you and then passing to an open teammate who is spotting up for an easier shot. This concept of unselfish one-on-one basketball, which creates openings for teammates, is team basketball at its best. All-time greats Bob Cousy, Julius Erving, Magic Johnson, Larry Bird, and Michael Jordan were unselfish one-on-one players who used offensive moves to draw-and-kick to open teammates to score.

Have a trained observer such as a coach, teacher, or a skilled player evaluate your ability to get open, your triple-threat stance, and your low-post and one-on-one moves and provide corrective feedback. Also, ask your coach to evaluate your decisions in reading your defender and reacting with the correct move.

LOW-POST MOVES

Offensive moves with the ball can be classified in two ways. Low-post moves are made with the

back to the hoop near the basket, inside the middle hash marks on the lane and below the

107

dotted semicircular line in the lane. The four basic low-post moves are the drop-step baseline power move, drop-step middle hook, front-turn baseline bank jump shot, and front-turn baseline crossover and hook.

When you are in the low post, try to seal off your defender (keep the defender to one side) by using your back, shoulder, and upper arm on that side. Do not allow your defender to get a foot in front of your foot. Strategies will vary, depending on whether you want to get open when denied or when fronted.

If your defender is in a denial position with a foot and hand in the passing lane between you and the ball, move a few steps away from the passer (figure 6.1). Quickly cut back on one side of your defender toward the ball. Work to get open—using short, quick steps—and get position in a strong, balanced stance, feet spread at least shoulder-width apart, knees flexed, back straight, and hands up and ball-width apart for a target.

On the pass, meet the ball, catching it with two hands. Use a jump stop landing outside the lane and above the box. The feet land at the same time on a jump stop, enabling you to use either one as a pivot foot. To keep from stepping forward after the catch, land with your weight initially back on your heels. After the landing, transfer your weight forward to the balls of your feet to get the balance you need to react and make an offensive move. Use a wide base and flex your knees. Protect the ball by keeping it in front of your forehead with your elbows out.

| Figure 6.1 | Getting Open for a Pass in the Low Post When Denied |

a *b* *c*

DEFENDER DENIES

1. Defender denies you the ball
2. Eyes on ball and opponent
3. Offensive stance
4. Hands up

MOVE AWAY, CUT BACK

1. Take defender away
2. Cut back to the ball
3. Keep hands up, ball-width apart

CATCH BALL

1. Catch ball with two hands
2. Protect ball in front of forehead
3. Keep elbows out
4. Jump stop and land in balance outside lane above box

If a defender completely fronts you, take the defender high by moving up the lane with short, quick steps to a position above the middle hash mark (figure 6.2). Seal your defender by keeping your forearm on defender's back. Signal for lob pass with hand closest to basket. Cut to the basket and catch lob pass that has been passed high toward the corner of the backboard. Jump stop and land in balance ready to score.

Figure 6.2	**Getting Open for a Pass in the Low Post When Fronted**

DEFENDER FRONTS

1. Defender fronts you
2. See ball and defender
3. Offensive stance
4. Hand up

TAKE DEFENDER HIGH

1. Take defender high (up lane)
2. Signal for lob pass with hand up
3. Cut to the basket on pass

CATCH LOB

1. Catch ball with two hands
2. Protect ball in front of forehead
3. Jump stop and land in balance ready to serve

Reading the defense means determining how your defender is playing you so you can react with the correct move. It involves seeing your opponent or feeling your defender's body against you. In the low post, you read the position by seeing or feeling whether your defender is on the *topside* (toward the foul line) or the baseline side. In both cases, you would drop step with the foot opposite the side of your defender. If you cannot locate your defender or are in doubt, use a front turn toward the baseline to face the basket and see your defender's position.

Before receiving the ball, you can anticipate your defender's position by recognizing where the pass will be coming from (that is, the corner, wing, or high-post area) and by being aware of your defender's position in trying to prevent the pass.

Drop-Step Baseline Power Move

After catching the ball in the low post and reading your defender's position on the topside, make a ball fake to the middle by showing the ball above your shoulder (figure 6.3). After the fake, move the ball to a protected position in front of your forehead with your elbows out. Drop step to the baseline with your inside foot, the one closer to the backboard. As you make the drop step, keep your weight on your pivot foot to avoid dragging it. Try to get your shoulders parallel to the backboard and your defender on your back. Maintain a strong, balanced stance with your back straight and the ball protected in front of your forehead, away from your defender. Make a power move toward the basket, jumping off both feet. Shoot the ball with two hands, keeping your shoulders parallel to the board and without opening up on the shot. Aim the ball high above the box. Land in balance, ready to rebound a possible miss with two hands. Go up again with as many power moves as it takes to score.

Figure 6.3	Low-Post Moves: Drop-Step Baseline Power Move

DEFENDER TOP SIDE

1. Jump stop as you catch the ball and land in a balanced stance
2. Protect the ball in front of your forehead
3. Keep elbows out
4. Read defender topside
5. Ball fake to the middle

DROP-STEP BASELINE

1. Drop step to the baseline and maintain a balanced stance
2. Protect the ball in front of your forehead
3. Keep elbows out
4. Fake the shot

POWER MOVE

1. Make the power move
2. Jump off both feet
3. Shoot with two hands
4. Follow through by landing in balance with your hands up, ready to rebound

Misstep

You land with a one-two stop and can use only one foot to pivot.

Correction

Land with a jump stop.

Drop-Step Middle Hook

After catching the ball in the low post and reading your defender's position on the *baseline side*, make a ball fake to the baseline by showing the ball above your shoulder (figure 6.4). After the fake, drop step to the baseline with your outside foot, the one away from the backboard. As you make the drop step, move the ball to hook shot position, with your shooting hand under the ball and your balance hand behind and slightly on top of the ball. Hold the ball back, protecting it with your head and shoulders rather than leading with it. Pivot in toward the basket. Shoot a hook shot. Land in balance, ready to rebound a possible miss with two hands, and use a power move to score.

| Figure 6.4 | Low-Post Moves: Drop-Step Middle Hook |

DEFENDER BASELINE

1. Jump stop as you catch the ball and land in balance
2. Protect the ball in front of your forehead
3. Keep elbows out
4. Read defender baseline side
5. Ball fake to the baseline

DROP-STEP MIDDLE

1. Drop step to the middle, maintaining a balanced stance
2. Get hands in hook shot position
3. Hold ball back and protect it with head and shoulders

HOOK SHOT

1. Shoot the hook shot
2. Keep two hands on the ball until release
3. Follow through by landing in balance, hands up, ready to rebound

Misstep

You rush into the move before reading the defender's position.

Correction

After receiving the pass in the low post, stop for at least one count to take time to read your defender's position. Then make your move.

Baseline Bank Jump Shot

If you cannot see or feel your defender after catching the ball in the low post your defender is behind you. Make a front turn to the baseline to see your defender. On the front turn, make an aggressive drive step and shot fake. A drive step is a short (8- to 10-inch) jab step with one foot straight at the basket. The drive step should make your defender react with a retreat step.

Keep your eye on the rim and your defender. Be a triple threat to shoot, pass, or drive. Hold the ball with your hands in shooting position. Be sure to keep your balance, and don't rush. Depending on your defender's reaction, you can then execute either a front-turn baseline bank jump shot (figure 6.5) or a front-turn baseline crossover and hook.

If the defender retreats on your drive step, shoot a bank jump shot. Aim for the top near corner of the box on the backboard. Land in balance, ready to rebound a possible miss with two hands, and use a power move to score.

| Figure 6.5 | Low-Post Moves: Front-Turn Baseline Bank Jump Shot |

DEFENDER BEHIND

1. Jump stop as you catch the ball, landing in a balanced stance
2. Protect the ball in front of your forehead
3. Keep elbows out
4. Defender behind you

FRONT-TURN BASELINE

1. Front turn to the baseline
2. Make drive step
3. See the rim and defender (defender's hands are down)
4. Fake the shot

BANK JUMP SHOT

1. Shoot bank jump shot
2. Aim for top near corner of box on backboard
3. Follow through by landing in balance, hands up, ready to rebound

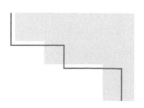

Misstep

Still in doubt about the defender's position, you front turn to the middle, which limits your moves to a jump shot in the middle or a crossover and hook from the baseline, both of which are difficult.

Correction

When in doubt, always front turn to the baseline so you can use the bank jump shot or use the crossover step to the middle and hook.

Front-Turn Baseline, Cross-over Middle and Hook

If your defender extends up on your shot fake, make a crossover step to the middle with the same foot you used for the drive step (figure 6.6). As you cross over to the middle, aggressively move the ball across the front of your body to hook shot position. Hold the ball back, protecting it with your head and shoulders. Pivot in toward the basket and shoot a hook shot. Land in balance, ready to rebound a possible miss with two hands, and use a power move to score.

Figure 6.6	Low-Post Moves: Front-Turn Baseline Crossover Middle and Hook

DEFENDER BEHIND

1. Jump stop as you catch the ball, landing in a balanced stance
2. Protect the ball in front of your forehead
3. Keep elbows out
4. Defender behind you

FRONT-TURN BASELINE, FAKE SHOT

1. Front turn to baseline
2. Drive step
3. See the rim and defender's hands up
4. Fake the shot

CROSSOVER MIDDLE

1. Crossover step to middle
2. Get hands in hook shot position
3. Hold ball back and protect it with head and shoulders

SHOOT HOOK SHOT

1. Pivot in toward basket
2. Shoot hook shot
3. Keep both hands on the ball until release
4. Follow through by landing in balance, hands up, ready to rebound

Misstep

You dribble the ball before making your move.

Correction

Make your move without dribbling. Learn to save the dribble until after your crossover step, when you can fake a hook and then either dribble by the defender or reverse dribble for a power move.

Low-Post Drill 1. *Low-Post Moves*

This drill covers the four low-post moves: the drop-step baseline power move, the drop-step middle hook, the front-turn baseline bank jump shot, and the front-turn baseline crossover and hook.

For each move, begin by tossing and catching the ball in the low post. Start under the basket and toss the ball so it will bounce at a low-post spot outside the lane and above the box on the lane line. Catch the ball with your back to the basket and make a jump stop, landing outside the lane and above the box. After catching the ball in the low post with your back to the basket, look to your baseline side to determine the position of your imaginary defender.

For the drop-step baseline power move, assume the defender is not on your baseline side. Make a shot fake to the middle and then protect the ball at your forehead. Make a drop step toward the baseline with your inside foot, the one closest to the basket, followed by another shot fake. Add a strong power move, jumping off both feet and keeping your shoulders parallel to the backboard as you shoot the ball with two hands. Aim the ball high above the box.

For the drop-step middle hook shot, assume the defender is on your baseline side. Make a shot fake to the baseline and then bring the ball to hook shot position with your shooting hand under the ball. Make a drop step toward the middle with your outside foot, the one farther from the basket, find the rim, and shoot a hook shot.

For the front-turn baseline bank jump shot, assume you must use a front turn to determine the position of the defender. Make a front turn to the baseline, drive step, and find the rim. On your drive step, show the ball, faking a jump shot high. Be a triple threat to shoot, pass, or drive. Aim for the top near the corner of the backboard box and shoot a bank jump shot.

For the front-turn baseline crossover and hook shot, make a front turn to the baseline and fake a shot, holding for a count of one before making your next move. Take a crossover step to the middle, aggressively moving the ball across the front of your body into hook shot position with your shooting hand under the ball, and shoot a hook shot.

On each move, land in balance, ready to rebound and go up again with as many power moves as necessary to score. Alternately toss the ball to the right, making each move on the right side of the basket, and to the left, making each move on the left side of the basket. Perform five repetitions of each move from each side.

Success Check

- Maintain triple-threat position, ready to pass, shoot, or drive.
- Take time to read the defender.
- Try to make five consecutive shots on each move from each side.

Score Your Success

Attempt to make five consecutive shots on each move from each side. Give yourself 1 point each time you make five consecutive shots.

Drop-step baseline power move from right ___; points earned ___

Drop-step baseline power move from left ___; points earned ___

Drop-step middle hook shot from right ___; points earned ___

Drop-step middle hook shot from left ___; points earned ___

Front-turn baseline bank jump shot from right ___; points earned ___

Front-turn baseline bank jump shot from left ___; points earned ___

Front-turn baseline crossover and hook shot from right ___; points earned ___

Front-turn baseline crossover and hook shot from left ___; points earned ___

Your score ___ (8 points maximum)

Low-Post Drill 2. *Read the Defense*

This drill gives you practice reading defenders in the low post and reacting with the correct move. Select a partner to be a defensive player. The defensive player defends you only until you read the defense and select the correct move, not while you make your move. After you catch the ball in the low post, the defender will vary defensive position—baseline side, topside, or off of you—to give you practice making the correct decision.

When you see or sense the foot opposite the side of your defender on the topside (toward the foul line) or on the baseline side, drop step with the foot opposite the side of the defender and make the appropriate move. If you cannot locate the defender or are in doubt, use a front turn toward the baseline to face the basket and see the defender's position. After the front turn, the defender will play you with hands up or hands down. If the defender's hands are down, make a bank jump shot. If the defender's hands are up, use a crossover step to the middle and shoot a hook shot. Continue the drill for 10 shots.

Success Check

- Read the defender and make the appropriate move.
- Use correct technique for each low-post move.

Score Your Success

Give yourself 1 point for each correct read of the defender and 1 point for each shot you make. Total your points to find your overall score.

Fewer than 11 points = 0 points

11 to 15 points = 1 point

16 to 20 points = 5 points

Your score ___

Low-Post Drill 3. *One-on-One in the Half Circle*

This competitive game develops your ability to read the defender and use fakes, pivots, and different low-post moves to score or draw a foul. It also develops defense and rebounding skills. You will play offense against a defender. Use the lower half of the free throw circle as a boundary. Your objective is to score with a low-post move. You may not dribble the ball, but you may take one step outside the lower half circle before shooting the ball.

The defender initiates play by getting in a defensive stance and then handing you the ball. You get 2 points each time you score. If you get fouled while making the shot, you get a free throw. If you get fouled but miss the shot, you get two free throws. If you miss the shot but get an offensive rebound, you may make a move and score from the spot where you rebounded the ball. Again, dribbling is not allowed. Continue play until you score or turn the ball over or until the defender gets the ball on a steal or rebound and dribbles back past the free throw line. Switch offensive and defensive roles. Play to 7 points.

As a variation, start on offense with a ball and your back to the basket. The defender initiates play by touching you. Another variation is to start with your back to the basket in the low post on either side of the lane.

Success Check

- Read the defender and use the best low-post move.
- Do not dribble the ball.
- Be aggressive.

Score Your Success

This is a competitive drill. The first player to score 7 points wins the game. Give yourself 5 points if you win the game.

Your score ___

ONE-ON-ONE PERIMETER MOVES

One-on-one moves are made on the outside or perimeter area, facing the basket. The six basic one-on-one moves are the drive-step jump shot, drive-step straight drive, drive-step crossover drive, straight-drive jump shot, crossover-drive jump shot, and step-back jump shot.

You may be a fine shooter and execute good offensive moves, but if you cannot get open to receive the ball when you are being defended, all this ability with the ball is worthless. When you move to get open, try to see the ball, the basket, and your defender. If you don't see a ball being passed to you, the result will be a turnover and a missed scoring opportunity.

Move to free yourself. You cannot stand still! Constantly change pace and direction. Creating space between players—an often neglected skill—is important. Work for 12 to 15 feet of space, enough to keep one defender from guarding two offensive players. Try to move to an open area or create an angle for an open passing lane between you and the passer. When the defender is denying you a passing lane on the perimeter, overplaying the passing lane between you and the passer, make a *backdoor cut* to the basket. If you still do not receive a pass after the backdoor cut, change direction and cut back to the outside. This is called a *V-cut*. Get open to receive the ball within your shooting range. Your *shooting range* is the distance within which you can consistently make an outside shot.

There are two methods for receiving the ball, depending on whether you are open or closely guarded. You read in step 4 about catching the ball when open in position to shoot (page 80). Catching the ball when you are closely guarded in the scoring area requires a different technique. When you are closely guarded, come to *meet the pass*. By meeting the pass you can beat your defender to the ball. Give the passer a good target. Your hands should be above your waist for straight passes, above your head for lob passes, and below your waist and above your knees for bounce passes. Catch the ball with your hands in a relaxed position, giving with the ball as you catch it. Land with a one-two stop. It is good to land first on your inside foot (the foot closer to the basket), establishing it as a pivot foot. You can then protect the ball with your body while you are in position to execute a reverse turn (drop step) with your opposite foot, if your defender overcommits when going for the pass. After receiving the ball, use a front turn, face the basket, and look to the rim. Focusing on the rim allows you to see the total picture, including whether your defender is playing you for the shot, drive, or pass. Hold the ball high with your hands in shooting position. Be a triple threat to shoot, drive, or pass.

When you receive the ball, face the basket and your defender (also called *squaring up*). Being square to the basket positions you well as a triple threat to shoot, pass, or drive (figure 6.7). Keep your eye on the rim and your defender. By focusing on the rim, you can see more of the court and whether a teammate is open in scoring position. You also can see your defender to read whether you are being played up close for a shot or back for a pass or drive. Hold the ball high with your hands in shooting position. You must first be a threat to shoot before the options of passing or driving become viable. Make an aggressive drive step (also called a *jab step*). A drive step is a short, quick step with your nonpivot foot straight toward your defender. Your weight should be on your pivot foot, with your knees flexed and your upper body erect. A drive step is used to fake a drive and force your defender to react with a retreat step.

| Figure 6.7 | Triple–Threat Position |

TRIPLE THREAT TO SHOOT, PASS, OR DRIVE

1. See the rim and defender
2. Head over waist
3. Back straight
4. Block-and-tuck hand position
5. Ball moving high
6. Knees flexed
7. Feet shoulder-width apart
8. Weight on pivot (back) foot
9. Short drive step with shooting foot

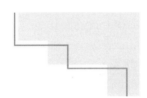

Misstep

You hold the ball too far from your body, allowing the defender to grab it.

Correction

Keep the ball high and close to your head and shooting shoulder.

Reading the defense when you are being guarded on the perimeter entails first determining how your defender reacts to your aggressive drive step and then reacting with the correct offensive move. From your triple-threat stance, you can make one of six basic one-on-one moves, all starting with the drive step: the drive-step jump shot, drive-step straight drive, drive-step crossover drive, straight-drive jump shot, crossover-drive jump shot, and step-back jump shot. Which move you choose depends on the defensive player's position in reaction to your drive step.

When your defender's hands are down, bring your drive-step foot back to shooting position and shoot a jump shot. When your defender has a hand up to play the shot, drive to the side of the raised hand. The weakness in a defender's stance is the lead foot (the foot that is forward or up). It is more difficult for a defender to stop a drive toward the lead foot because it necessitates a long drop step with that foot while reverse pivoting on the back foot. A drive toward the defender's back foot necessitates only a short retreat step. In a normal defensive stance, the defender's hand that is up will be on the same side as the lead foot. Rather than looking down to check which foot is up, simply look at which hand is up and drive to that side. Whichever hand is up is on the side of your defender's lead foot and weakness. When the defender's hand is up on the side of your drive step, use a straight drive. When the defender's hand is up on the side away from your drive step, use a crossover drive.

Being a triple threat, making a drive step, and reading your defender's reaction and hand position are all extremely important. Do not rush. Keep your balance physically, mentally, and emotionally. Only by maintaining control and reading your defender can you successfully execute a one-on-one offensive move.

Drive-Step Jump Shot

If the defender's hands are down, quickly bring your drive-step foot back into a balanced shooting stance and make a jump shot (figure 6.8).

Figure 6.8   Perimeter Moves: Drive–Step Jump Shot

TRIPLE-THREAT

1. Triple-threat stance
2. See the rim and defender
3. Short drive step
4. Read defender; hand is down

SHOOT JUMP SHOT

1. Bring drive-step foot back
2. Shoot jump shot

FOLLOW-THROUGH

1. Land in balance
2. Hold follow-through until ball reaches basket
3. Be ready to rebound or get back on defense

Misstep

You dribble the ball before making your move.

Correction

Make your move without dribbling first. Learn to save your dribble.

Drive-Step Straight Drive

If the defender's hand is up on the side of your drive step, take a longer step with your drive-step foot past the defender's lead foot (figure 6.9). Take a long dribble with your outside hand, the one away from the defender, and then push off your pivot foot, keeping your head up with your eyes on the basket. The ball must leave your hand before you lift your pivot foot off the floor or you will commit a traveling violation. Having your weight on your pivot foot during your drive step helps prevent traveling. Protect the ball with your inside hand and your body.

Drive in a straight line to the basket, close to your defender. Cut off your defender's retreat by closing the gap between your body and your defender's retreat step. After driving past your defender, look to the basket and be alert for defensive help. You may decide to finish the play by going strong to the basket for a layup, exploding on your takeoff and protecting the ball with two hands. If a teammate's defender attempts to pick you up, pass to an open teammate who can score.

Figure 6.9 | Perimeter Moves: Drive–Step Straight Drive

a 3 1 *b* *c* 3

STRAIGHT DRIVE

1. Drive step, then long step past defender's lead foot
2. Dribble ball past defender with outside hand
3. Push off pivot foot
4. Protect ball with inside hand

CLOSE GAP

1. Close gap between your body and defender's retreat step
2. Pick up ball at shooting knee
3. Have shooting hand on top of ball

SHOOT LAYUP

1. Shoot layup or pass to teammate
2. Protect ball with two hands until release
3. Land in balance, ready to rebound

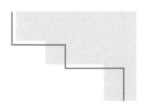

Misstep

You make your drive step too long or you lean, putting weight on your drive-step foot. This limits your ability to quickly move your lead foot in reaction to how the defender plays you.

Correction

Keep your weight on your pivot foot as you execute the drive step. This enables you to move your lead foot quickly to shoot, pass, or use a straight or crossover drive.

Drive-Step Crossover Drive

This one-on-one move is similar to the straight drive except that you cross the ball over in front of your chest and crossover step with your drive-step foot past your defender's lead foot (figure 6.10). Then take a long dribble with your outside hand and continue as in the straight drive.

Figure 6.10 | Perimeter Moves: Drive-Step Crossover Drive

TRIPLE-THREAT

1. Triple-threat stance
2. See the rim and defender
3. Short drive step
4. Read defender; hand is up on side away from drive step

CROSSOVER DRIVE

1. Crossover step past defender's lead foot
2. Dribble past defender with outside hand
3. Push off pivot foot
4. Protect ball with inside hand

CLOSE GAP

1. Close gap between your body and defender's retreat step
2. Pick up ball at shooting knee
3. Have shooting hand on top of ball

SHOOT LAYUP

1. Shoot layup or pass to a teammate
2. Protect ball with two hands until release
3. Land in balance, ready to rebound

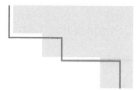

Misstep

On a drive to the basket, you dribble too wide, allowing the defender more time to recover against your drive.

Correction

Dribble behind the defender to close the gap and cut off the defender's retreat step.

Straight-Drive Jump Shot

From a triple-threat stance, make an aggressive drive step (figure 6.11). Stop and read the defender's hand position. If the defender's hand is up on the *same side* as your drive step, take a longer step with your drive-step foot past your defender's lead foot. Take one long dribble with your outside hand, the one away from the defender, and then push off your pivot foot. Aim the dribble for a spot past the defender's body, keeping your eyes on the basket. Protect the ball with your inside hand and your body.

Move under the defender's arm and jump stop behind the defender's body. This move makes it difficult for the defender to block your shot without fouling you. If you go too wide, the defender will have time and space to block the shot. Pick up the ball in front of your shooting knee with your shooting hand on top of the ball and your balance hand under the ball. Protect the ball with your head and shoulders and move it away from the defender's reach as you shoot a jump shot.

Figure 6.11   **Perimeter Moves: Straight-Drive Jump Shot**

a

b

c

STRAIGHT DRIVE	**JUMP STOP**	**SHOOT JUMP SHOT**
1. Take long step past defender's lead foot	1. Move under defender's arm	1. Protect ball with head and shoulders
2. Dribble ball behind defender's body with outside hand	2. Jump stop behind defender's body	2. Move ball away from defender
3. Push off pivot foot	3. Pick up ball at shooting knee	3. Expect to be fouled
4. Protect ball with inside hand	4. Have shooting hand on top of ball	4. Shoot jump shot

Basketball: Steps to Success

Misstep
On a one-dribble jump shot, you dribble too wide, allowing the defender time and space to block the shot.
Correction
Move under the defender's arm and jump stop behind the defender's body, making it difficult for the defender to block your shot without fouling you.

Crossover-Drive Jump Shot

The crossover-drive one-dribble jump shot is similar to the straight-drive one-dribble jump shot. If the defender's hand is up on the side *away* from your drive step, cross the ball over in front of your chest before the dribble (figure 6.12). Crossover step with your drive-step foot past your defender's lead foot.

Figure 6.12 **Perimeter Moves: Crossover-Drive Jump Shot**

a

b

TRIPLE-THREAT
1. Triple-threat stance
2. See the rim and defender
3. Short drive step
4. Read defender; hand is up on side away from drive step

CROSSOVER DRIVE
1. Crossover step past defender's lead foot
2. Dribble ball behind defender's body with outside hand
3. Push off pivot foot
4. Protect ball with inside hand

(continued)

Figure 6.12 *(continued)*

c

d

JUMP STOP	**SHOOT JUMP SHOT**
1. Move under defender's arm	1. Protect ball with head and shoulders
2. Jump behind defender's body	2. Move ball away from defender
3. Pick up ball at shooting knee	3. Expect to be fouled
4. Have shooting hand on top of ball	4. Shoot jump shot

Misstep

You rush into your move before reading your defender's position.

Correction

After receiving a pass, take time to read the defender's position. Then make your move.

Step-Back Jump Shot

If the defender makes a retreat step, take a quick step back away from the defender on the same foot used for the drive step (figure 6.13). Dribble back with your strong hand, jump behind the ball, and pick it up in front of your shooting knee with your shooting hand on top of the ball. Shoot a jump shot. Maintain balance by picking up the ball at your knee and exaggerating the follow-through of your shoulders, head, and shooting hand toward the basket to counter any tendency to lean back or step back on your shot.

| Figure 6.13 | **Perimeter Moves: Step–Back Jump Shot** |

a

b

c

TRIPLE-THREAT

1. Triple-threat stance
2. View of rim and defender
3. Short drive step
4. Read defender's retreat on drive step

STEP BACK DRIBBLE

1. Step back with drive-step foot
2. Dribble ball back with strong hand
3. Push off pivot foot
4. Protect ball with nondribbling hand
5. Pick up ball at shooting knee with shooting hand on top of ball

SHOOT JUMP SHOT

1. Shoot jump shot
2. Exaggerate the follow-through
3. Land in balance, hand up until the ball reaches the basket, ready to rebound

Misstep

When dribbling back, you lean your head and shoulders back causing you to fade back and miss short on your shot.

Correction

Use a low dribble back and keep your head and shoulders forward.

Perimeter Drill 1. *One-on-One Moves off Toss to Elbow*

This drill practices the six one-on-one moves off a drive step: the drive-step jump shot, drive-step straight drive, drive-step crossover drive, straight-drive jump shot, crossover-drive jump shot, and step-back jump shot. Position a chair inside the left elbow to serve as an imaginary defender. Start at the left box and toss the ball so it bounces at the left elbow and behind the chair. You are passing the ball to yourself; use a tossback if one is available. Catch the ball with a one-two stop. Your inside foot, the one closer to the basket, should land first, becoming your pivot foot. Make a front turn to the middle, drive step, and look for the rim. Assume a triple-threat stance to shoot, pass, or drive.

For the drive-step jump shot, after taking the drive step, assume the defender's hands are down and make a jump shot.

For the straight drive, after taking the drive step, assume the defender's inside hand, the one closest to the middle, is up. Make an aggressive shot fake and then take a straight step past the chair with the same foot you used for the drive step. Dribble beyond the chair with the hand away from the defender, drive to the basket, and shoot a layup, making sure your pivot foot doesn't leave the floor before you release the ball on the dribble. Use your inside hand for protection, and keep your body close to the chair to cut off the imaginary defender's retreat step. After shooting a layup, land in balance, ready to rebound and make as many power moves as necessary to score.

For the crossover drive, after taking the drive step, assume the defender's outside hand, the one away from the middle, is up. Make an aggressive shot fake and then crossover step past the chair with the same foot you used for the drive step. On the crossover step, aggressively move the ball across the front of your body. Dribble beyond the chair with the hand away from the defender, drive to the basket, and shoot a layup. From this point, continue as with the straight drive.

For the straight-drive jump shot, after taking the drive step, assume the defender's inside hand, the one closest to the middle, is up. Make an aggressive shot fake and then take a straight step past the chair with the same foot you used for the drive step. Aim the dribble behind the chair. Dribble with the hand away from the defender, jump behind the ball, and pick it up at your shooting knee with your shooting hand on top. Shoot a jump shot. Imagine that you are driving under the defender's arm, and keep your body close to the imaginary defender to prevent your shot being blocked. Use your head and shoulders to protect the ball, and try to draw a foul as you shoot for a possible three-point play. After shooting, land in balance, ready to rebound and make as many power moves as it takes to score.

For the crossover-drive jump shot, after taking the drive step, assume the defender's outside hand, the one away from the middle, is up. Make an aggressive shot fake and then crossover step

past the chair with the same foot you used for the drive step. On the crossover step, aggressively move the ball across the front of your body, aiming the dribble for a spot behind the chair. Continue as in the straight-drive jump shot.

For the step-back one-dribble jump shot, after taking the drive step, assume that the defender takes a retreat step. Take a quick step back away from the chair with the same foot used for the drive step. Dribble back with your strong hand and jump behind the ball. Shoot a jump shot. Make sure to pick up the ball in front of your knee with your shooting hand on top of the ball, and exaggerate the follow-through of your shoulders, head, and shooting arm to counter any tendency to lean back or step back on the shot.

Alternately toss the ball to the left, making each move at the left elbow, and to the right, making each move at the right elbow. Perform 10 repetitions of each move to each side.

Success Check

- Be a triple threat to pass, shoot, or drive.
- Read the defender and react with the best move.
- Use correct shooting technique.

Score Your Success

Perform 10 attempts for each move and each side. Record the number of shots you make off each move to each side. Give yourself 1 point if you make at least 8 out of 10 attempts.

Drive-step jump shot, left elbow ___; points earned ___

Drive-step jump shot, right elbow ___; points earned ___

Drive-step straight drive, left elbow ___; points earned ___

Drive-step straight drive, right elbow ___; points earned ___

Drive-step crossover drive, left elbow ___; points earned ___

Drive-step crossover drive, right elbow ___; points earned ___

Straight-drive jump shot, left elbow ___; points earned ___

Straight-drive jump shot, right elbow ___;
   points earned ___

Crossover-drive jump shot, left elbow ___;
   points earned ___

Crossover-drive jump shot, right elbow ___;
   points earned ___

Step-back jump shot, left elbow ___;
   points earned ___

Step-back jump shot, right elbow ___;
   points earned ___

Your score ___ (12 points maximum)

Perimeter Drill 2. *Read the Defense*

This drill gives you one-on-one practice at reading how a defender is playing you and reacting with the correct move. Select a partner to be a defender. The defender defends you only until you read the defense and select the correct move, not while you make your move.

After you catch the ball at the free throw line, the defender varies the defensive position—hands down or one hand up—to give you practice making the correct decision. If the defender's hands are down, shoot a jump shot. If the defender's hand is up, drive to the side of the raised hand with the appropriate straight drive or crossover drive. If the defender retreats on your drive step, use the step-back jump shot. Continue the drill until you have taken 10 shots.

Success Check

- Read the defender and make the correct decision.
- Use proper technique for each one-on-one move and each shot.

Score Your Success

Keep track of the number of times you make a correct read of the defense and the number of shots you make. Each element is worth 1 point. After you finish the drill, tally your points to find your overall score.

Fewer than 11 points = 0 points

11 to 15 points = 1 point

16 to 20 points = 5 points

Your score ___

Perimeter Drill 3. *One-on-One in the Free Throw Circle (One Dribble)*

This competitive game develops the ability to read the defender and use fakes, pivots, and one-on-one moves to score or draw a foul. It also develops defense and rebounding skills. You will play offense against a defender. Your objective is to score with a one-on-one move. Use the top half of the free throw circle as a boundary. You may dribble once and may take one step outside the top half of the circle before releasing the shot.

The defender initiates play by getting in a defensive stance inside the free throw line and handing you the ball at a position above the free throw line. You get 2 points each time you score. If you get fouled on a successful shot, you get a free throw. If you get fouled but the shot misses, you get two free throws. If you miss the shot but get an offensive rebound, make a move and score from the spot where you rebounded the ball. Again, only one dribble is allowed. Continue play until you score or turn over the ball or until the defender gets the ball on a steal or rebound and dribbles back past the free throw line. Switch offensive and defensive roles. Play to 7 points.

Success Check

- Read the defender and use the best one-on-one move.
- Do not dribble the ball more than once.
- Be aggressive.

Score Your Success

This is a competitive drill. The first player to score 7 points wins the game. Give yourself 5 points if you win the game.

Your score ___

Perimeter Drill 4. *Close Out One-on-One (Three Dribbles)*

This competitive game also develops the ability to read a defender and use fakes, pivots, and one-on-one moves to score or draw a foul. Again, it develops defense and rebounding skills. Your objective is to score with a one-on-one move. Start on the perimeter within shooting range. The defender starts under the basket.

The defender tosses a ball to the offensive player to begin the drill. The defender closes out on defense (runs at the offensive player and gets into a defensive stance within touching distance of the offensive player). The offensive player may use three dribbles. You get 2 points each time you score. If you get fouled on a successful shot, you get a free throw. If you get fouled but the shot misses, you get two free throws. If you miss the shot but get an offensive rebound, make a move and score from the spot where you rebounded the ball. Again, only three dribbles are allowed. Continue play until you score or turn over the ball or until the defender gets the ball on a steal or rebound and dribbles

back past the free throw line. Switch offensive and defensive roles.

For variety, the offensive player can start at a different position, such as the top, wing, or either corner, within the player's shooting range.

Success Check

- Read the defender and use the best one-on-one move.
- Do not dribble the ball more than three times.
- Be aggressive.

Score Your Success

This is a competitive drill. The first player to score 7 points wins the game. Give yourself 5 points if you win the game.

Your score ___

Perimeter Drill 5. *Block the Shot*

This drill requires two players, one on offense and one on defense. Start as the offensive player. Be in position to catch and shoot at the three-point line or within your shooting range. The defender starts under the basket.

The defender starts the drill by making a chest pass to your shooting hand. The defender then runs past you, attempting to block your shot. As the defender runs past you, fake the shot, then take one dribble step away from the shot blocker and shoot a jump shot. Score a point each time you make a successful shot. After each attempt, switch offensive and defensive roles. Each player makes 10 attempts.

Success Check

- Be prepared to catch and shoot in one smooth motion.
- Use only one dribble to move away from the defender after the fake.

Score Your Success

This is a competitive drill. Try to score more points than your partner, and give yourself 5 points if you succeed.

Your score ___

Perimeter Drill 6. *Dribble One-on-One*

This drill requires two players, one on offense and one on defense. The defender starts under the basket and makes a chest pass to the offensive player before quickly moving to a defensive position.

As the offensive player, dribble at the defender and use a footfire dribble (page 45) as you meet. The footfire dribble normally causes a defender to freeze for a second, giving you time to gain balance, read the defender's position, then make the appropriate one-on-one move.

You get 2 points each time you score. If you get fouled on a successful shot, you get a free throw. If you get fouled but the shot misses, you get two free throws. If you miss the shot but get an offensive rebound, make a move and score from the spot where you rebounded the ball. Continue play until you score or turn over the ball or until the defender gets the ball on a steal or rebound. Switch offensive and defensive roles. Play to 7 points.

Success Check

• Read the defender and use the best one-on-one move.

• Use the footfire dribble to freeze the defender.

• Be aggressive.

Score Your Success

This is a competitive drill. The first player to score 7 points wins the game. Give yourself 5 points if you win the game.

Your score ___

RATE YOUR SUCCESS

Become a triple threat to score, pass, or drive by perfecting movement with the ball. Learn to take on a defender one-on-one and win, opening up offensive opportunities for your team. In this step, we have covered various moves with the ball that will turn you into a triple threat.

In the next step, we will look at moving without the ball. Before going to step 7, however, look back at how you performed the drills in this step. For each of the drills presented in this step, enter the points you earned, then add up your scores to rate your total success.

Low-Post Drills

1. Low-Post Moves	___ out of 8
2. Read the Defense	___ out of 5
3. One-on-One in the Half Circle	___ out of 5

Perimeter Drills

1. One-on-One Moves off Toss to Elbow	___ out of 12
2. Read the Defense	___ out of 5
3. One-on-One in the Free Throw Circle (One Dribble)	___ out of 5
4. Close Out One-on-One (Three Dribbles)	___ out of 5
5. Block the Shot	___ out of 5
6. Dribble One-on-One	___ out of 5
TOTAL	___ out of 55

If you scored 40 or more points, congratulations! You have mastered the basics of this step and are ready to move on to step 7, moving without the ball. If you scored fewer than 40 points, you may want to spend more time on the fundamentals covered in this step. Practice the drills again to develop mastery of the techniques and increase your scores.

Moving Without the Ball

Basketball is a team game. Having the most talented players does not guarantee that your team will win. To win, you must play as a team. A team's success depends on all players working together so all team members fully utilize their offensive talents. On offense, the goal is to score. This means helping each other create opportunities to get the best shot possible each time your team has possession of the ball. Only one of the team's five players can have the ball at a time, so about 80 percent of the time you will be playing without the ball.

To help your team create scoring opportunities, you must be able to move without the ball. Moving without the ball includes helping yourself or a teammate get open by setting or cutting off a screen and keeping your defender focused on your movements away from the ball, limiting defensive help on the ball.

When you learn to move without the ball, you will not only make yourself a better player, but will also have more fun. The knowledge that you are helping your teammates brings its own satisfaction in addition to the acknowledgment you receive from an appreciative coach, teammates, and fans.

No matter how good your offensive skills with the ball are, they will not help if you cannot get open to use them. First, you must move to get open to receive the ball where you can be in position as a triple threat to shoot, drive, or pass. You also must move without the ball to provide opportunities for the shots you and your teammates want, such as an inside post-up, a one-on-one drive, or a jump shot that you can shoot in rhythm and range. Before shooting, you or your teammate must get open. Moving without the ball includes not only getting yourself open, but also setting and moving off screens to enable your teammate to get open.

Moving without the ball is also important when you are away from the ball. When uncertain of your position, your defender will not be as alert to giving defensive help to a teammate guarding the player with the ball.

Some specific opportunities for moving without the ball are to

- use various maneuvers to get open to receive the ball in position to be a triple threat to shoot, pass, or drive;

- set a screen on or off the ball, enabling a teammate to get open or forcing a switch that will get you open;

- cut off a screen to get yourself open or to force a switch that will get the screener open;

- keep moving away from the ball to make it difficult for your defender to see both you and the ball or to be in position to give defensive help to a teammate guarding the player with the ball;

- be alert to go after loose balls or to change from offense to defense when your team loses possession; and

- move on a shot to get in offensive rebound position or get back on defense.

Have a trained observer such as a coach, teacher, or a skilled player evaluate and provide corrective feedback on your ability to move without the ball and execute two- and three-person plays.

V-CUT

When your defender has a foot and hand in the passing lane to deny you the pass, take your opponent toward the basket and then sharply change direction, cutting back to the outside. This is called a *V-cut* (figure 7.1) and is the most commonly used way to get open. You can use a V-cut from any position on the floor if an opponent is overplaying the passing lane between you and the passer.

The effectiveness of a V-cut depends on deception, timing, and changing direction sharply from cutting toward the basket to cutting back out. When you take a defender toward the basket, be deceptive before changing direction to cut back to the outside. Time your cut back out to coincide with the delivery of the pass.

As you change direction, use a two-count move. Step first with your inside foot and then with your outside foot, without crossing your feet. On your first step, use a three-quarter step rather than a full step and flex your knee as you plant your foot firmly to stop your momentum.

Turn on the ball of your inside foot and push off toward the outside. Shift your weight and take a long step with your outside foot, toes pointing to the outside. Continue to move out, going to meet the ball as it is passed.

When you move to get open, keep the ball, the basket, and the defender in view. Failing to see the ball being passed to you usually results in a turnover and a missed scoring opportunity. After making the V-cut, get your lead hand up as a target for the pass. Beat your defender to the ball by going to meet the pass, and catch it with two hands.

Land with a one-two stop. Land first on your inside foot, the one closer to the basket, establishing it as your pivot foot. You can then protect the ball with your body and still be in position to execute a reverse turn (drop step) with your opposite foot if your defender overcommits going for the pass. After receiving the pass, use a front turn to the middle, face the basket, look for the rim, and be a triple threat to shoot, drive, or pass.

Figure 7.1 | V-Cut

a

b

c

CUT TO BASKET

1. Cut to basket, using a three-quarter step with the Inside foot
2. Use deception and timing and a two-count move
3. Flex your knee

V-CUT OUT

1. Turn on ball of foot and push off to outside
2. Shift weight and take a long step with outside foot
3. Have outside hand up as a target
4. Continue cut to outside

CATCH AND FRONT TURN

1. Meet the pass and catch it with both hands
2. Use one-two stop, landing on inside foot first
3. Front turn to middle
4. Keep the rim and defender in view
5. Get in triple-threat stance

Misstep

You circle your change of direction rather than making a sharp cut.

Correction

Use a two-count move, first taking a three-quarter step and flexing your knee to pivot sharply and push off in the direction you want to go. Shift your weight and take a long second step.

BACKDOOR CUT

When your defender has a foot and hand in the passing lane to deny you the pass to the outside, change direction and cut behind the defender toward the basket. This is called a *backdoor cut* (figure 7.2). You can use the backdoor cut from any position on the floor if an opponent is overplaying the passing lane between you and the passer.

With experience, you will be able to use a backdoor cut automatically any time you are denied a pass on the outside. Also use this move when you see your defender's head turned away from you and toward the ball. That momentary loss of vision can cause your defender to miss seeing you cut backdoor to the basket for a pass and possible layup.

The success of a backdoor cut comes from communicating with the passer and sharply changing direction to the basket. The passer may throw the ball away when a backdoor cut is not made. Eliminate guesswork by using a designated key word to indicate to the passer that you are going backdoor. This key word signals that, once you start, you will continue your backdoor cut to the basket. A sharp, two-syllable word (for example, *New York, LA,* or *ice cream*) works well because it coincides with your two-count footwork. Set up the backdoor cut by taking your defender high. On the wing, take the defender at least a step above the foul line extended; at the point, take the defender a step above the free throw circle. Shout the key word to indicate your backdoor cut just before changing direction and cutting to the basket. Use a two-count move to change direction, stepping first with your outside and then with your inside foot (see the V-cut to review how).

The backdoor cut appears to be a relatively simple move but requires concentrated practice to execute sharply and effectively. Concentrate on a two-count move. When changing direction from right to left, you would concentrate on a two-count *right-left*; when going from left to right, you would concentrate on a two-count *left-right*.

As with the V-cut, when you cut backdoor, keep the ball, the basket, and other defenders in view. You also must be alert for help-side defenders rotating to you and possibly trying to draw a charge after your cut. After making your backdoor cut, get your lead hand up as a target. After receiving the pass, look to shoot, drive to the basket for a layup, or if picked up by another defender, pass to the teammate who has been left open.

Figure 7.2   Backdoor Cut

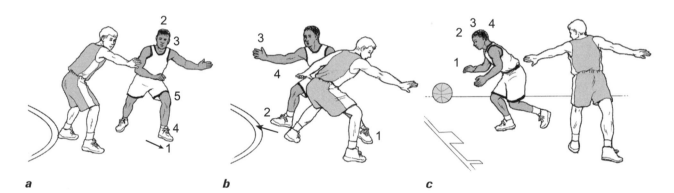

a   b   c

TAKE DEFENDER HIGH

1. Take defender high
2. Concentrate on two-count move
3. Shout key word for backdoor cut
4. Take three-quarter step with outside foot
5. Flex your knee

CUT TO BASKET

1. Turn on ball of foot and push off to inside
2. Shift weight and take long step with inside foot
3. Have inside hand up as target
4. Continue cut to basket

CATCH THE PASS

1. Catch ball with two hands
2. Shoot layup or pass
3. Protect ball with two hands until release
4. Follow through by landing in balance, ready to rebound

Misstep

You do not have enough space on your backdoor cut to get open.

Correction

Take the defender high. On the wing, take the defender at least a step above the foul line extended; at the point, take the defender a step above the free throw circle.

Backdoor Cut Drill. *Two-on-Zero*

This drill requires two players. Start with the ball at a box outside the lane and with your back to the basket. Pass to yourself by tossing the ball diagonally across the lane to the opposite elbow. Catch the ball with a one-two stop with your inside foot landing first. Pivot to the middle, find the rim, and take a drive step. Be a triple threat to shoot, pass, or drive.

On your toss of the ball, your teammate runs to the opposite box, makes a sharp change of direction, and runs up the lane line to the elbow on the side opposite you. On reaching the elbow, your teammate assumes that a defender is denying a pass at the elbow (a chair can represent a defender) and makes a backdoor cut to the basket, giving a verbal signal just before the backdoor cut. A two-syllable word such as *eyeball* or *onion* is recommended to coincide with the sharp two-step change of direction needed to make a successful backdoor cut. Make a bounce pass to your teammate, who will receive the pass and shoot a layup.

Follow the shot to rebound a possible miss and make a power move to score. Change positions and continue the drill, with each player making five backdoor cuts and five layups on each side.

Success Check

- Use a one-two stop when you catch the ball, landing on your inside foot first.
- Verbally signal the backdoor cut to your teammate.
- Get in triple-threat position when you have the ball.

Score Your Success

Give yourself 1 point for each successful backdoor cut and each successful layup on each side, for a total of 20 points maximum. A score of 16 to 20 points is excellent.

Your score ___

GIVE-AND-GO

The give-and-go, the most basic play in basketball, has been part of the game since it was first played. The name comes from the action: You give (pass) the ball to your teammate and go (cut) to the basket, looking to receive a return pass for a layup. The give-and-go exemplifies team play. By passing the ball and then moving without it, you create an opportunity to score on a return pass. Even if you do not get open on the cut, you at least give your teammate a better opportunity to initiate a one-on-one move because your defender will be in a less advantageous position to give defensive help.

After initiating the give-and-go with a pass, be sure to read the defender's position before cutting to the basket. If the defender moves with you, continuing to guard you closely, simply make a hard cut to the basket. But if your opponent drops off you, moving toward the ball on your pass (as most players learn to do), set up your defender with a fake before you cut. Fake by taking a step or two *away* from the ball, as though you are not involved in the play. As the defender moves with you, make a sharp change of direction and *front cut* to the basket (figure 7.3). You also can fake by taking a step or two *toward* the ball, as though you are going to set a screen for or take a handoff from the player with the ball. Then, as the defender moves with you, make a sharp change of direction and *backdoor cut* to the basket (figure 7.4). As you gain experience in executing the give-and-go, you will learn to read your defender, use deception, and time your cut.

Figure 7.3   Give-and-Go: Fake Away and Front Cut

PASS

1. Pass to teammate

a

FAKE AWAY

1. Fake with step away from ball

b

FRONT CUT

1. Change direction and front cut to basket
2. Have lead hand up
3. Catch ball with two hands
4. Shoot layup

c

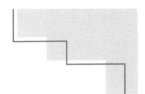

Misstep

You do not have enough space to get open.

Correction

At the point, start the give-and-go at least a step above the free throw circle. On the wing, start the give-and-go a step above the foul line extended.

Figure 7.4　　Give-and-Go: Step to Ball and Backdoor Cut

PASS

1. Pass to teammate

a

FAKE TOWARD BALL

1. Fake with step toward ball

b

BACKDOOR CUT

1. Change direction and backdoor cut all the way to basket
2. Have lead hand up
3. Catch ball with two hands
4. Shoot layup

c

Misstep

After starting your backdoor cut, you stop cutting causing the pass to be thrown away.

Correction

On a backdoor cut, you must cut all the way to the basket. The passer will only pass if you are open. This will eliminate a turnover on the pass.

Give-and-Go Drill. *Two-on-Zero*

Select a teammate to be your partner. Start with the ball at a box outside the lane and with your back to the basket. Your partner starts at the opposite box across the lane. Pass to yourself by tossing the ball diagonally across the lane to the opposite elbow. Catch the ball with a one-two stop with your inside foot landing first. Pivot to the middle, find the rim, and make a drive step. Be a triple threat to shoot, pass, or drive.

On your toss of the ball, your teammate runs to the opposite box, makes a sharp change of direction, and runs up the lane line to the elbow on the side opposite you. You make a chest pass to your teammate and cut to the basket (give-and-go). Your teammate makes a return bounce pass to you as you cut. Receive the pass and shoot a layup. Your teammate follows to rebound a possible miss and make as many power moves as necessary to score.

Change positions and continue the drill, with each player cutting and shooting five layups on each side, for a total of 10 layups for each player.

Success Check

- Use a one-two stop, landing on your inside foot first.
- Get in triple-threat position when you have the ball.

Score Your Success

Fewer than 5 made layups = 0 points

5 to 6 made layups = 1 point

7 to 8 made layups = 3 points

9 to 10 made layups = 5 points

Your score ___

SCREENING

Setting a screen (also called a *pick*) is a maneuver to position yourself to block the path of a teammate's defender. Screens may be set for a player with or without the ball.

The pass and screen away is basic to team play in basketball. It involves at least three players: screener, cutter, and passer. You set a screen for a teammate, who cuts off the screen to get open to receive a pass for a shot or drive. If your defender switches to your cutting teammate, you will be momentarily open and on the ball side of the defender whom you screened.

Screening involves four steps: setting the screen, seeing the screen, using the screen, and freeing the screen.

Setting the screen. When setting a screen, align the center of your body on your teammate's defender at an angle that can prevent the defender from going through it. Taking a few steps toward the basket before setting the screen enables you to get a better angle on your teammate's defender. To avoid an illegal moving block, use a wide two-footed jump stop to establish a stationary position. You will be taking the blow of your teammate's defender moving into

you, so you need good balance, with your feet more than shoulder-width apart and your knees flexed. While your teammate uses the screen, you are not allowed to move any body part into the defender. Keep one arm in front of your crotch and the other in front of your chest for protection.

Seeing the screen. Wait until the screen is set to prevent an illegal moving block. Be patient. Allow time for the screen to be set and to read how the defense is playing it. Most mistakes in using screens occur either because you do not read the defense or because you move too fast without setting up the defense.

Using the screen. When you are cutting off a screen, approach it with control, but then make an explosive move. You can actually walk your defender into the screen while gaining a good angle for cutting off the screen. First, move slowly in the direction your defender plays you before cutting hard off the screen in the opposite direction. As you cut off the screen, go shoulder to shoulder with the screener so your defender cannot get between you and the screen. Be sure to cut far enough away from the screen so that one defender cannot guard both you and the screener and so you create space for a pass to the screener when there is a defensive switch.

Freeing the screen. Setting a good screen will have one of two outcomes: either you or your teammate using the screen will be open. If your teammate cuts off your screen correctly, your defender's usual reaction is to give defensive help or switch. This momentarily gives you inside position on the defender who has given defensive help or, after a switch, on your new defender.

You can keep your open position by using a roll. A roll is executed by pivoting on your inside foot and opening your body in the direction of the ball, putting your defender on your back. If your teammate cuts to the outside, you will be free to roll in toward the basket and receive a pass for an inside shot. If your teammate cuts to the basket, you will be free to step back and receive a pass for an outside shot.

You can also fake a screen and cut (called *slipping the pick* or *early release*). This maneuver is effective if your defender decides to give help by stepping out hard to slow your teammate's cut off your screen. If your defender leaves you to step out toward the cutter as you go to set the screen, make a quick cut to the basket to receive a pass for an inside shot.

If both defenders are trying to take the cutter, move to an open area. After receiving the pass, you will have the defense outnumbered and be in position to drive or pass to a teammate for an open shot.

You have four basic options for cutting off a screen, depending on how it is defended: pop-out, curl, backdoor cut, and fade. As you and your teammates practice the screen away, you will learn to read the defense and react with the best option to create an opening for a shot. Properly executed, the screen away is a beautiful example of teamwork. By setting a screen for your teammate away from the ball, you create an opportunity for your teammate or you to score.

When the screener's defender drops back to allow your defender to slide behind the screen, pop out to receive a chest or overhead pass for a *catch-and-shoot* jump shot in your rhythm and range (figure 7.5).

Figure 7.5 — Cutting off a Screen: Pop-Out

DEFENDER GOES UNDER SCREEN

1. Screener sets screen
2. Jump stop with a wide base
3. Keep arms in
4. Cutter fakes in, waiting for screen
5. Defender goes under screen

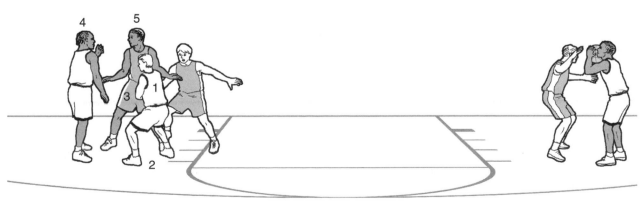

a

(continued)

Figure 7.5   *(continued)*

POP-OUT

1. Defender slides under screen
2. Cutter reads defense and pops out
3. Screener rolls in toward basket

b

CATCH AND SHOOT

1. Ball is passed to open cutter
2. Cutter shoots jump shot

c

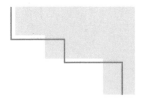

Misstep

As you cut off the screen, you do not create enough space to get open and you allow the screener's defender to guard you and the screener.

Correction

Cut far enough past the screen to create operating space for you or the screener to get open.

If the defender *trails* your body over the top of the screen, curl (cut in front and completely around the screen) toward the basket to receive an overhead or bounce pass for an inside baby hook shot (figure 7.6). Signal this move by putting your arm around the screener's body as you curl. If the screener's defender helps slow your cut, the screener will then pop out for an open catch-and-shoot jump shot.

Figure 7.6   Cutting off a Screen: Curl

DEFENDER TRAILS CUTTER

1. Screener sets screen
2. Cutter jump stops with a wide base
3. Cutter's arms are in
4. Cutter fakes in, waiting for screen

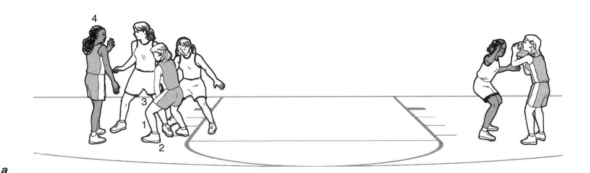

a

CURL

1. Defender trails cutter's body around screen
2. Cutter reads defense
3. Cutter signals curl with arm around screener
4. Cutter curls in toward basket

b

(continued)

Figure 7.6 *(continued)*

CATCH AND SHOOT

1. Screener pops out
2. Ball is passed to open cutter on curl
3. Cutter shoots baby hook shot

c

Misstep

You predetermine the cut when a screen is set for you and do not read your defender's position. For example, you pop out when you should curl.

Correction

The success of your cut depends on reading the defense and reacting to how your defender plays the screen. Do not predetermine or rush your cut. If your defender drops back, pop out. If your defender trails you, curl to the basket. If your defender steps out, anticipating your cut, use a backdoor cut. If your defender takes a shortcut behind the screener and the screener's defender, fade.

If your defender *tries to anticipate* your move over the top of the screen before you make your cut, step out above the screen with your outside foot and sharply change direction for a backdoor cut—behind the screen toward the basket—to receive a lob or bounce pass for a layup (figure 7.7). Signal the backdoor cut before your jab step with a key two-syllable word such as *eyeball*. At the same time, provide a passing target with your inside hand pointing toward the basket for a bounce pass or pointing up in the air for a lob pass. If the screener's defender helps on the backdoor cut, the screener will then pop out and be open for a catch-and-shoot jump shot in rhythm and range.

Figure 7.7 **Cutting off a Screen: Backdoor Cut**

DEFENDER STEPS OUT

1. Screener sets screen
2. Cutter waits for screen
3. Defender steps out to deny pass
4. Cutter shouts key word for backdoor cut
5. Cutter fakes out

a

BACKDOOR CUT

1. Defender steps out to deny pass
2. Cutter reads defense
3. Cutter executes backdoor cut to basket
4. Screener pops out

b

CATCH AND SHOOT

1. Backdoor cutter receives bounce pass or lob pass
2. Cutter shoots layup

c

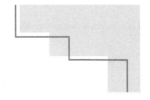

Misstep

You do not set a strong pick, and the defender is able to stay with the cutter.

Correction

Set your screen at an angle that makes the defender go under you. Use a wide base with your knees flexed to maintain balance. Keep one arm in front of your crotch and the other in front of your chest for protection as the defender fights to get through your pick.

If your defender takes a shortcut to your anticipated cut by moving behind the screener's defender on the basket side of the screen, fade (flare) away from the screen (figure 7.8). Signal this move by putting your hands on your screener's hip before you fade. Prepare to receive an overhead skip pass to the far side of the screen for a catch-and-shoot jump shot in your rhythm and range. If the screener's defender switches out to pressure your shot, the screener cuts in for post-up or rebound position.

Figure 7.8   **Cutting off a Screen: Fade**

DEFENDER SHORTCUTS

1. Screener sets screen
2. Cutter waits for screen
3. Defender takes shortcut under both screener and screener's defender
4. Cutter reads defense
5. Cutter signals fade with hands on screener's hips
6. Cutter shouts key word *fade*

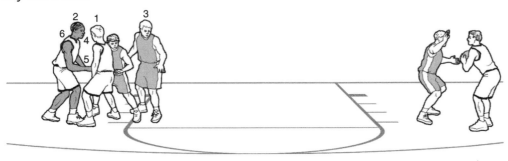

a

FADE

1. Defender shortcuts
2. Cutter fades away from ball
3. Screener pops out

b

(continued)

Figure 7.8   *(continued)*

CATCH AND SHOOT

1. Ball is passed to open cutter on fade
2. Cutter shoots jump shot

c

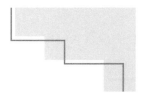

Misstep

After you set the screen and a defensive switch occurs, you roll the wrong way, taking your eyes off the ball and failing to see a possible pass.

Correction

On a defensive switch, use a reverse pivot on your inside foot. Open your body to the ball as you roll so you will be able to see the pass.

PICK-AND-ROLL

The pick-and-roll is another basic play that has been part of basketball since the game was first played. Its name, like the give-and-go, comes from the action of the play. You set a pick (screen) for a teammate, who dribbles by it for an outside shot or drive. If your defender switches to your teammate, you will momentarily be inside the defender you picked and free to roll toward the basket, looking to receive a return pass from the dribbler for a layup. When a pick is set for you, you should use at least two dribbles going by the pick to create space for a pass to the picker, who rolls to the basket after a defensive switch.

The basic pick-and-roll presents other options, depending on how it is defended, including the pick-and-pop, slip (early release), and stretch-the-trap. On the basic pick-and-roll play, your pick is defended by a defensive switch. To combat that switch, you roll to the basket for a pass and layup (figure 7.9).

As you and your teammates become experienced in executing the pick-and-roll, you will learn to read how the pick is being defended and react with a roll, pop-out, or stretch dribble to create an opening for a shot. Properly executed, the pick-and-roll can create the opportunity for your teammate or you to score. It is another example of fine teamwork.

Figure 7.9   Pick-and-Roll

DEFENDERS SWITCH

1. Screener sets pick
2. Cutter waits for pick
3. Defenders switch
4. Offensive players read defense

a

DRIVE OFF PICK

1. Drive off pick shoulder to shoulder
2. Take two dribbles past pick
3. Picker rolls to basket

b

PICKER ROLLS TO BASKET

1. Bounce or lob pass to picker
2. Picker rolls to basket for layup

c

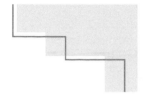

Misstep

You are called for a foul because you move your body or body part into the path of the defender as your teammate dribbles off your pick.

Correction

Use a wide, two-footed jump stop before your teammate dribbles to avoid an illegal moving block. Keep your arm and knee in as the defender fights to get through your pick.

Pick-and-Roll Drill 1. *Two-on-Zero*

This drill requires two players. Start with the ball at a box outside the lane and with your back to the basket. Pass to yourself by tossing the ball diagonally across the lane to the opposite elbow. Catch the ball with a one-two stop with your inside foot landing first. Pivot to the middle, find the rim, and make a drive step. Be a triple threat to shoot, pass, or drive.

On your toss of the ball, your teammate runs to the opposite box, makes a sharp change of direction, and runs up the lane line to the elbow on the side opposite you. Make a chest pass to your teammate and set a screen on the inside (lane side) of your teammate's imaginary defender. Your teammate uses the screen, brushing your outside shoulder to prevent a defender from getting over the screen and staying with the dribbler.

Your teammate dribbles at least twice in moving past your screen to create space for a pass as you roll to the basket. Execute the roll by opening to the ball with a reverse pivot on your inside foot, the one closer to the basket, and seal out an imaginary defender. Your teammate makes a bounce or lob pass to you as you cut to the basket. Shoot a layup. Your teammate follows to rebound a miss,

making a power move to score. Change positions and continue the drill. Each player should execute five pick-and-rolls and five layups on each side.

To Increase Difficulty

- Add a third player, a defender, to the drill. After executing the chest pass, set a screen on the inside (lane side) of the receiver's defender.

Success Check

- Use a one-two stop when you catch the ball, landing on your inside foot first.
- Get in triple-threat position when you have the ball.
- When using the screen, brush the screener's outside shoulder to keep a defender from getting over the screen.

Score Your Success

Award yourself 1 point for each correct, successful screen-and-roll or layup from each side, for a maximum of 20 points. A score of 16 points is excellent.

Your score ___

Pick-and-Roll Drill 2. *Switching Defense (Two-on-Two)*

This drill provides practice in executing the pick-and-roll against a switching defense. The drill requires four players, two on offense and two on defense. Start with the ball at a box outside the lane and with your back to the basket. Pass to yourself by tossing the ball diagonally across the lane to the opposite elbow. Catch the ball with a one-two stop with your inside foot landing first. Pivot to the

middle, find the rim, and make a drive step. Be a triple threat to shoot, pass, or drive.

On your toss of the ball, your teammate runs to the opposite box, makes a sharp change of direction, and runs up the lane line to the elbow on the side opposite you. Make a chest pass to the other offensive player and set a screen on the inside (lane side) of your teammate's defender. The

145

defender should switch as your partner dribbles past your screen. Roll to the basket. If the defender you screen defends your roll by quickly spinning around the pick toward the basket, rather than rolling in, you may pop out to receive a pass for a jump shot.

Each basket is worth 2 points. If an offensive player is fouled and the shot goes in, a free throw is awarded. An offensive player who is fouled on a missed shot gets two free throws. If the offensive side recovers the rebound on a missed shot, they may continue playing offense until they score or turn over the ball or until the defense gets the ball on a steal or rebound and dribbles back past the free throw line. Switch sides. Play until one team scores 7 points.

Success Check

- Use a one-two stop when you catch the ball, landing on your inside foot first.
- Go after the rebounds and keep playing until the defense gets the ball or you make the shot.
- Communicate with your partner.

Score Your Success

This is a competitive drill. The first team to score 7 points wins the game. Give yourself 5 points if your team wins the game.

Your score ___

The *pick-and-pop* (figure 7.10) is used when your defender opens (drops back) to allow the defender you screened to slide under your pick. Rather than rolling in, you can pop out to receive a pass for a jump shot. You can also do this when the defense switches and the defender you screen quickly spins around your pick toward the basket.

Figure 7.10 Pick-and-Pop

DEFENDERS OPEN AND GO UNDER

1. Screener sets pick
2. Cutter waits for pick
3. Picker's defender opens (drops back) and your defender slides under pick
4. Offensive players read defense

(continued)

Figure 7.10 *(continued)*

DRIVE OFF PICK

1. Drive off pick, shoulder to shoulder
2. Take at least two dribbles past pick
3. Picker pops out

b

PICKER POPS FOR JUMP SHOT

1. Pass back to picker
2. Picker shoots jump shot

c

Misstep

As you drive off pick you do not create enough space, allowing one defender to guard both you and picker.

Correction

Take at least two dribbles past pick to create space for you to shoot, or pass back to picker for open shot.

Pick-and-Pop Drill. *Open and Slide Under Defense (Two-on-Two)*

In this drill, you will practice executing the pick-and-pop against a sliding defense. This drill resembles the switching defense drill in the pick-and-roll section except the two defenders use a sliding defense rather than switching. The screener's defender opens (drops back) to allow the defender being screened to slide under the screen and stay with the dribbler. After dropping back, the first defender recovers to a defensive position on the screener.

When you set a pick and your defender opens (drops back), allowing the screened defender to slide under your pick, rather than rolling in, pop out to receive a pass for a jump shot. Your partner can either make a jump shot or pass to you for a jump shot if your defender fails to recover after dropping back.

Each basket is worth 2 points. If an offensive player is fouled and the shot goes in, a free throw is awarded.

An offensive player who is fouled on a missed shot gets two free throws. If the offensive side recovers the rebound on a missed shot, they may continue playing offense until they score or turn over the ball or until the defense gets the ball on a steal or rebound and dribbles back past the free throw line. Switch sides. Play until one team scores 7 points.

Success Check

- After setting the pick, pop out for the return pass.
- Communicate with your partner.

Score Your Success

This is a competitive drill. The first team to score 7 points wins the game. Give yourself 5 points if your team wins the game.

Your score ____

Slip (early release) the pick when your defender reacts to the pick-and-roll by stepping out hard to make your teammate using your screen veer out (figure 7.11). If your defender leaves you to step out toward the dribbler as you go to set the pick, slip (release early) and make a basket cut for a pass from your teammate.

Figure 7.11   Slip the Pick

PICKER'S DEFENDER STEPS OUT

1. Screener sets pick
2. Cutter waits for pick
3. Picker's defender steps out
4. Offensive players read defense

a

(continued)

Figure 7.11 *(continued)*

SLIP THE PICK

1. Picker slips the pick and cuts to basket
2. Overhead lob pass to picker
3. Picker shoots a layup

b

Misstep

You do not read your defender and you slip the pick before your defender steps out, enabling your defender to stay with you.

Correction

Read your defendeer. Wait for your defender to step out before you slip the pick and cut to the basket.

Slip the Pick Drill. *Help-and-Recover Defense (Two-on-Two)*

This drill requires four players, two on offense and two on defense. The two defenders use a help-and-recover defense as an offensive player dribbles past the screen set by the other offensive player.

Start with the ball at a box outside the lane and with your back to the basket. Pass to yourself by tossing the ball diagonally across the lane to the opposite elbow. Catch the ball with a one-two stop with your inside foot landing first. Pivot to the middle, find the rim, and make a drive step. Be a triple threat to shoot, pass, or drive.

On your toss of the ball, your teammate runs to the opposite box, makes a sharp change of direc-tion, and runs up the lane line to the elbow on the side opposite you. Make a chest pass to your partner and set a screen on the inside (lane side) of your teammate's defender. Your defender will help the defender being screened by stepping out on the dribbler. After stepping out, the first defender recovers to a defensive position on the screener. Your teammate can then drive to the basket for a layup, shoot a jump shot, or pass back to you if your defender fails to recover after giving help. Another option you have is to slip the pick (early release). If your defender decides to defend the pick-and-roll by stepping out early to slow down your teammate before the dribble, slip the pick and make a basket cut for a pass from your teammate.

Each basket is worth 2 points. If an offensive player is fouled and the shot goes in, a free throw is awarded. An offensive player who is fouled on a missed shot gets two free throws. If the offensive side recovers the rebound on a missed shot, they may continue playing offense until they score or turn over the ball or until the defense gets the ball on a steal or rebound and dribbles back past the free throw line. Switch sides. Play until one team scores 7 points.

Success Check

- Use a one-two stop when you catch the ball, landing on your inside foot first.
- Communicate with your partner.
- Read the defense and react to what the defenders are doing.

Score Your Success

This is a competitive drill. The first team to score 7 points wins the game. Give yourself 5 points if your team wins the game.

Your score ___

When both defenders react to the pick-and-roll by trapping the player with the ball as you set the pick, a different adjustment, called *stretch the trap* (figure 7.12), is advantageous. When the trap occurs, the player with the ball should retreat dribble to stretch the defense and create space. The dribbler can then split the trap or pass to the picker moving to an open area. You will have the defense outnumbered and be in position to drive or pass to a teammate for an open shot.

Figure 7.12   Stretch the Trap

DEFENDERS TRAP BALL

1. Screener sets pick
2. Cutter waits for pick
3. Defenders trap ball
4. Offensive players read defense

a

(continued)

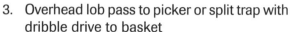

Figure 7.12 *(continued)*

STRETCH THE TRAP

1. Retreat dribble to stretch trap (at least two dribbles)

2. Picker cuts to open area and calls for the ball

3. Overhead lob pass to picker or split trap with dribble drive to basket

b

Misstep

You stop your dribble and allow yourself to be trapped.

Correction

Make at least two dribbles past the pick to create operating space for you to shoot or pass to the picker on a roll or pop-out. Keep your dribble alive using a retreat dribble to stretch the trap and create space to pass to picker or split trap with dribble drive.

Stretch the Trap Drill. *Two-on-Two*

This drill requires four players, two on offense and two on defense. The two defenders use a trap against your pick.

Start with the ball at a box outside the lane and with your back to the basket. Pass to yourself by tossing the ball diagonally across the lane to the opposite elbow. Catch the ball with a one-two stop with your inside foot landing first. Pivot to the middle, find the rim, and make a drive step. Be a triple threat to shoot, pass, or drive.

On your toss of the ball, your teammate runs to the opposite box, makes a sharp change of direction, and runs up the lane line to the elbow on the side opposite you. Make a chest pass to your partner and set a screen on the inside (lane side) of your teammate's defender. The screener's defender traps the dribbler as the pick is being set. If both defenders trap the dribbler during the screen, you should adjust by stretching the trap. Your teammate should retreat dribble to stretch the defense. The dribbler can split trap with a dribble drive or pass to the picker moving to an open area. After receiving the pass, you will have the defense outnumbered and be in position to drive to the basket.

Each basket is worth 2 points. If an offensive player is fouled and the shot goes in, a free throw is awarded. An offensive player who is fouled on a missed shot gets two free throws. If the offensive side recovers the rebound on a missed shot, they may continue playing offense until they score or turn over the ball or until the defense gets the ball on a steal or rebound and dribbles back past the free throw line. Switch sides. Play until one team scores 7 points.

Success Check

- Use a one-two stop when you catch the ball, landing on your inside foot first.
- Communicate with your partner.
- Stretch the defense.

Score Your Success

This is a competitive drill. The first team to score 7 points wins the game. Give yourself 5 points if your team wins the game.

Your score ___

FLASH AND BACKDOOR CUT

A flash is a quick cut toward the ball. The flash and backdoor cut (figure 7.13) involves three players: a passer, an overplayed receiver who is being denied the ball, and a player who will flash. When a defender is denying a teammate from catching the ball and you are the next closest player to the denied receiver, you should automatically flash to an open area between the passer and your overplayed teammate. Flashing to the ball relieves defensive pressure on your two teammates by giving the passer another outlet. A flash can not only prevent a possible turnover, but also can create a scoring opportunity when you combine it with the overplayed receiver's well-timed backdoor cut.

As you flash, signal the cut with the key word *flash*. On the flash, go hard with two hands up to receive the pass. When you receive the ball, use a one-two stop to land with your inside foot, the one closer to the basket, landing first. Catch the ball and look for your overplayed teammate, who should be setting up to make a backdoor cut toward the basket. Use a reverse pivot and make a bounce pass to your teammate cutting backdoor for a layup. If your teammate is covered on the backdoor cut, front turn into a triple-threat position for a possible shot, drive, or pass.

You should automatically flash whenever you see a teammate being overplayed. Usually you will flash high when your teammate is prevented from receiving a pass on the perimeter. You can also flash to the high post when a teammate is being fronted in the low post, or you can flash to the low post when a teammate is being denied at the high post.

The success of the flash and backdoor cut is based on communication between teammates and the timing of the overplayed receiver's backdoor cut. Using the key word signals to the passer that you are flashing and alerts your overplayed teammate to cut backdoor after you receive the pass. Your overplayed teammate should set up the defense by taking a step away from the basket before the backdoor cut. The flash and backdoor cut requires alertness and timing to execute sharply and effectively.

Figure 7.13   Flash and Backdoor Cut

SEE TEAMMATE DENIED

1. See overplayed teammate
2. Fake away

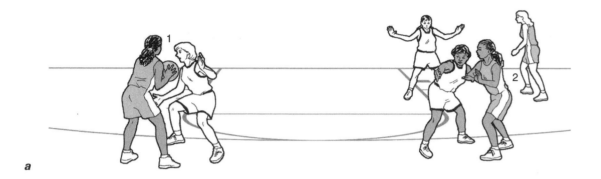

a

FLASH

1. Shout "Flash!" and flash to ball
2. Catch the pass
3. Make a one-two stop, landing on inside foot first
4. Overplayed teammate steps high

b

BACKDOOR

1. Overplayed teammate executes a backdoor cut
2. Reverse pivot
3. Bounce pass to backdoor cutter

c

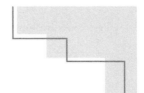

Misstep

The backdoor cut is made too soon.

Correction

The backdoor cut can be timed correctly by stepping away from the basket just as the ball is caught by the flash cutter and then cutting backdoor.

Flash and Cut Drill 1. *Pass and Cut (Three-on-Zero)*

This drill requires three players. Player 1 starts with the ball at the point position at the top of the free throw circle. Players 2 and 3 start at the right and left wing positions (foul line extended), respectively. Player 1 passes to either player 2 or player 3 and takes one or two steps away from the ball toward the weak-side wing. Player 1 then executes a sharp change of direction and cuts toward the basket. As player 1 cuts to the basket, the weak-side wing replaces him at the point. The wing who received the pass may bounce pass to player 1 as he cuts to the basket, and player 1 may pass to the player now occupying the point. If the ball is passed to the point, player 1 moves to the open wing position that was vacated when the player moved to the point. Continue the drill: The player at the point passes to either wing and cuts to the basket, and the wing fakes a pass to the cutter before passing back to the point. Make at least five passes before passing the ball to a player cutting from the point to the basket for a layup. Continue the drill for a total of 30 passes and layups without error.

Success Check

- Pass and cut with precision.
- Run the drill smoothly and continuously.
- Try to complete 30 consecutive passes and layups without error.

Score Your Success

Fewer than 20 passes and layups without error
  = 0 points

20 to 24 passes and layups without error
  = 1 point

25 to 29 passes and layups without error
  = 3 points

30 passes and layups without error
  = 5 points

Your score ___

Flash and Cut Drill 2. *Pass and Screen Away (Three-on-Zero)*

This drill requires three players. Begin in the same positions as in the pass and cut drill. When you pass to the player at either wing, fake a cut to the basket before setting a screen away from the ball on the inside of an imaginary defender on the weak-side wing (a chair can represent the defender). The weak-side wing has four options when using the screen: the front cut, backdoor cut, pop-out, or fade. If the weak-side wing uses your screen by cutting to the basket with a front cut or backdoor cut, you should pop back to the ball. If the weak-side wing pops out toward the ball to receive a possible pass for an outside jump shot, you should roll in to the basket by opening to the ball with a reverse pivot on your inside foot, the one closer to

the basket, and sealing out an imaginary defender. If the weak-side wing fades away from the ball, you can pop out or roll to the basket, depending on how you imagine the defense is being played.

The wing who receives the pass can make a bounce pass to the player cutting to the basket, pass to the player popping out, throw a skip pass (a pass that bypasses the next closest receiver) to the player fading, or pass or dribble the ball out to the point. A player receiving the pass on a cut to the basket should shoot a layup, rebounding any miss and scoring with a power move. After a pop-out or fade, the receiver may take the outside shot or pass back to the point to restart the pass and screen play.

Change positions and continue the drill. Each player should execute five screen aways and reactions to how the screen is used.

Success Check

- Communicate with teammates.
- Use proper screening technique.
- Make the right decision in reaction to what your teammates are doing and what the defense is doing.

Score Your Success

Award yourself 1 point for each correct screen away and for each correct reaction to use of the screen.

3 or fewer points = poor

4 to 5 points = fair

6 to 7 points = good

8 to 10 points = excellent

Your score ___

Flash and Cut Drill 3. Flash Backdoor (Three-on-Zero)

Begin as in the two previous flash and cut drills. After passing to either the right or left wing, fake a screen away before cutting to the basket. The weak-side wing moves out to replace you at the point. Assume that an imaginary defender is denying a swing pass back toward the weak-side point and flash to the ball-side elbow to receive a pass, shouting the *flash* signal. When you receive the pass at the elbow after you flash, the player at the point should make a backdoor cut to the basket. Reverse pivot on your inside foot and make a bounce pass to your teammate, who is cutting backdoor to the basket. On receiving the pass, the cutter shoots a layup, rebounding any miss and scoring with a power move.

Change positions and continue the drill. Each player passes and cuts from the point, flashes from the weak side, and reverse pivots for a bounce pass to the backdoor cutter on each side.

Success Check

- Verbally signal your teammates when you flash to the ball-side elbow.
- Make the right decision in reaction to what your teammates are doing and what the defense is doing.

Score Your Success

Award yourself 1 point for each flash and for each correct reverse pivot and bounce pass to the backdoor cutter.

13 or fewer points = poor

14 to 15 points = fair

16 to 17 points = good

18 to 20 points = excellent

Your score ___

DRIBBLE SCREEN AND WEAVE

A dribble screen occurs when you dribble toward your teammate to hand the ball off while you screen your teammate's defender. To execute the play, dribble to the inside of your teammate. Your teammate fakes in and then cuts to the outside and behind you to receive the handoff. To hand off the ball, pivot on your inside foot, the one closer to the basket, placing your body in the path of your teammate's defender. Be prepared for contact during the handoff. Maintain a strong, balanced stance and use your body and two hands to protect the ball. After receiving the handoff, your teammate should be a triple threat to shoot, drive, or pass. After you make the handoff, read the defense and either roll to the basket, pop out, or move away from the ball to an open area.

The dribble screen is used to execute a *weave*, another basic basketball play. In a weave, at least three players set dribble screens for each other. For example, you start the weave with a dribble screen and hand off to your teammate. The recipient of the handoff has several options: shoot from behind the screen, drive to the basket, or continue the weave by dribbling toward another teammate for a dribble screen and handoff (figure 7.14). The weave continues until someone takes advantage of an opening for a shot or drive to the basket.

With experience, you and your teammates will learn to read how the weave is being defended so you can choose whether to react with a handoff, fake handoff, or backdoor cut to create an opening for a shot. The weave creates a variety of scoring opportunities and is yet another beautiful example of teamwork.

Figure 7.14   Weave: Shoot, Drive, or Continue Weave

DEFENDERS OPEN AND GO UNDER

1. Dribbler starts weave by dribbling inside teammate, setting a dribble screen
2. Receiver steps away before cutting to dribbler's outside for handoff
3. Dribbler's defender opens (drops back) and receiver's defender slides under screen
4. Offensive players read defense
5. Dribbler hands off ball to receiver

a

SHOOT, DRIVE, OR WEAVE

1. Receiver shoots jump shot, drives to basket, or continues weave
2. Screener cuts away from ball

b

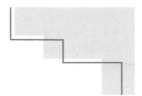

Misstep

As you dribble toward your teammate to set the dribble screen, you bump into each other.

Correction

To prevent bumping into each other, remember that the dribbler goes to the inside and the receiver cuts behind the dribbler and to the outside.

One way to defend either the dribble screen or weave is getting in the path of the receiver to prevent the handoff (figure 7.15). When you are the potential receiver and a defender gets in your path, take a step to the outside and make a backdoor cut to the basket for a possible pass and layup.

Figure 7.15 | Weave: Cut Backdoor

DEFENDER DENIES HANDOFF

1. Dribbler starts weave by dribbling inside teammate, setting a dribble screen
2. Receiver steps away before cutting to dribbler's outside for handoff
3. Receiver's defender denies handoff
4. Offensive players read defense
5. Receiver shouts key word for backdoor cut

a

BACKDOOR

1. Receiver cuts backdoor
2. Dribbler makes overhead pass to backdoor cutter

b

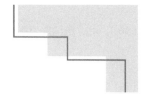

Misstep

When a dribble screen is set for you, you do not read the defense. For example, your defender steps in the path of the handoff and you fail to make a backdoor cut.

Correction

Success on the weave depends on reading and reacting to how the defense plays it. Learn to read how the dribble screen is being defended and react with a handoff, a fake handoff, a backdoor cut, or a retreat dribble to create an opening for a shot.

A second defense is to jump switch into the path of the receiver (figure 7.16). A jump-switch is an aggressive early switch made to draw a charge or to change the direction of the player receiving the ball. To combat a jump switch, make a short 5- to 10-foot cut to an open area after you hand off and look for a quick return pass. When you anticipate a jump switch, you can also fake the handoff and drive to the basket.

| Figure 7.16 | **Weave: Fake Handoff and Drive** |

DEFENDERS JUMP SWITCH

1. Dribbler starts weave by dribbling inside teammate, setting a dribble screen
2. Receiver steps away before cutting to dribbler's outside for handoff
3. Defenders jump switch
4. Offensive players read defense

a

FAKE HANDOFF AND DRIVE

1. Dribbler fakes handoff while continuing to dribble
2. Dribbler drives between defenders to basket

b

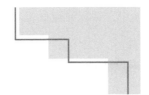

Misstep

When you set the dribble screen, you get knocked off balance.

Correction

Expect to be bumped, and maintain your balance by widening your base and flexing your knees as you hand off.

Another way to defend the weave is to have both defenders trap the player receiving the handoff (figure 7.17). When the opponents trap, your teammate should retreat dribble to stretch the defense and then pass to you while you make a short 5- to 10-foot cut to an open area. After receiving the pass, you will outnumber the defense and be in position to drive or pass to a teammate for an open shot.

| **Figure 7.17** | **Weave: Stretch Trap** |

DEFENDERS TRAP

1. Dribbler starts weave by dribbling inside teammate, setting a dribble screen
2. Receiver steps away before cutting to dribbler's outside for handoff
3. Defenders trap receiver
4. Offensive players read defense

a

STRETCH THE TRAP

1. Receiver retreat dribbles to stretch trap
2. Screener makes short cut to open area
3. Screener calls for ball
4. Overhead lob pass to cutter or split trap with dribble drive

b

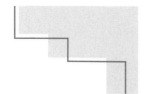

Misstep

You stop your dribble and allow yourself to be trapped.

Correction

Keep your dribble alive using a retreat dribble to stretch the trap and create space to pass to cutter or split trap with dribble drive.

Weave Drill. *Three-on-Zero*

This drill requires three players. Start as player 1 with the ball at the point position at the top of the free throw circle. Players 2 and 3 start at the right and left wing positions (foul line extended), respectively.

Begin the weave by dribbling toward one of the wings. Screen the wing's defender and dribble to the inside. The wing cuts to the outside and behind you to receive the handoff. The wing should then be a triple threat to shoot, drive, or pass.

After the handoff, imagine how the defense is playing the move and roll to the basket, pop out, or move away from the ball to an open area. The recipient of the handoff has the option of shooting from behind the screen, driving to the basket, or continuing the weave by dribbling toward another teammate for a dribble screen and handoff.

The weave continues until a member of your team takes advantage of an opening for a shot or a drive to the basket. Make at least five handoffs before passing to a player cutting to the basket for a layup. Continue the drill for a total of 30 correct handoffs and layups.

To Increase Difficulty

• Add a defender.

Success Check

• Read the defense.
• Communicate with your teammates.
• Use the correct technique when doing the weave.

Score Your Success

Fewer than 15 correct consecutive handoffs and layups = 0 points

15 to 19 correct consecutive handoffs and layups = 1 point

20 to 24 correct consecutive handoffs and layups = 3 points

25 to 30 correct consecutive handoffs and layups = 5 points

Your score ___

Moves Without the Ball Drill. *Half-Court Offense Versus Passive Defense (Three-on-Three)*

This drill requires six players, three on offense and three on defense, to play a half-court three-on-three game. The three defenders will play passive (half-speed) defense to allow the offense to practice executing offensive options in a three-on-three situation. Having the defense play at half speed helps the offensive players recognize which defense is being played, react with the correct offensive option, and develop confidence. The offensive options are to pass and cut (give-and-go), pass and screen away, pass and go to the ball

for a pick-and-roll, flash backdoor, or weave. The defensive options are to switch, slide, help and recover, or trap.

The drill starts when the defensive team gives the offensive team the ball at half-court. The offensive team gets 1 point each time it scores. If the defense commits a foul, the offense gets the ball and starts again. If an offensive player misses a shot and a teammate gets an offensive rebound, continue playing. The defense gets 1 point if it gets the ball on a steal or rebound and makes an outlet pass past the free throw line or if it forces the offense into a violation. The first team to score 5 points wins the game. The defense then goes to offense and the offense goes on defense.

To Increase Difficulty

- Practice against an active (full-speed) defense.
- Practice the drill without dribbling, creating more opportunities to practice passing and cutting, especially using the backdoor cut and flash backdoor.

Success Check

- Read and react to the defense.
- Communicate with teammates.
- Go after rebounds to keep the ball alive.

Score Your Success

This is a competitive drill. The first team to score 5 points wins the game. Give yourself 5 points if your team wins the game.

Your score ___

RATE YOUR SUCCESS

Moving effectively without the ball will make you a productive team player. You will increase your team's chances of winning the game if you can move without the ball, getting in position for a pass.

In the next step, we will look at executing the fast break. Before going to step 8, however, look back at how you performed the drills in this step. For each of the drills presented in this step, enter the points you earned, then add up your scores to rate your total success.

Backdoor Cut Drill

    1. Two-on-Zero   ____ out of 20

Give-and-Go Drill

    1. Two-on-Zero   ____ out of 5

Pick-and-Roll Drills

    1. Two-on-Zero   ____ out of 20

    2. Switching Defense (Two-on-Two)   ____ out of 5

Pick-and-Pop Drill

    1. Open and Slide Under Defense (Two-on-Two)   ____ out of 5

Slip the Pick Drill

    1. Help-and-Recover Defense (Two-on-Two)   ____ out of 5

Stretch the Trap Drill

    1. Two-on-Two   ____ out of 5

Flash and Cut Drills

   1. Pass and Cut (Three-on-Zero)   ___ out of 5

   2. Pass and Screen Away (Three-on-Zero)   ___ out of 10

   3. Flash Backdoor (Three-on-Zero)   ___ out of 20

Weave Drill

   1. Three-on-Zero   ___ out of 5

Moves Without the Ball Drill

   1. Half-Court Offense Versus Passive Defense (Three-on-Three)   ___ out of 5

TOTAL   ___ *out of 110*

If you scored 90 or more points, congratulations! You have mastered the basics of this step and are ready to move on to step 8, fast break. If you scored fewer than 90 points, you may want to spend more time on the fundamentals covered in this step. Practice the drills again to develop mastery of the techniques and increase your scores.

Fast Break

The fast break is exciting for both players and fans. The objective of the fast break is to advance the ball up the court for a high-percentage shot, either by outnumbering the defense or by denying the defense an opportunity to get set. The fast break places a premium on physical conditioning, fundamentals, teamwork, and intelligent decisions.

The fast break is important for several strategic reasons. It creates the easiest way to score. A team that has to work hard for every shot against a set five-on-five half-court defense will have trouble beating a team that consistently gets fast-break baskets. Creating an easy scoring opportunity by numerical advantage is the first objective of the fast break. The two-on-one and three-on-two, the most common numerical advantages, often result in a layup. The four-on-three usually leads to an inside post-up shot. The five-on-four often allows for an easy swing of the ball away from the side of defensive pressure and for a possible open shot on the weak side.

A second objective is to attack before the opponents are set to play team defense or rebound. The fast break works well against zone defenses because the defenders do not have time to get set in their positions. A fast-breaking team's advantage over a half-court team is in combating pressing defenses. A fast-breaking team is better prepared to inbound the ball quickly before the press is set. A fast-breaking team is more experienced in passing on the move and generally looks to score against the press rather than just getting the ball past half-court, posing a greater threat to the pressing team. A fast-break attack can also create mismatches against man-to-man defenses.

Another important objective of playing fast-break basketball is motivating the fast-breaking team to play tough defense and to rebound. Good defense and rebounding are the best ways to start the fast break. A fast-breaking team also discourages its opponents from sending too many players to rebound an offensive board for fear of not having players back to defend against the break. A fast-break style is very demanding and encourages a team to be in top physical condition.

The fast break places a premium on physical conditioning, fundamentals, teamwork, and intelligent decisions. Have a trained observer such as a coach, teacher, or a skilled player subjectively evaluate your skills and decision making at different fast-break positions.

THREE-LANE FAST BREAK

The most common fast-break attack is the controlled three-lane fast break. In the controlled fast break, fundamental execution and good decision making matter more than speed. The controlled fast break has three phases: starting the fast break, getting into position, and finishing the break with the correct scoring option.

To start the fast break, you must first gain possession of the ball, which requires good defense and rebounding. Aggressive defense creates opportunities to get the ball after missed or blocked shots, steals, interceptions, or violations by an opponent. Rebounding the ball quickly after an opponent scores from the field or on a free throw also provides an opportunity to start the fast break.

After gaining possession, yell a key word such as *ball*. Immediately look upcourt for the possibility of passing ahead to an open teammate for an uncontested breakaway layup. When the opportunity for a quick pass ahead is not there, a quick outlet pass to the point guard (the best ball handler and playmaker) is needed. As shown in figure 8.1, the rebounder (5) uses the outlet pass to get the ball to the point guard (1). Players 2 and 3 sprint ahead to fill the outside lanes. The quicker you outlet the ball, the better, provided the pass is completed. If there is too much congestion or you are trapped under your opponent's basket when rebounding, use one or two strong power dribbles up the middle and then look to complete an outlet pass to the point guard. If the point guard is not open, pass to another teammate on the weak side of the court.

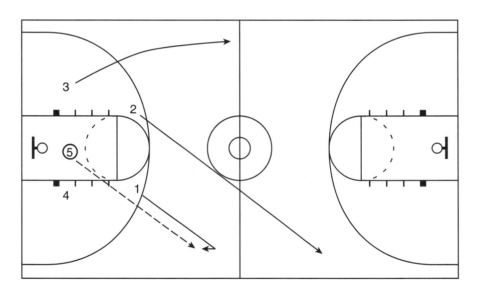

Figure 8.1 Fast break: Rebounder outlets to point guard.

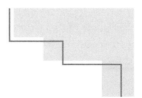

Misstep

As the point guard receiving an outlet pass, you dribble before looking upcourt.

Correction

Catch the ball with a one-two stop, pivot to the middle, see the rim, and then look to advance the ball up the court quickly with a pass or dribble.

The point guard will handle the ball in the middle of the fast break. The point guard should get open to receive an outlet pass in the area between the top of the circle and half-court on the side the ball was rebounded, calling for the ball by using a key word such as *outlet*. If denied a pass in this area, the point guard should look to make a backdoor cut toward your basket. As shown in figure 8.2, the point guard (1) makes a backdoor cut when denied the pass. When the

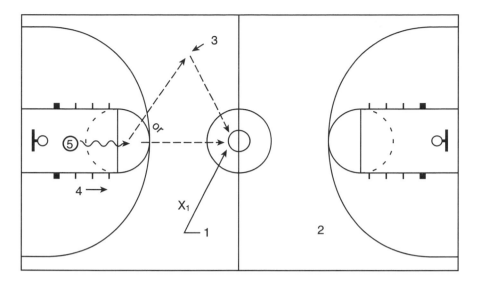

Figure 8.2 Fast break: Point guard cuts backdoor when denied the pass.

rebounder is in a congested area or trapped, the rebounder (5) power dribbles up the middle and makes an outlet pass to player 1 or 3. When the point guard is denied, a teammate, particularly a player on the weak-side wing, should flash back to the ball, then pass to the point guard on a backdoor cut toward the basket or on a front cut toward the ball. If the rebounder is in trouble and cannot make an outlet pass, the point guard should come back to that player to receive a short pass or handoff. The point guard should demand the ball and come to meet the pass, catching the ball with a one-two stop. The point guard should pivot to the middle, locate the rim, and then look to advance the ball quickly up the court with either a pass or a dribble.

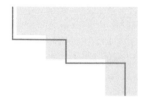

Misstep

As the point guard, you are denied receiving the outlet pass.

Correction

When you are denied, make a backdoor cut toward your basket. Signal your backdoor cut with a key word such as *eyeball*. If the rebounder is in trouble, come back to the ball for a short pass or handoff, calling out "Ball!" to demand the ball.

After receiving the outlet pass, immediately look upcourt for the possibility of passing ahead to an open teammate for an uncontested breakaway layup or a two-on-one scoring opportunity. When you are the point guard and a quick pass ahead is not there, push the dribble upcourt into the middle of the floor. Signal your move by yelling "Middle!" When you are not the point guard and a quick pass ahead is not there, look to pass the ball to the point guard in the middle of the floor.

To execute the controlled three-lane fast break (figure 8.3), think of the court as divided by imaginary lines into three lanes. During the fast break, the point guard (number 1) will handle the ball in the middle lane, signaling this with the key word *middle*. The shooting guard (number 2) will be a wing and fill one of the outside lanes, and the small forward (number 3) will also be a wing and fill the other outside lane.

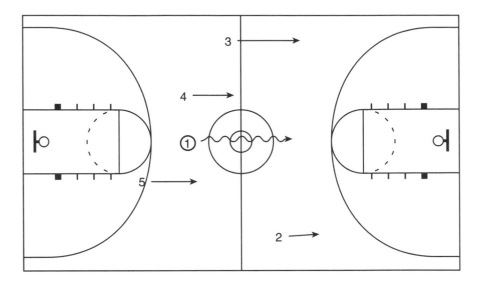

Figure 8.3 Filling lanes on the fast break.

Misstep

A player other than the best ball handler dribbles middle, resulting in a possible turnover and missed scoring opportunity.

Correction

The point guard should demand the ball and, if necessary, take the ball out of a teammate's hands.

If two players find themselves in the same lane, whoever gets there second must cut across to the lane on the other side of the court. The lanes should be called out. The player filling the right lane yells "Right!" and the player filling the left lane yells "Left!" The wings should stay wide, about five feet from the sideline, and run ahead of the ball. The remaining players, usually the power forward (number 4) and center (number 5), will be trailers. The first trailer (usually your best post-up player) takes a position several feet to the rear and left side of the middle player and yells "Trailer left!" The second trailer (usually the best passer and outside shooter among your big players) follows the play upcourt, serving as a defensive safety.

Three-Lane Fast-Break Drill 1. *Parallel Lane Passing*

This drill requires three players. Get in three lanes evenly spaced along the baseline. The player in the middle lane starts with the ball. The middle player tosses the ball high on the backboard and rebounds with two hands while yelling "Ball!" On the rebound, the wing on the right runs to an outlet position past the foul line extended while yelling "Outlet!" The rebounder makes a two-handed overhead outlet pass to the right wing beyond the foul line extended. The rebounder sprints up the middle while yelling "Middle!" and receives a return chest pass. The left wing sprints up the court while yelling "Left!" The player in the middle makes a chest pass to the left wing, who has sprinted ahead. Continue the drill up the court with each player passing and sprinting in parallel lanes while calling out lanes.

When the ball is received above the free throw line in the scoring area, the middle player makes a bounce pass to the weak-side wing for a bank jump shot. At the foul line extended, each wing should cut at a sharp 45-degree angle to the basket. The wing who receives the pass shoots a bank jump shot from 15 to 18 feet. The other wing should follow in, prepared to rebound a possible miss and score with a power move. After a score, switch lanes: The middle player moves to the right, the right player moves to the left, and the left player moves to the middle. Continue the drill back down the court. Each player should attempt three bank jump shots from each side of the basket, for a total of six bank jump shots each.

Success Check

- Verbally communicate lanes with your teammates.
- Maintain proper spacing in the lanes.
- Make accurate passes.

Score Your Success

Give yourself 1 point for each made bank jump shot from each side, for a maximum of 6 points. A score of 5 to 6 points is excellent.

Your score ___

Three-Lane Fast-Break Drill 2. Pass and Go Behind

This drill requires three players, who set up as in the three-player parallel lane passing drill. After making a two-handed overhead outlet pass to the player in the right lane, the rebounder follows the pass by sprinting behind the player passed to, filling the right lane and yelling "Right!" The player in the left lane then sprints to the middle lane and yells "Middle!" The player in the right lane makes a chest pass to the player now in the middle, follows the pass by sprinting behind the player passed to, filling the left lane and yelling "Left!" Continue the drill up the court with each player passing and going behind the player who receives the pass, making a weave pattern and filling and calling out a lane. When the ball is received above the free throw line in the scoring area, the middle player makes a bank jump shot. At the foul line extended, each wing should cut at a sharp 45-degree angle to the

basket, continuing as with the first drill. Each player should have three bank jump shot opportunities from each side, for a total of six bank jump shots for each player.

Success Check

- Verbally communicate lanes with your teammates.
- Maintain proper spacing in the lanes.
- Make accurate passes.

Score Your Success

Give yourself 1 point for each made bank jump shot from each side, for a maximum of 6 points. A score of 5 to 6 points is excellent.

Your score ___

TWO-ON-ONE FAST BREAK

The two-on-one fast break is a quick way to move the ball upcourt and should result in a scoring layup. When executed properly, the two-on-one is a fine example of teamwork and one of the most exciting plays in basketball. When you gain possession of the ball, you should immediately look upcourt, read the offensive situation, and react to it. See whether the two-on-one fast break, a quick scoring option, is available.

When you and a teammate recognize a two-on-one fast-break situation, you should immediately alert each other by yelling "Two-on-one!"

Move the ball upcourt, quickly passing back and forth to each other while maintaining lane-wide position (about 12 feet apart, or the width of the free throw lane). Being wider than that results in longer passes that are more easily intercepted and creates a slower break. Being any narrower than that, however, allows the defender to guard both offensive players more easily.

When you have the ball as you reach the scoring area just above the top of the circle, you must decide whether to pass or drive. Good decisions come from reading the defense. When the defender attacks you and is in your driving line, pass to an open teammate cutting to the basket (figure 8.4). Use a quick inside-hand bounce pass with a smaller player and a sure two-handed lob with a taller teammate or someone with great leaping ability. Both the bounce and lob passes have less chance of being intercepted than a chest pass.

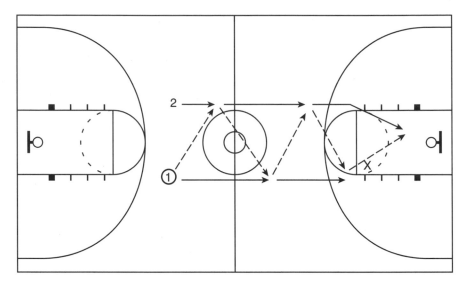

Figure 8.4 Two-on-one fast break: Player 1 sees defender in driving line and passes to cutting teammate.

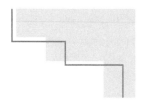

Misstep

In the scoring area, you penetrate past the foul line before passing, which creates congestion and allows one defender to guard two players or results in an interception or charging foul.

Correction

Only penetrate past the foul line to score if the defense gives you an open driving line to the basket.

When the defender is off the driving line, drive to the basket (figure 8.5). The usual defensive adjustment is to stop the ball high, a step above the foul line. On a pass to the cutter, a larger defender will react by trying to block the shot behind the shooter's head. A smaller player will

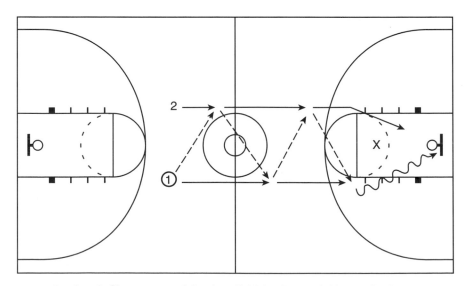

Figure 8.5 Two-on-one fast break: Player 1 sees defender off driving line and drives to basket.

168

attempt to draw a charge or steal the ball. As you drive to the basket, you should react to the defense and take the ball to the basket with a strong two-handed layup. Your teammate should follow, prepared to rebound a possible miss and score with a power move.

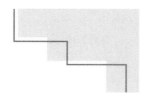

Misstep

When you reach the scoring area just above the top of the circle, you fail to read the defense and make a poor decision on whether to pass or drive.

Correction

Read the defense when you reach the scoring area. If your defender is on your driving line, pass to the cutter. If your defender is off your driving line, drive to the basket.

Within the scoring area, penetrate past the foul line to score only if the defense gives you an open driving line to the basket. Penetrating past the foul line and then attempting to pass creates congestion and allows one defender to guard two players. This can result in an interception or charging foul.

Two-on-One Fast-Break Drill. *Two-on-One*

This drill requires three players, two on offense and one on defense. The two offensive players start at the boxes outside the lane on their defensive end, and the defensive player starts with the ball just inside the foul line. The defender starts the drill by passing to one of the offensive players and then sprinting back to the free throw line in the scoring area.

Both offensive players yell "Two-on-one!" and move the ball upcourt, quickly passing back and forth while maintaining positions 12 feet apart (the width of the free throw lane). If you have the ball as you reach the scoring area just above the top of the circle, read the defense and decide whether to pass or drive. If the defender attacks you in your driving line, pass to the teammate who is cutting to the basket. Use a quick, inside-hand bounce pass with a smaller player or a two-handed lob with a taller player or one with great leaping ability.

When the defender is off the driving line, drive to the basket, scoring with a strong two-handed layup. The offense should not only get an open shot, but should also establish offensive rebounding position.

When you play on defense, stop the ball high, a step above the foul line. React on a pass to the cutter by trying to block the shot behind the shooter's head, draw a charge, or steal the ball. Change positions after a made shot or a turnover by the offense. Play to 5 points.

Success Check

- Offensive players should communicate with each other as they move upcourt.
- The defender should try to stop the ball high.
- Offensive players should react to the defender's actions and make the correct decision on whether to pass or drive to the basket.

Score Your Success

The offense scores 1 point when either offensive player makes a basket. The defensive player scores 1 point each time he stops the two offensive players from scoring. This is a competitive drill. The first team to score 5 points wins the game. Give yourself 5 points if your team wins the game.

Your score ___

THREE-ON-TWO FAST BREAK

The three-on-two is a classic fast-break situation. The point guard should have the ball and should read the situation when the fast-breaking team enters the scoring area (normally a step outside the three-point line). Correct decisions are needed on whether to penetrate to the basket or pass to the wing. The point guard should penetrate past the foul line and drive for a score only if the defense gives an open driving line to the basket. Otherwise, it is always better to stop above the foul line. Too much penetration causes congestion and may result in a charging foul.

The two defenders normally will be in tandem, with the top defender meeting the player with the ball slightly ahead of the foul line. When the wings reach the foul line extended, they should cut toward the basket at a 45-degree angle (figure 8.6). When attacked by the top defender, the point guard should pass to the open wing player and cut to the ball-side elbow. In turn, the wing player should catch the pass in position to shoot and react to the defense. If the back defender does not come out, the wing should be in position for a catch-and-shoot bank jump shot, a short drive

for a pull-up bank jump shot in rhythm and range, or a drive to the basket.

As shown in figure 8.6, the wings (players 2 and 3) make sharp 45-degree cuts to the basket at the foul line extended. The point guard (1) bounce passes to the open wing (2) and then cuts to the ball-side elbow. Player 4 trails the play, then spots up at the weak-side elbow. Player 5 trails and acts as the defensive safety.

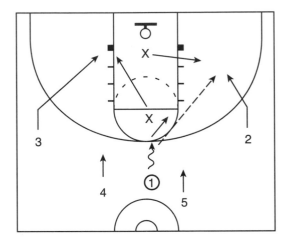

Figure 8.6 Three-on-two fast break.

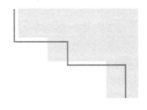

Misstep

The wings cut to the corners, making for a difficult corner jump shot rather than an easier bank jump shot.

Correction

The wings should cut at a 45-degree angle to be in position for a catch-and-shoot bank jump shot, a short drive for a pull-up bank shot in rhythm and range, or a drive to the basket.

The normal defensive adjustment is for the back player to yell "Ball!" and cover the pass to the wing while the top player yells "You have help!" and drops back to give help on a drive or block out on a shot. When this occurs, reverse the ball to the point guard, who may shoot or pass to the weak-side wing for a jump shot. The offense should not only get an open shot, but should also establish offensive rebounding position.

Three-on-Two Fast-Break Drill 1.   *Three-on-Two*

This drill requires five players, three on offense and two on defense. The defensive players start at half-court and sprint in tandem to the defensive positions just inside the free throw line in the scoring area. The offensive players are evenly spaced

along the baseline in three lanes. The offensive player in the middle lane has the ball. The middle player starts the drill by tossing the ball high on the backboard and rebounding it with two hands while yelling "Ball!" On the rebound, the right wing runs to an outlet position past the foul line extended and yells "Outlet!" The rebounder makes a two-handed overhead outlet pass to the right wing beyond the foul line extended, sprints up the middle while yelling "Middle!" and receives a return chest pass. The left wing sprints up the court while yelling "Left!" The middle player makes a chest pass to the left wing, who has sprinted ahead. Continue the drill up the court, with each player passing and sprinting in parallel positions and calling out their lanes.

Defensive players should be in tandem, one on top and one behind. The top defensive player defends the player with the ball, yelling "I've got the ball!" The bottom defender near the basket yells "I've got the hole!" On a pass to the wing, the bottom defender takes the ball and the top defender retreats to defend the basket or block out the weak side wing and rebound a possible missed shot.

At the foul line extended, each wing should cut at a sharp 45-degree angle to the basket. The offensive player in the middle makes a bounce pass to one of the wings for a bank jump shot from 15 to 18 feet or makes a driving layup. The other wing follows in, prepared to rebound a miss and score with a power move. The middle player stays back for a swing of the ball, in case the wing decides not to shoot or for defensive balance on a shot. After a score, switch lanes: The middle player moves to the right, the right player moves to the left, and the left player moves to the middle. Continue the drill back down the court. Play to 5 points.

Success Check

- Offensive players should communicate with each other as they move upcourt.
- Wings cut at a 45-degree angle to the basket at the foul line extended.
- Offensive players, especially the middle player, should read the defenders' actions.

Score Your Success

The offense earns 1 point each time they make a basket. The defense earns 1 point each time they stop the three offensive players from scoring. This is a competitive drill. The first team to score 5 points wins the game. Give yourself 5 points if your team wins the game.

Your score ___

Three-on-Two Fast-Break Drill 2. *Continuous Three-on-Two, Two-on-One*

This drill requires at least 5 and no more than 15 players. Two defensive players start in tandem just inside the free throw line in the scoring area (figure 8.7). Three offensive players are evenly spaced along the baseline in three lanes. The offensive player in the middle lane has the ball. The middle player starts the drill by tossing the ball high on the backboard and rebounding it with two hands while yelling "Ball!" On the rebound, the right wing runs to an outlet position past the foul line extended and yells "Outlet!" The rebounder makes a two-handed overhead outlet pass to the right wing beyond the foul line extended. After the rebound and a two-handed outlet pass, the three offensive players move up the court to the scoring area, where they attempt to score against the two defenders. When either the offense scores or the defense obtains possession via an interception or rebound, the original two defenders and one original offensive player start a two-on-one fast break. The other two original offensive players remain back as the defense for the next three-on-two fast break. When the offense scores or the defense obtains possession via an interception or rebound, a three-lane fast break begins in the other direction with the two offensive players and the original defender or with three new players. The drill becomes a three-on-two and two-on-one continuous fast-break drill. Play to 5 points.

Success Check

- Offensive players should communicate with each other as they move upcourt.
- Offensive players should read the defenders' actions and make the right decisions.
- Aggressively go for the rebounds.

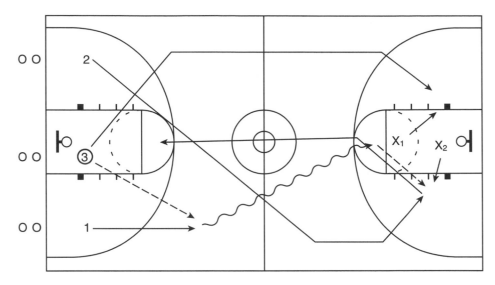

Figure 8.7 Continuous three-on-two, two-on-one fast-break drill.

Score Your Success

The offense earns 1 point each time they make a basket. The defense earns 1 point each time they stop the three offensive players from scoring. This is a competitive drill. The first team to score 5 points wins the game. Give yourself 5 points if your team wins the game.

Your score ___

Three-on-Two Fast-Break Drill 3. *Three-on-Two With Defensive Trailer*

This drill requires at least 9 but no more than 15 players. Group players into three or more teams with three players on each team. Team 1 starts on offense, its three players evenly spaced along the baseline in three lanes (figure 8.8). The middle player has the ball. Team 2 starts out of bounds at half-court, ready to jump in on defense. The remaining teams wait their turn.

The middle player on team 1 starts the drill by tossing the ball high on the backboard and rebounding it with two hands. As the ball is rebounded, two defensive players from team 2 run and touch a foot in the center circle before sprinting back to tandem defensive positions just inside the free throw line in the scoring area. The three offensive players move up the court to the scoring area and attempt to score. After one of the offensive players crosses half-court, the remaining defensive player from team 2 is allowed to run and touch the center circle and sprint back as a defensive trailer. After team 1 scores or team 2 obtains possession via an interception or a rebound, team 1 gets off the court and becomes the last team waiting out of bounds at half-court.

Team 2, the original defensive team, now starts a three-lane fast break in the other direction. Two players from team 3 run and touch a foot in the center circle and sprint back on defense. The third player from team 3 runs and touches a foot in the center circle after a player from the offensive team crosses half-court. The drill becomes a continuous three-on-two with a defensive trailer fast break. The first team to score 7 points wins the game.

To Increase Difficulty

- Any team that scores is allowed to press up to half-court.

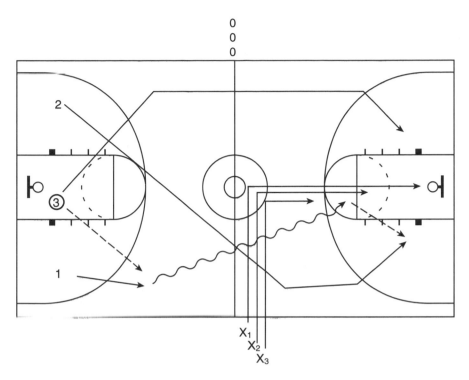

Figure 8.8 Three-on-two with defensive trailer drill.

Success Check

- Communicate with the players on your team.
- On offense, read and react to the defenders' actions.
- On defense, work hard to deny the pass and deny the drive.

Each made basket is worth 1 point. This is a competitive drill. The first team to score 7 points wins the game. Give yourself 5 points if your team wins the game.

Your score ___

FOUR-ON-THREE FAST BREAK

The four-on-three fast break (figure 8.9) uses the first trailer. When the defense gets three players back, the wing player should dribble to the corner and look to pass to the first trailer cutting to the ball-side box. The wing player should keep the dribble alive until able to pass to the trailer or reverse the ball to the middle. The first trailer should cut to the weak-side elbow and then make a diagonal cut to a post-up position above the ball-side box, looking to receive a pass from the wing. After beating the defense to the box, the trailer should seal a retreating defender on the topside and look for a pass from the baseline side. The wing should then pass to the trailer with a sidearm bounce pass from the baseline side.

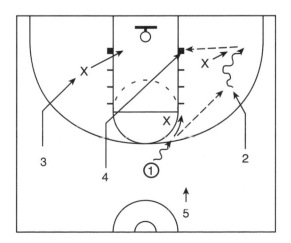

Figure 8.9 Four-on-three fast break.

As shown in figure 8.9, the point guard (1) bounce passes to the open wing (2) and then cuts to the ball-side elbow. Wing 2 dribbles to the corner, then makes a sidearm bounce pass to the trailer. Wing 3 prepares to rebound the ball. The first trailer (4) makes a diagonal cut to the low post at the ball-side block. The second trailer (5) follows as a defensive safety.

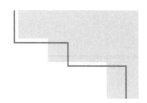

Misstep

The wing stops dribbling, is unable to pass to the trailer or back to the point guard, and is vulnerable to being trapped in the corner.

Correction

The wing player should keep the dribble alive until she can pass to the trailer or reverse the ball back to the point guard.

Four-on-Three Fast-Break Drill. *Four-on-Three With Defensive Trailer*

This drill requires 12 to 16 players grouped into three or four teams, each with four players. Team 1 starts on offense (figure 8.10). Team 2 starts on defense. The action is similar to the three-on-two with defensive trailer drill. Three players from team 2 run and touch a foot in the center circle before sprinting back to defensive position as the offensive players of team 1 move up the court. Again, as one of the offensive players crosses half-court, the remaining defensive player runs and touches a foot in the center circle and sprints back as a defensive trailer. The drill becomes a continuous four-on-three with defensive trailer fast break. The first team to score 7 points wins the game.

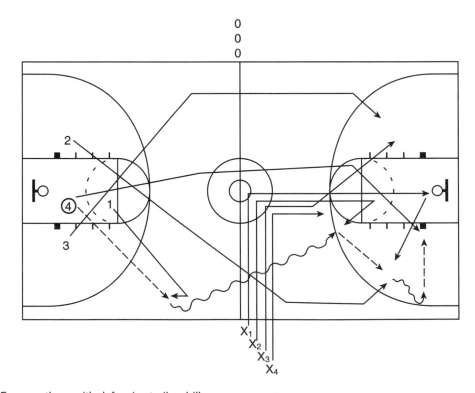

Figure 8.10 Four-on-three with defensive trailer drill.

- Communicate with the players on your team.
- On offense, read and react to the defenders' actions.
- On defense, work hard to deny the pass and deny the drive.

Each made basket is worth 1 point. This is a competitive drill. The first team to score 7 points wins the game. Give yourself 5 points if your team wins the game.

Your score ___

FAST-BREAK SWING

In the fast-break swing, the second trailer receives a pass and swings the ball from the ball side to the weak side. When the defense gets four or five players back and the wing player cannot pass to the first trailer in the post, each of the other players should spot up within shooting range to swing (reverse) the ball to the weak side (figure 8.11). The point guard should spot up above the ball-side elbow while the second trailer spots up above the weak-side elbow. Meanwhile, the weak-side wing should maintain spacing at the imaginary foul line extended. After receiving a swing pass, each perimeter player's options, in order, are to pass inside to the post-up player moving across the lane, swing the ball to the weak side, and shoot the outside shot. During the swing of the ball, the post-up player should move on each pass across the lane to the weak-side box.

The second trailer has an important role during the swing. If the defense denies him the first swing pass, the point guard should either cut through to the weak-side corner or pull out to the ball-side sideline (figure 8.12). As this happens, the second trailer must immediately flash to the ball-side elbow to receive a pass from the wing. After receiving the pass, the second trailer's options, in order, are to pass to the weak-side wing, pass inside, and shoot.

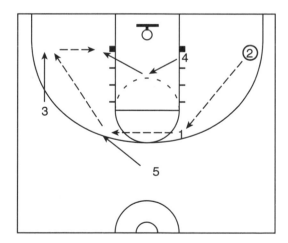

Figure 8.11 Fast-break swing: Post-up player (4) moves from block to block as ball is passed (swings) to players spotting up on perimeter.

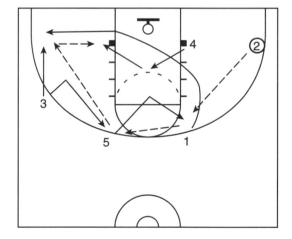

Figure 8.12 Fast-break swing: Defense denies first swing pass, so point guard (1) cuts through or pulls and second trailer (5) flashes to ball side.

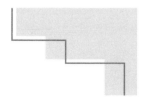

Misstep

On a swing of the ball, the perimeter players first look to shoot, rather than looking inside first and weak side second.

Correction

The swing players' options, in order, are to look to pass inside, to look weak side to continue the swing of the ball, and finally, to look to shoot.

When a swing of the ball to the weak side does not produce an open inside or outside shot, the team can get into a passing game offense or the point guard can demand the ball and run a set play.

Complete Fast-Break Drill 1. *Five-on-Zero Fast-Break Options*

This drill requires 5 to 15 players grouped into one or more teams of 5 players each. Each team will run the fast break using a different scoring option down the court each time. The scoring options include

- passing to the strong-side wing for a bank jump shot.
- passing to the weak-side wing for a bank jump shot.
- passing to the strong-side wing, who then passes to the first trailer at the strong-side box for a low-post move.
- passing to the strong-side wing, who then passes back to the point guard at the strong-side elbow for a jump shot.
- passing to the strong-side wing. The point guard either cuts through to the weak-side corner or pulls out to the ball-side sideline, and the strong-side wing then passes to the second trailer, who is flashing to the ball-side elbow for a jump shot.
- passing to the strong-side wing. The point guard either cuts through to the weak-side corner or pulls out to the ball-side sideline, and the strong-side wing then passes to the second trailer flashing to the ball-side elbow, who then passes inside to the first trailer for a low-post move.
- passing to the strong-side wing. The point guard either cuts through to the weak-side corner or pulls out to the ball-side sideline, and the strong-side wing then passes to the second trailer flashing to the ball-side elbow, who then passes to the weak-side wing. The weak-side wing takes a jump shot or passes inside to the first trailer, who moves high across the lane on each pass from the strong-side box to the weak-side box.

The drill starts with the fast-breaking team in defensive position at the defensive end. Either the center or power forward tosses the ball to the backboard, rebounds it, and makes an outlet pass to the point guard. The selected scoring option is then executed. Repeat each scoring option twice.

Success Check

- Use the correct technique for the scoring option being executed.
- Communicate with teammates during the fast break.

Score Your Success

Each trip down the court can result in 2 points, 1 point for correctly executing the fast-break scoring option and 1 point for making the shot at the end of the scoring option. If more than one team is playing, make it a competitive game. The first team to score 14 points wins. If only one team is playing, try to make 12 out of 14 points. If you are playing a competitive game against another team, give yourself 5 points if your team wins. If you are playing with only one team, give yourself 5 points if you make 12 to 14 points, 3 points if you make 10 to 11 points, and 0 points if you make fewer than 10 points.

Your score ___

Complete Fast-Break Drill 2. *Five-on-One Deny the Point Guard*

This drill requires 5 to 15 players grouped into one or more teams of 5 players each. Select a player from one of the teams to play defense on the middle player (point guard). Only the point guard is allowed to score. The point guard can practice moving without the ball (cutting through to the weak-side corner or pulling out to the ball-side sideline) while being denied from receiving a return pass at the ball-side elbow. The other offensive players practice options for when the point guard is denied the ball, such as flashing to the ball.

Each offensive team will run a fast-break swing option, looking to get the ball inside to the first trailer. The offensive team will swing the ball. Each perimeter player looks to pass inside to the point guard, who attempts to get open by moving high across the lane on each pass from the strong-side box to the weak-side box. After receiving a pass, the point guard attempts to score with a low-post move. Play to 5 points.

To Increase Difficulty

• Make the drill a five-on-two fast-break drill by using two defenders. The two defenders can be put on the point guard and the first trailer, on the two wings, or on any other two offensive players. Only the defended players may score.

Success Check

• Each perimeter player looks first to pass inside to the point guard.

• The offensive team swings the ball around the perimeter until the point guard gets open.

Score Your Success

The fast-breaking team earns 1 point for each shot made by the point guard. This is a competitive drill. The first team to score 5 points wins the game. Give yourself 5 points if your team wins the game.

Your score ___

Complete Fast-Break Drill 3. *Five-on-(Two Plus One Plus Two) Fast Break*

This drill is used to give a fast-breaking team practice at reading and reacting to various defensive options. The drill requires 10 players, 5 on offense and 5 on defense. As the offensive team runs a fast break, the defensive team will choose defensive options to defend it.

Divide the full court into three equal areas: area I (initial area), area II (secondary area), and area III (scoring area) (figure 8.13). The defense spreads into a two-one-two alignment with two defenders in area I, one defender in area II, and two defenders in area III. The drill starts with a coach, teacher, or extra player intentionally missing a shot. The players on the fast-breaking team start in defensive positions, block out their two opponents, and rebound the ball. The defenders in area I can go for the rebound, trap the rebounder, steal the ball from the rebounder, drop back to deny a passing lane to the favorite or other potential outlet receiver, or intercept the outlet pass.

Once the fast-breaking team advances the ball into area II, the secondary area, the single defender in area II can overplay the outlet receiver and deny the outlet pass, allow the outlet pass and pop up on the offensive player who receives the ball with the intent of drawing a charge, pressure the dribbler to delay the fast break, allow the dribbler to go by, or try to steal the ball by flicking it from behind.

Once the fast-breaking team advances the ball into area III, the scoring area, the two defenders in area III can trap the player with the ball, play a tandem defense inside the free throw lane, pressure the shooter, or rebound a possible missed shot.

The offensive team gets 1 point each time it scores. If the defense commits a foul, the offense gets the ball and starts again. If an offensive player misses a shot and a teammate gets an offensive rebound, play continues. The defense gets 1 point if it steals the ball or rebounds it or if it forces the offense into a violation. Play to 5 points, then switch roles.

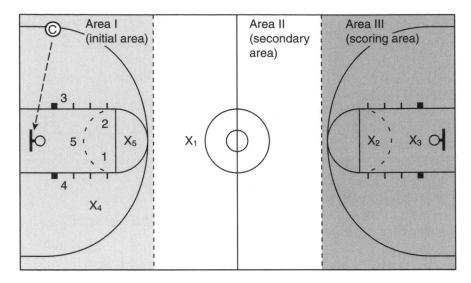

Figure 8.13 Five-on-(two plus one plus two) fast-break drill.

Success Check

- On offense, read the defense's actions and react accordingly.
- On defense, choose the best option and communicate with teammates.

Score Your Success

This is a competitive drill. Try to win more games than your opponent, playing each game to 5 points. Give yourself 5 points if your team wins the most games.

Your score ___

Complete Fast-Break Drill 4.   *Five-on-Five Fast Break*

In this drill, the offensive team practices running a fast break and the defensive team practices defending against the fast break. This drill requires 10 players grouped into two teams of 5 players each. One team plays offense and the other plays defense.

To defend against the fast break, the defensive team should have the player nearest the rebounder pressure the outlet pass. They should also have a defender deny a passing lane to the favorite or other potential outlet receiver. The other defenders should quickly retreat to the scoring area by sprinting back on the ball side of the floor while calling out their individual assignments in order. The first player back takes the most dangerous offensive player, usually the one near the basket. The second player back takes the second most

dangerous player, usually the player with the ball. The third player back takes the third most dangerous player, the other team's best shooter. (Instead, you can choose to have your defensive center always take the offensive center.) Once two defensive players are back, a defensive guard can attack the offensive player who receives the ball with the intent of pressuring the dribbler to delay the fast break.

The offensive team gets 1 point each time it scores. If the defense commits a foul, the offense gets the ball and starts again. If an offensive player misses a shot and a teammate gets an offensive rebound, play continues. The defense gets 1 point if it steals the ball or rebounds it or if it forces the offense into a violation. Play to 5 points, then switch roles.

Success Check

- On defense, pressure the rebounder and the outlet pass.
- Communicate your defensive assignment.
- On offense, read the defense and react with the best option.

Score Your Success

This is a competitive drill. Try to win more games than your opponent, playing each game to 5 points. Give yourself 5 points if your team wins the most games.

Your score ___

RATE YOUR SUCCESS

A well-executed fast break is an exciting play to watch and participate in. You can swing the momentum of a game in your favor if you and your teammates can run the fast break effectively.

In the next step, we will look in more detail at team offense. Before going to step 9, however, look back at how you performed the drills in this step. For each of the drills presented in this step, enter the points you earned, then add up your scores to rate your total success.

Three-Lane Fast-Break Drills

1. Parallel Lane Passing ____ out of 6
2. Pass and Go Behind ____ out of 6

Two-on-One Fast-Break Drill

1. Two-on-One ____ out of 5

Three-on-Two Fast-Break Drills

1. Three-on-Two ____ out of 5
2. Continuous Three-on-Two, Two-on-One ____ out of 5
3. Three-on-Two With Defensive Trailer ____ out of 5

Four-on-Three Fast-Break Drill

1. Four-on-Three With Defensive Trailer ____ out of 5

Complete Fast-Break Drills

1. Five-on-Zero Fast-Break Options ____ out of 5
2. Five-on-One Deny the Point Guard ____ out of 5
3. Five-on-(Two Plus One Plus Two) Fast Break ____ out of 5
4. Five-on-Five Fast Break ____ out of 5

TOTAL ____ *out of 57*

If you scored 45 or more points, congratulations! You have mastered the basics of this step and are ready to move on to step 9, team offense. If you scored fewer than 45 points, you may want to spend more time on the fundamentals covered in this step. Practice the drills again to develop mastery of the techniques and increase your scores.

Team Offense

At its best, basketball is a team game played by five players moving the ball, moving without the ball, and making quick, intelligent decisions, especially with regard to shot selection. Team offense depends on the sound execution of fundamentals, including moving the ball and moving without the ball. It also depends on intelligent and unselfish play.

Have a trained observer, such as a coach, teacher, or skilled player, subjectively evaluate your ability to execute the basic actions and your decision-making skills when you play the passing game.

MAN-TO-MAN OFFENSE (PASSING GAME)

The passing game, or motion offense, is one of the most popular man-to-man offenses in basketball. In the passing game, players are guided more by principles than by a strict set of specific assigned responsibilities. Every player should learn to execute the passing game because it teaches team play and is an offense used by many teams.

The passing game can be started from a variety of offensive formations, or sets, including the 3-2, 2-3, 1-3-1, 2-1-2, and 1-4. The 3-2 open set (figure 9.1), also called the spread formation, is the most basic formation for learning to play team offense. It involves three perimeter players and two baseline players. The point position (player 1 in figure 9.1) is above the top of the circle. The wing positions (players 2 and 3) are at the imaginary foul line extended on each side. The baseline positions (players 4 and 5) are at the midpoint between the corner and the basket on each side.

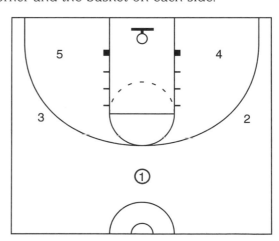

Figure 9.1 3-2 open set or spread formation.

181

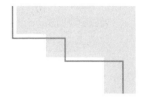

Misstep

Players on your team tend to crowd together near the ball or too close to the basket.

Correction

Maintain spacing and balance in an open formation, spread 15 to 20 feet apart. Keep the middle open. When you cut to the basket and do not receive a pass, continue through and fill a spot on the side with fewer players.

The 3-2 open set encourages versatility rather than forcing players into restricted roles as center, power forward, small forward, shooting guard, or point guard. It gives each player the opportunity to handle the ball, cut, screen, and move outside and inside. The 3-2 set provides initial structure and spacing that allow players to execute basic two- and three-person plays and plays involving all five players, such as a five-player weave or five-player give-and-go offense.

When executing the passing game, keep in mind these basic principles of good teamwork.

Talk. Communication is key to all aspects of team offense. The passing game is not a set play offense, and players are not assigned a specific set of responsibilities. Therefore, continual communication between players becomes especially important when executing the passing game.

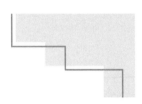

Misstep

You and your teammates get confused about what each other is doing.

Correction

Talk! The passing game is not a set play offense in which each player has a specific assignment or set of responsibilities. Communication is especially important in a passing game, so use designated key words for basic passing game actions.

See the rim. By having the rim in view, you see the entire court. When you have the ball, keep the rim in view and look for teammates cutting to the basket, posting up, and cutting off screens. When you do *not* have the ball, you should have the rim and the player with the ball in view.

Maintain spacing and court balance. Start in an open formation with players spread 15 to 20 feet apart. Space yourselves high at the top, wide on the wing, and at the midpoint between the basket and corner on the baseline.

Backdoor cut when overplayed. When overplayed by a defender who denies you the pass, make a backdoor cut all the way to the basket. When backdoor cuts are used frequently, the passing game becomes a great offense for beating pressure defenses.

Flash between the passer and overplayed receiver. When a defender denies your teammate the pass and you are the next player away from the receiver, automatically flash to an open area between the passer and the overplayed receiver. Flashing to the ball helps relieve defensive pressure on your teammates by giving the passer

another outlet. A flash can not only prevent a possible turnover, but also can create a scoring opportunity if the overplayed receiver combines it with a well-timed backdoor cut.

Keep the middle open. When you cut to the basket and do not receive a pass, you should continue on through and fill an open spot on the side of the court with fewer players. This will keep the middle open and the floor balanced. Do not stay in the post area for more than one count.

Move to a vacated spot quickly. When you are the next player away from a cutting player, quickly move to the vacated spot. It is especially important to replace a player who has cut from the point or top position. To replace the player at the point, cut high above the three-point line, creating a better passing angle to receive a swing pass from a wing and a better angle to reverse the ball to the weak side. This will also force the defense to cover more of the court, thus providing more space for cutting, driving, and posting up.

Know your options at the wing position. When you are on the wing, your options are to catch and shoot within your rhythm and range or to continue your cut out wide. When you catch the ball outside of your range, look to pass inside to a cutter or player posting up. On the wing, hold the ball for a count or two to give cutters and post-up players time to get open. If you are unable to pass to an open teammate cutting or posting up, look to penetrate and pass (draw-and-kick) or try to balance the court by quickly dribbling to the point. Look to pass to a baseline player only if that teammate is open for a catch-and-shoot jump shot within rhythm and range or can make an easy pass to a player cutting inside or posting up. You can move the ball more quickly if you swing it from wing to point to wing and keep it off the baseline.

Know your options at the point position. When you are at the point position, your options, in order, are to reverse the ball quickly to the weak side, look inside for a pass to a post-up player, penetrate and pass (draw-and-kick), or fake a pass to the weak side and make a quick snapback pass to the wing on the side from which you received the pass.

Know your options at the baseline position. When you are at a baseline position, look to set up your defender for a cut off a down screen or set a back pick for a wing player. On the baseline, you should be especially alert to flash to the ball when a wing is denied the pass. Look to receive a pass on the baseline only when you are in an open catch-and-shoot position within your rhythm and range or can make an easy pass to a player cutting inside or posting up. The ball can be moved more quickly if it is kept off the baseline.

Know your options as a post-up player. When you receive the ball in the low post, read the defense and look to score before passing out to a perimeter player. When you do not receive a pass in the low post, look to set a back pick for a perimeter player. After setting the pick, pop out to receive a pass on the perimeter for a possible jump shot within your rhythm and range.

Maintain rebounding and defensive balance. On a shot inside, players should rebound, while the point guard and another outside player should get back for defensive balance. When you take a shot outside of the lane area, you should get back for defensive balance. Any time the player at the point drives to the basket, players at the wings should get back for defensive balance.

A member of your team, usually the point guard, signals the start of the passing game with a simple verbal call such as "Passing game" or "Motion" or with a hand signal such as circling one finger upward. The best way to start is to pass the ball to the wing and then work together, using basic passing game actions. After receiving a pass on the wing, you should be a triple threat to pass, shoot, or drive to the basket. On a drive, look to score or to penetrate and pass (draw-and-kick) inside or outside to an open teammate.

When the ball is at the point, the closest wing player should initiate movement by cutting through to create an open area for a baseline player, who will cut to the wing for a pass from the point (figure 9.2). When you are at the point and cannot pass to the wing, initiate movement by dribbling at the wing and using a dribble screen or weave action (figure 9.3).

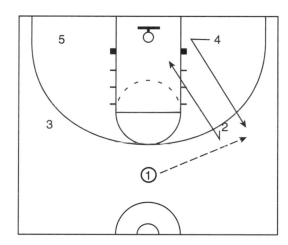

Figure 9.2 Start of passing game: Wing player 2 cuts through to create opening for player 4.

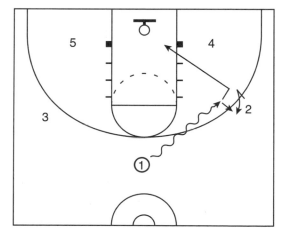

Figure 9.3 Start of passing game: Player at point (1) sets dribble screen for wing 2 and then cuts to basket.

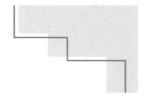

Misstep

You and your teammates have difficulty seeing each other when you get open on a cut, off a screen, or when posting up.

Correction

Players with the ball should see the rim and the entire court. When you see the rim, you can see when your teammates are open.

Some of the basic actions used in the passing game are the backdoor cut, flash, give-and-go, dribble screen or weave, down screen, back pick, elbow curl, cross screen, pick-and-roll, and draw-and-kick.

Backdoor Cut

You should automatically use a backdoor cut any time you are overplayed by a defender and prevented from receiving a pass. You should also use a backdoor cut when your defender's head is turned away from you, causing a momentary loss of visual contact. Use a designated key word such as *eyeball* to signal the passer that you are going backdoor. The designated word indicates that you will continue your backdoor cut to the basket once you start it. When you are on the wing, set up your defender by taking a step above the foul line extended (figure 9.4), or when you are at the point, by taking a step above the free throw circle (figure 9.5). After receiving the pass, look to shoot, drive to the basket for a layup, or penetrate and pass (draw-and-kick).

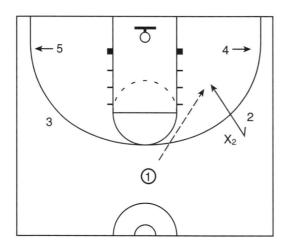

Figure 9.4 Backdoor cut: Player 2 denied pass at wing, cuts backdoor.

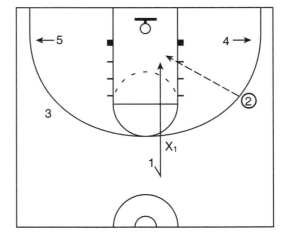

Figure 9.5 Backdoor cut: Player 1 denied pass at top, cuts backdoor.

Misstep

Your team has difficulty moving the ball from the ball side to the weak side, resulting in your swing passes being intercepted easily.

Correction

When you are replacing the point from the weak side, cut high above the circle to receive a pass and swing the ball. A shallow cut gives your defender a good angle at which to deny and intercept a pass. If you cut high and your defender continues to go with you, cut backdoor.

Flash

Any time you see a teammate being denied the pass and you are the next player away, you should automatically flash to an open area between the passer and overplayed receiver. Flashing to the ball relieves defensive pressure on your teammates by giving the passer another outlet. A flash can not only prevent a possible turnover, but combined with a well-timed backdoor cut by the overplayed receiver, can also create a scoring opportunity. Signal your flash cut with the key word *flash*. As you receive the pass, look to pass to your overplayed teammate cutting backdoor to the basket. If your teammate is covered on the backdoor cut, front turn into a triple-threat position for a possible shot, drive to the basket, or pass.

Flash high when your teammate is prevented from receiving a pass on the perimeter (figure 9.6). You can also flash to the high post when your teammate is being fronted in the low post (figure 9.7), and you can flash to the low post if your teammate is being denied at the high post (figure 9.8).

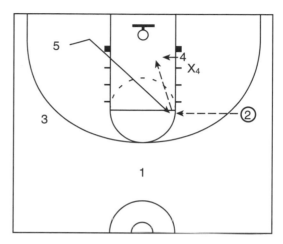

Figure 9.7 Flash: Player 5 sees low post 4 being denied, flashes high, receives pass from player 2, and passes to 4, who is cutting to the basket.

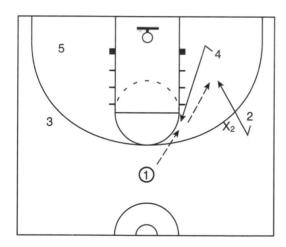

Figure 9.6 Flash: Player 4 sees wing 2 being denied, flashes high, receives pass from player 1, and passes to 2, who is cutting backdoor.

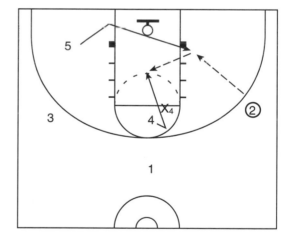

Figure 9.8 Flash: Player 5 sees high post 4 being denied, flashes to low post, receives pass from player 2, and passes to 4, who is cutting backdoor.

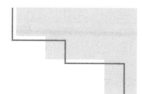

Misstep

Pressure defense prevents you and your teammates from getting open to receive a pass.

Correction

When your defender overplays you and denies you from receiving a pass, make a backdoor cut to the basket. When you see a defender denying your teammate from receiving a pass, you should automatically flash.

Give-and-Go

The give-and-go (figure 9.9) is the most basic play in basketball. Give (pass) the ball to your teammate and go (cut) to the basket, looking to receive a return pass for a layup. Read and set up your defender with a well-timed fake before the cut. Fake by taking a step or two away from the ball (as if you are not involved in the play). Then, as your defender moves with you, change direction sharply and use a front cut to the basket. Another way to fake is by taking a step or two toward the ball as if you are going to set a screen for or take a handoff from the player with the ball. As your defender moves with you, change direction sharply and make a backdoor cut behind (refer to figures 7.3 and 7.4 on pages 134 and 135). Figure 9.9 shows a five-player give-and-go offensive pattern.

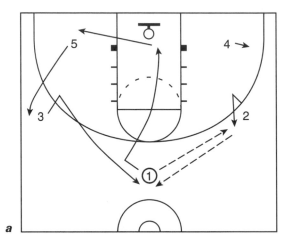
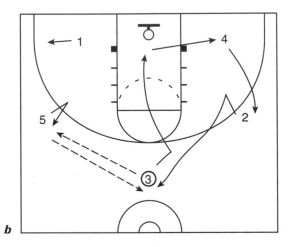

Figure 9.9 Five-player give-and-go: *(a)* To start the give-and-go, the point player (1) passes to wing 2 and cuts to the basket. The weak-side wing (3) quickly replaces the point and receives the pass from 2. *(b)* Player 3 passes to opposite wing 5 and cuts to the basket. The weak-side wing (2) quickly replaces the point and receives the pass from 5.

Give-and-Go Drill 1. *Five-on-Zero, No Dribble*

This drill requires five players. Set up in a 3-2 open set with three perimeter players and two baseline players. This is the most basic formation and is good for learning to play team offense. Run the give-and-go (pass-and-cut) offense against an imaginary defense. The offense may not dribble the ball except on a drive to the basket.

A team member, usually the point guard, signals the start of the offense with a simple verbal call, such as "Pass-and-cut" or "Give-and-go." When the ball is at the point, the closest wing player should initiate movement by cutting through to create an open area. Then a baseline player can cut to the wing for a pass from the point. Pass the ball to your teammate and cut to the basket, looking to receive a return pass for a layup.

Use your imagination, deception, and timing before cutting. Set up a fake either by taking a step or two away from the ball or by taking a step or two toward the ball before sharply changing direction and cutting to the basket. After receiving a pass on the wing, be a triple threat. As you cut to the basket, the weak-side wing replaces you at the point and the weak-side corner replaces the weak-side wing.

After receiving the pass, the wing may make a bounce pass to a player cutting to the basket, pass to the player now occupying the point, or cut to the basket. If the ball is passed to the point, the cutter moves to the open corner position that has been vacated.

Continue the drill with the player at the point passing to either wing, cutting to the basket, and having the wing fake a pass to the cutter before passing back to the point. Make at least five passes before passing to the cutter or driving to the basket. On a drive from the wing, look to score by using the draw-and-kick. Also use your imagination! At times, assume defensive pressure and use the backdoor cut and flash backdoor options. Continue the drill for a total of 30 passes and layups without error.

Success Check

- Communicate verbally with teammates using key words.
- When in possession of the ball, be a triple threat to pass, drive, or shoot.
- Imagine the defense and use fakes to get open or help a teammate get open.
- Pass at least five times before driving to the basket.

Fewer than 15 consecutive passes and layups without error = 0 points

15 to 19 consecutive passes and layups without error = 1 point

20 to 24 consecutive passes and layups without error = 3 points

25 to 30 consecutive passes and layups without error = 5 points

Your score ___

Give-and-Go Drill 2.   Five-on-Two, No Dribble

This drill requires 10 players, divided into two teams of 5 players each. One team is on offense, the other on defense. Select two players from the defensive team to play defense on two selected players from the offensive team. Only the defended players are allowed to score. This drill gives the two offensive players practice in moving without the ball, such as cutting backdoor, and all players practice the flash backdoor.

Use a backdoor cut automatically any time a defender overplays and prevents you from receiving a pass. Use a designated key word such as *eyeball* to indicate to the passer that you are going backdoor. A flash-and-backdoor cut is also effective against a defender denying a teammate from catching the ball when you are the next closest player. Flash to an open area between the passer and overplayed receiver. As you flash, signal your cut with the key word *flash*. Catch the ball and look for your overplayed teammate, who should make a backdoor cut toward the basket.

The offensive team may not dribble the ball. If the ball bounces to the floor on a missed or deflected

pass, it is not counted as a dribble. The offensive team is awarded 1 point for a made basket. The defensive team is awarded 1 point for each steal, turnover, or defensive rebound. Change from offense to defense after a made basket or after the defense obtains possession. Rotate in new defensive players after each made basket or after the defense obtains possession. Play to 3 points.

Success Check

- Communicate verbally with teammates using key words.
- Read the defenders and use fakes to get open or help a teammate get open.
- Only the players who are defended can score.

This is a competitive drill. The first team to score 3 points wins the game. Give yourself 5 points if your team wins the game.

Your score ___

Give-and-Go Drill 3.   Five-on-Five, No Dribble

This drill requires 10 players divided into two teams of 5 players each. One team will play offense and the other will play defense.

The offense may not dribble the ball. If the ball bounces to the floor on a missed or deflected pass, it is not counted as a dribble. This drill gives the offense practice at moving without the ball and

using the give-and-go, backdoor cut, and flash backdoor. When the defensive team is instructed to pressure the ball and deny all passes, it also becomes an extremely challenging team defensive drill.

The offensive team gets 1 point each time it scores. If the defense commits a foul, the offense gets the ball and starts again. If an offensive player misses a shot and a teammate gets an offensive rebound, play continues. The defense gets 1 point if it gets the ball on a steal or rebound or if it forces a violation. Play to 5 points. Teams then switch roles.

Success Check

* The offense may not dribble the ball.

* Communicate verbally with teammates.
* Read the defenders and use the right move to get open.

Dribble Screen or Weave

A dribble screen is set by dribbling toward a teammate and screening the defender while handing off the ball to a teammate (refer to figures 7.14 through 7.17, beginning on page 156). On a dribble screen, the defensive reaction usually will be for the screener's defender to give defensive help or switch.

Before receiving the handoff, read the defensive positioning. When your defender attempts to prevent the handoff by getting in your path, make a backdoor cut to the basket. After you receive a handoff on a dribble screen, read the defense. If the defenders do not switch and your defender is slow getting over the screen, turn the corner and drive to the basket. If your defender slides behind the screen, look to take the outside shot. If your teammate's defender switches to you as you receive the handoff for an outside shot, go at least two dribbles past the screen and pass back to the screener, either rolling to the basket or popping out.

One way to defend the dribble screen is for the dribble screener's defender to jump switch into the path of the receiver with the intent of drawing a charge or changing the direction of the player receiving the ball. To combat the jump switch after the handoff, make a short, 5- to 10-foot cut to an open area and look for a quick return pass. If you anticipate a jump switch, fake the handoff and drive to the basket.

Another way the defense may try to overcome the dribble screen is for both defenders to trap the player receiving the ball on the handoff. If the defenders trap you, retreat dribble to stretch the defense and then pass to your teammate, making a short, 5- to 10-foot cut to an open area. The defense will then be outnumbered, and the player with the ball will be able to drive or pass to an open teammate for a shot.

The dribble screen is used to execute a weave, a basic play in basketball. A weave (figure 9.10) involves at least three players who set dribble screens for each other. It starts with a dribble

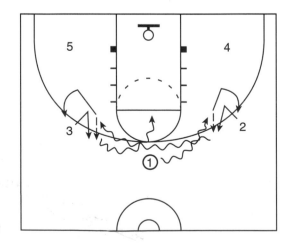 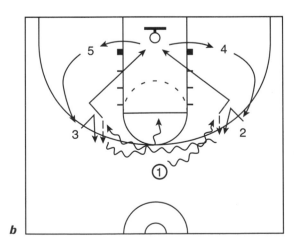

Figure 9.10 Dribble screen: *(a)* Three-player weave; *(b)* five-player weave.

screen and handoff to your teammate. After receiving the handoff, shoot from behind the screen, drive to the basket, or continue the weave by dribbling toward another teammate

for another dribble screen and handoff. The weave continues until you or a teammate can take advantage of an opening for a shot or drive to the basket.

Weave Drill 1. *Five-on-Zero Weave*

This drill requires five players. Set up in a 3-2 open set, or spread formation, with three perimeter players and two baseline players. Run a weave offense against an imaginary defense.

A member of the team, usually the point guard, signals the start of the weave with a simple verbal call such as "Weave" or "Figure." The point guard initiates the weave by dribbling to the inside of one of the wings. The wing should create an opening by faking away and then cutting to the outside of the dribbler for a handoff. The point guard hands off and cuts to the basket, looking to receive a return pass for a layup.

Use imagination, deception, and timing before cutting. As the point player cuts to the basket, the weak-side wing replaces the point and the weak-side corner replaces the weak-side wing. After receiving the handoff, the wing should be a triple threat and can bounce pass to the cutter, shoot, drive, or continue to weave by dribbling to the inside of the player now occupying the point. If the weave is continued, the cutter moves to the vacated open corner position.

Continue the weave, making a least five handoffs before passing to a player cutting or driving to the basket. On a drive or after receiving a pass after a cut, look to score or draw-and-kick. Use your imagination to mix in various offensive options off

the weave. You might assume your defender is attempting to get in your path to prevent the handoff and make a backdoor cut before the handoff. After the handoff, you might assume the defense is jump switching or trapping and make a short, 5- to 10-foot cut to an open area, look for a quick return pass, and drive to the basket. Continue the drill for a total of 30 handoffs and layups without error.

Success Check

- Make at least five handoffs before driving to the basket.
- Communicate verbally with teammates.
- Imagine various defensive tactics and use fakes and moves to overcome them.

Score Your Success

Fewer than 15 consecutive handoffs and layups without error = 0 points

15 to 19 consecutive handoffs and layups without error = 1 point

20 to 24 consecutive handoffs and layups without error = 3 points

25 to 30 consecutive handoffs and layups without error = 5 points

Your score ___

Weave Drill 2. *Five-on-Five Weave*

This drill requires 10 players divided into two teams of 5 players each. One team plays offense and the other plays defense.

This drill gives the offense practice executing the weave against various defensive strategies. Practice different defensive options against the weave, such as opening up and sliding, pressuring the ball and denying all passes, jump switching, and trapping.

The offensive team gets 1 point each time it scores. If the defense commits a foul, the offense gets the ball and starts again. If an offensive player misses a shot and a teammate gets an offensive rebound, play continues. The defense gets 1 point if it gets the ball on a steal or rebound or if it forces the offense into a violation. Play to 5 points. Teams then switch roles.

Success Check

- Communicate verbally with teammates during the weave.
- Read the defenders and react to how they are playing the weave.
- Have the rim and the players on the court in view.

This is a competitive drill. The first team to score 5 points wins the game. Give yourself 5 points if your team wins the game.

Your score ___

Down Screen

A screen set by a player screening down for a teammate is called a down screen. By setting a down screen for a teammate, you create a scoring opportunity. Your teammate can cut off your down screen to get open to receive a pass for a shot or drive. If your defender switches to your cutting teammate, you will be on the ball side of the defender you screened, momentarily open. Taking a few steps toward the basket before setting the screen enables you to get a better angle on the defender. You want the defender to go under the pick. As you set the down screen, communicate with your teammate by using a designated key word such as *down*.

Use one of the four basic options for cutting off a screen, depending on how it is defended: pop-out, curl, backdoor cut, and fade (see figures 7.5 through 7.8, beginning on page 137). Be patient. Wait until the screen is set to prevent an illegal moving block, and read how the defense is playing it. Before using the screen, slowly set up your move off it. Set a good angle for cutting off the screen by first moving slowly in the direction your defender plays you and then cutting hard off the screen in the opposite direction. Cut far enough away from the screen so that one defender cannot guard both you and the screener. This creates space for a pass to the screener if there is a defensive switch.

When you cut off a screen correctly, the screener's defender usually will give defensive help or switch. If you cut to the outside, the screener will be free to roll in toward the basket and receive a pass for an inside shot. If you cut to the basket, the screener becomes free to pop out and receive a pass for an outside shot (figure 9.11).

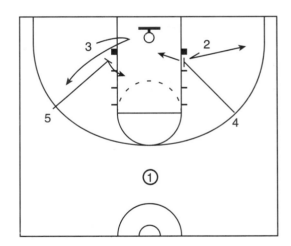

Figure 9.11 Down screen, pop and fade options. Players 5 and 4 set down screens for players 3 and 2. Cutter 3 pops out and screener 5 rolls. Cutter 2 fades and screener 4 cuts to the basket.

Misstep

Fouls are called on you and your teammates for setting illegal screens.

Correction

Be patient. When setting a screen, use a jump stop to prevent moving when your teammate uses your screen. When a screen is being set for you, wait until it is set before using it. You can be late to cut or dribble off a screen, but you should never be early. Waiting for the screen to be set prevents an illegal moving screen and gives you time to read the defense.

Back Pick

When you screen for a teammate by setting a pick behind the teammate's defender, it is called a *back pick* or up screen (figure 9.12). By setting a back pick for a teammate, you create the opportunity for either the teammate or you to score. Your teammate can cut off your back pick to get open to receive a pass for a layup or drive. If your defender switches to the cutter, you will be on the ball side of your teammate's defender, free to pop out to the ball to receive a pass for a jump shot. Take a few steps toward the basket to get a better angle on the defender you will back pick, communicating to your teammate by shouting a designated key word such as *up*.

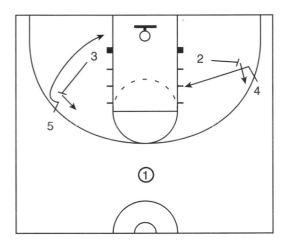

Figure 9.12 Back pick or up screen. Players 2 and 3 set back picks for players 4 and 5. Cutter 5 goes backdoor and screener 3 pops out. Cutter 4 front cuts and screener 2 pops out.

Make sure you set a legal screen. With a back pick, you are not allowed to be closer than a normal step from a stationary opponent if that opponent is unaware of your screen. You also may not be so close that a moving opponent cannot avoid contact without changing direction or stopping. Your opponent's speed determines what your screening position may be. This position will vary and might be one to two normal steps away.

As with the down screen, wait until the back pick is set before cutting off it to prevent an illegal screen and to read the defense. Slowly set up your move off the screen for a good angle before you cut hard off it in the opposite direction. If you cut

to the basket with a front cut or backdoor cut, the screener will be free to pop out and receive a pass for an outside shot. If you fake a cut to the basket and pop out, or if you fake to receive a pass for an outside shot, the screener should cut to the basket. The four basic options for cutting off a back pick, depending on how it is defended, are the front cut, backdoor cut, pop-out, and fade.

Elbow Curl

When you set a down screen for a teammate positioned at the elbow, your teammate should look to curl off your down screen. On an elbow curl (figure 9.13), your defender usually will give defensive help or switch. This momentarily frees you to pop out and receive a pass for a jump shot. The elbow curl is best used when a smaller player sets a down screen at the elbow for a bigger player. The bigger player can curl to the basket and the smaller player can pop out for a catch-and-shoot jump shot. To set the screen for an elbow curl, again take a few steps toward the basket to get a better angle on the defender. Signal to your teammate to curl off your down screen by shouting the key word *curl*.

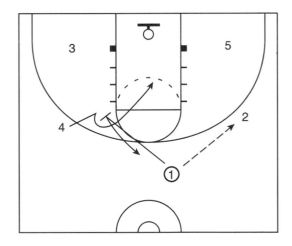

Figure 9.13 Elbow curl. Player 1 sets an elbow screen for player 4. Cutter 4 curls and screener 1 pops out.

Cross Screen

A cross screen (figure 9.14) is set by starting on one block and screening across the lane for a teammate at the opposite block. On a cross screen, the screener's defender usually reacts by giving defensive help or switching.

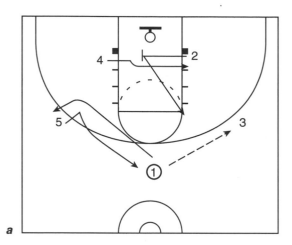

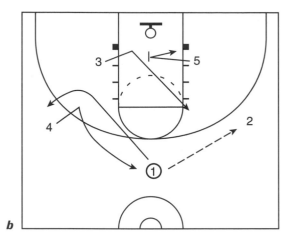

Figure 9.14 Cross screen: *(a)* Player 2 sets a cross screen for 4. Cutter 4 cuts low to the block and screener 2 rolls high. *(b)* Player 5 sets a cross screen for 3. Cutter 3 cuts high and screener 5 rolls low to the block.

When you cut off a cross screen, you should read the defensive positioning and cut either over or under the screen. When you set a cross screen and your teammate cuts low to the block by cutting over or under the cross screen, you should pop out high to the elbow area and receive a pass for an outside shot. If your teammate flashes high to the elbow to receive a pass for an outside shot, you should roll back to the ball-side block.

Pick-and-Roll

The pick-and-roll (figure 9.15), another basic basketball play, gets its name from the action. You set a pick (screen) for your teammate, who dribbles past it for an outside shot or drive. If your defender switches to your teammate, you will momentarily be inside the defender you

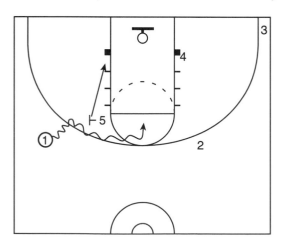

Figure 9.15 Pick-and-roll. Player 5 sets a pick for player 1 and rolls to the basket.

screened and free to roll toward the basket, looking to receive a return pass from the dribbler for a layup. Four options with the pick-and-roll, depending on how it is defended, are pick-and-roll, pick-and-pop, slip (early release), and stretch-the-trap (see figures 7.9 through 7.12, beginning on page 144). Figure 9.15 shows the basic option when defenders switch.

Draw-and-Kick

When you penetrate past a defender and a teammate's defender leaves to give defensive help on you, an open passing lane to your teammate is created. This action of penetrating and passing is called *draw-and-kick*. Always be alert for an opportunity to drive past a defender to score or create an open shot for a teammate whose defender is drawn to you. Also look for an opening or gap between two defenders to penetrate with one or two dribbles and draw the defenders to you.

Effective use of the draw-and-kick depends on judging well when and where to penetrate. But it also depends on players without the ball moving to open spots. Because the passing game depends primarily on moving the ball, overdribbling becomes counterproductive. The draw-and-kick is best used from the wing after a swing of the ball from ball side to weak side. Penetrating options include driving to the basket, shooting an in-between runner (pull-up jump shot), penetrating and passing inside (draw-and-kick in, figure 9.16), and penetrating and passing outside (draw-and-kick out, figure 9.17).

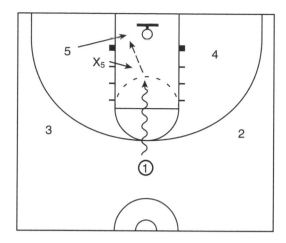

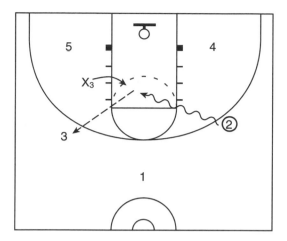

Figure 9.16 Draw-and-kick in. Player 1 penetrates, drawing the defender off player 5, and passes (kicks in) to player 5, who is cutting to the basket.

Figure 9.17 Draw-and-kick out. Player 2 penetrates, drawing the defender off player 3, and passes (kicks out) to player 3, who is spotting up outside.

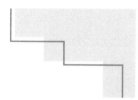

Misstep

You and your teammates overuse the dribble without a plan. You do not move the ball and players enough to break down the defense.

Correction

The passing game is most effective when there is both ball and player movement. Too much dribbling is counterproductive. Reverse the ball to the weak-side wing before using the draw-and-kick.

Passing Game Drill 1. *Five-on-Zero*

This drill requires five players. Set up in a 3-2 open set, or spread formation, with three perimeter players and two baseline players. Run a passing game offense against an imaginary defense.

One player, usually the point guard, signals the start of the drill with a simple verbal call such as "Passing game" or "Motion" or a hand signal such as circling one finger upward. The point passes the ball to the wing, and the other players work together using basic passing game actions. After receiving a pass on the wing, the wing should be a triple threat. On a drive, the wing looks to score or draw-and-kick. When the ball is at the point, the closest wing player should initiate movement, cutting through to create on open area for a baseline player to cut to the wing for a pass from the point. When the point cannot pass to the wing, the point can initiate movement by dribbling at the wing and using a dribble screen or weave action.

Use your imagination to mix in various offensive options, such as the backdoor cut, flash backdoor, give-and-go, weave, down screen, back pick, cross screen, elbow curl, pick-and-roll, and draw-and-kick. Work on the basic options for cutting off a screen: pop-out, curl, backdoor cut, and fake. Practice communicating by using designated key words such as *flash, down, up, cross, pick,* and *weave.* Continue for a total of 30 passes without error.

Success Check

- Communicate with teammates using key words.
- Use different offensive options, including the backdoor cut, flash, give-and-go, weave, down screen, and cross screen.

Score Your Success

Fewer than 15 consecutive passes without error = 0 points

15 to 19 consecutive passes without error = 1 point

20 to 24 consecutive passes without error = 3 points

25 to 30 consecutive passes without error = 5 points

Your score ___

Passing Game Drill 2. *Five-on-Two*

This drill requires 10 players divided into two teams of 5 players each. One team plays offense and the other plays defense. Select two players from the defensive team to play defense on two selected offensive players. Only the defended players may score.

This drill focuses on the two offensive players as they practice executing various passing game options and the basic options for cutting off a screen. Again, practice communicating to teammates with designated key words. The two defenders can practice pressuring the ball, strong-side denial, weak-side help, and combating screens with a slide, jump switch, or trap. Change from offense to defense after a made basket or after the defense obtains possession. Rotate in new defensive players after each made basket or after the defense obtains possession. The offense is awarded 1 point for each basket made by a defended player. The defense is awarded 1 point for each steal, turnover, or defensive rebound. Play to 5 points.

Success Check

• Communicate with teammates using designated key words.

• On offense, use various passing game options and methods for cutting off a screen.

• On defense, work on pressuring the ball, strong-side denial, weak-side help, and beating screens.

Score Your Success

The offensive team earns 1 point for each successful shot made by a defended player. The defensive team earns 1 point for each steal, turnover, or defensive rebound. This is a competitive drill. The first team to score 3 points wins the game. Give yourself 5 points if your team wins the game.

Your score ___

Passing Game Drill 3. *Five-on-Five*

This drill requires two teams of five players each. One team plays offense and the other plays defense.

The offensive team practices executing various passing game options, using basic options for cutting off a screen, and communicating with designated key words. The defense practices pressuring the ball, strong-side denial, weak-side help, and combating screens with a slide, jump, switch, or trap.

The offensive team gets 1 point each time it scores. If the defense commits a foul, the offense gets the ball and starts again. If an offensive player misses a shot and a teammate gets an offensive rebound, play continues. The defense gets 1 point if it gets the ball on a steal or rebound or if it forces the offense into a violation. Play to 5 points. Teams then switch roles.

Success Check

• On offense, read the defense and use the right option to create a good scoring opportunity.

• On defense, use various options to combat the screen and pressure the ball.

• Communicate with teammates using key words.

Score Your Success

This is a competitive drill. The first team to score 5 points wins the game. Give yourself 5 points if your team wins the game.

Your score ___

ZONE OFFENSE

In zone defenses, defenders are assigned to a designated area of the court rather than an individual offensive opponent. When you attack zone defenses, you should understand the type of zone you are playing against. Different zones employ different strategies, from sagging inside to pressuring outside shots, overplaying passing lanes, or trapping the ball. Zone defenses are named according to the alignment of players from the top toward the basket and include the 2-1-2, 2-3, 1-2-2, 3-2, and 1-3-1 zones.

Several common set offenses are used against zones. One method of attacking a zone is to use an offset alignment. Attack a zone that has an even front (two players) with an odd front (one player), and vice versa. This allows you to get into the gaps or seams of the zone, the areas between defensive players, where the defenders may be indecisive or late in covering. Other set attacks against the zone include sending a cutter or cutters through to open areas on the weak side and inside and overloading a zone area.

The basic principles for attacking zones are more important than those for a set zone offense:

- Fast break. Beat the zone upcourt and attack it before the defenders get to their zone positions.

- Use good spacing. Spread the zone. Three-point shooters should spot up behind the three-point line.

- Move the ball. The ball can move faster than the zone can shift. Pass the ball from the ball side to the weak side. Move the ball inside, then out.

- Reverse the ball. Pass the ball to make the defense move in one direction, then quickly reverse the ball back (snapback) to the opposite side.

- Be a triple threat. Square up to the basket and be a threat to score. Make use of shot fakes and pass fakes.

- Split the zone. Outside players should move into the gaps or seams of the zone (between defenders) and within shooting range.

- Draw-and-kick. Penetrate between defenders to draw your teammate's defender to you and create an open passing lane to your teammate.

- Use cuts. Send a cutter or cutters through to the weak side or to the inside behind the defense. It is very difficult for the defense to have visual contact with both the ball and an offensive player cutting through and from behind.

- Show patience, poise, and good shot selection. When you are patient, the defense can become fatigued and make mistakes.

- Attack the offensive boards. Although better rebounders can be positioned in the inside zone areas, they have a more difficult time matching up to block out aggressive offensive rebounders.

Zone Offense Drill. *Draw-and-Kick Shell Drill*

This drill is a good offensive drill for establishing a triple-threat position and being able to penetrate and pass (draw-and-kick). Divide eight players into two teams of four players each, one offensive team and one defensive team. The offensive team starts with two guards at the top of the circle and two forwards at the wing positions. Any offensive player with the ball is allowed one penetrating dribble. When the defender nearest the ball moves to help stop penetration, the offensive player with the ball passes out to whichever player the helping defender left. The offensive player receiving the pass should be a triple threat to shoot, pass, or drive.

The offensive team gets 1 point for each basket made. If the defense commits a foul, the offense gets the ball and starts again. If an offensive player misses a shot and a teammate gets an offensive rebound, keep playing. The defense gets 1 point when it gets the ball on a steal or rebound or when it forces the offense into a violation. Play to 5 points. Teams then switch roles.

Success Check

- The offensive player who receives the pass must be a triple threat.
- The offensive player with the ball must be aware of which teammate is open when the defensive player moves to help stop the penetration.

Score Your Success

This is a competitive drill. The first team to score 5 points wins the game. Give yourself 5 points if your team wins the game.

Your score ___

RATE YOUR SUCCESS

After you master individual skills, you are ready to apply them in a team environment. Basketball is the ultimate team game, and a well-executed team offense will lead to more point production and better teamwork.

In the next step, we will look in more detail at team defense. Before going to step 10, however, look back at how you performed the drills in this step. For each of the drills presented in this step, enter the points you earned, then add up your scores to rate your total success.

Give-and-Go Drills

   1. Five-on-Zero, No Dribble   ___ out of 5

   2. Five-on-Two, No Dribble   ___ out of 5

   3. Five-on-Five, No Dribble   ___ out of 5

Weave Drills

   1. Five-on-Zero Weave   ___ out of 5

   2. Five-on-Five Weave   ___ out of 5

Passing Game Drills

   1. Five-on-Zero   ___ out of 5

   2. Five-on-Two   ___ out of 5

   3. Five-on-Five   ___ out of 5

Zone Offense Drill

   1. Draw-and-Kick Shell Drill   ___ out of 5

TOTAL   ___ *out of 45*

If you scored 35 or more points, congratulations! You have mastered the basics of this step and are ready to move on to the final step, team defense. If you scored fewer than 35 points, you may want to spend more time on the fundamentals covered in this step. Practice the drills again to develop mastery of the techniques and increase your scores.

Team Defense

You win with defense. Even more than skill, defense requires desire and intelligence. The best defensive players play with heart, giving maximum effort every second on the court. Defense is mostly desire, but the desire to play defense is limited by physical conditioning. As fatigue sets in, you lose your ability to execute skills, which leads to a more harmful loss in the desire to compete. You also have to be smart to play winning defense. Coaches look for good decision makers who will stay in position, avoid fouling, help teammates, and wisely choose their opportunities for charges, steals, and shot blocks.

Good defense inhibits an opponent by limiting uncontested open shots. Good team defense not only reduces scoring opportunities for an opponent, but also creates them for your team. An aggressive pressure defense leads to steals, interceptions, and missed shots that enable your team to create scoring opportunities. More often than not, steals and interceptions lead to high-percentage shots at the end of fast breaks.

Playing tough defense seldom brings the public acclaim afforded to successful offense, but most coaches recognize the value of defensive stoppers and tough team defense. You can make your team better by being a great defender, even if your offensive skills haven't developed. Defensive skills take less time to develop, but they require hard work.

Teams with less than average offensive talent can be successful by playing hard, intelligent team defense. Defense is more consistent than offense because it is based mostly on desire and effort, whereas offense is based on a high degree of skill. The ball might not be dropping for you in a given game, but with sufficient effort, you'll never have an off game defensively.

Striving on defense not only helps you become a better player, but also helps you contribute to your team's success. Enthusiasm, intelligence, and maximum effort on defense can be contagious. It can foster a greater team defensive effort and team spirit. The old saying is true: Defense wins championships.

FACTORS OF CHAMPIONSHIP DEFENSE

The common attributes of top defenders can be broken down into emotional, mental, and physical factors.

The primary emotional factors are desire and aggressiveness. The **desire** to play great defense is most important. Offense is mostly fun. Defense, although hard work, can also be fun, as you stop what your opponent wants to do. Desire in defense means giving maximum effort and concentration on each play. Playing defense with intensity involves great effort, such as running at full speed in transition from offense to defense, maintaining a defensive stance with your hands up at all times, drawing the charge, diving for loose balls, blocking out for defensive rebounds, and communicating to your teammates by using key defensive words.

Defense is a battle. When playing offense, you have the advantage of knowing what your next move will be. When playing defense, the tendency is to react to the offensive player's moves. This is a negative view. Take the positive approach of **being aggressive on defense,** thereby forcing the offensive player to react. Being an aggressive defender means that your attitude is to dominate your opponent in all ways. You do not allow the moves your opponent wants to make. You take the initiative. Aggressive defense forces your opponent to react to what you do. For example, an aggressive defender pressures the dribbler, fights over the top of screens, pressures the shooter, denies passes and goes for interceptions, takes the charge, dives for loose balls, and rebounds missed shots.

Mental skills such as discipline, toughness, knowledge, anticipation, concentration, alertness, and judgment are important to great defense as well. Great desire is a start, but you must **discipline yourself** to stick with your goal of becoming a great defensive player. The hard work of developing superior physical conditioning, practicing defensive skills, and playing tough defense in games requires continuous self-discipline. Defense cannot be part-time. It must be played hard all the time. This requires discipline, and tough defenders commit to doing that.

The physical demands of aggressive defense can exhaust even the most highly conditioned athlete. The progressive discomfort of defensive movements, plus the physical pain of fighting over screens, drawing the charge, diving for loose balls, and battling for rebounds, can take a toll. Tough defenders overcome this physical discomfort and pain. They bounce up from the floor each time they're knocked down. Your **mental toughness** can inspire teammates and fans.

Successful defense requires **analyzing your opponent** and your opponent's team offense. Prepare by studying scouting reports, watching videos, and observing your opponent during the game's early stages. Judge your opponent's quickness and strength. What are the opponent's offensive tendencies? Does your opponent want to shoot or drive? What are your opponent's offensive moves and which direction is preferred? From a team standpoint, would your opposition rather beat you on fast breaks or with a set offense? Which plays will the opposing team run against your team, and which plays will they run when they need a key basket? Who are their outside shooters, drivers, and post-up players? Study both your individual opponent and the team. Know what your opponent does best and work to take it away.

Anticipation means knowing tendencies and adjusting to each situation to gain an advantage. Playing offense gives you the advantage of knowing your next move, but when playing defense you must react to the offensive player's move, unless you use anticipation. If you know your opponent's tendencies beforehand, you can adjust accordingly and anticipate the next move. You should not guess on defense, but you should make a calculated move based on intelligent study of your individual opponent and opponent's team.

To concentrate is to focus completely on the assignment and not be distracted. Potential distractions are an opponent's trash talk, the action of fans, an official's call, and your own negative thoughts. When you recognize that you are being distracted or are thinking negatively, interrupt the distraction by saying a key word such as **stop** to yourself. Then replace the distraction with a positive statement. Concentrate on your defensive assignment rather than allowing yourself to be distracted.

Alertness involves being in a state of readiness, able to react instantly, at all times. On the ball, be ready to defend your opponent's shot, drive, or pass, and remain alert to being screened. Off the ball, keep the ball and your opponent in sight. Be alert to stop a cut, defend a screen, go for an interception, dive for a loose ball, or rebound a missed shot.

Judgment is the ability to size up the game situation and decide on the appropriate action. Numerous situations on defense call for good judgment. One example is deciding whether to pressure the ball on the perimeter or to drop back to prevent a pass inside. Decisions on the defensive end will involve comparing your ability with your opponent's, knowing the tempo of the game, knowing the score, and being aware of the time remaining. Using good defensive judgment is particularly important near the end of close games.

Physical factors such as conditioning and quickness and balance also play a role. A high level of **physical conditioning** is a prerequisite to good defense. Throughout a game, your desire to compete will be proportional to your level of physical conditioning. Defensive playing shape develops through specific physical conditioning programs and, even more, through expending great effort in both practice and games. Dominating an opponent requires strength, muscular endurance, and circulatory-respiratory endurance. Work to improve your total body strength so you can withstand the body contact when defending a low-post player. You must also improve the muscular endurance of your legs. It is not just how quickly you can move, but whether you can move quickly throughout the game.

Quickness refers to speed of movement when performing a skill, not simply running speed. Being able to move the feet quickly is the most important physical skill for a defensive player, and you must develop that ability. Being able to change direction laterally is also very important. Although making great improvements in quickness is difficult, three factors can help. First, you can improve speed through footwork drills and by jumping rope. Second, you can be mentally quick, using intelligence to anticipate your opponent's offensive moves and thus move more quickly to the right place at the right time. Knowing and anticipating your opponent can compensate for mediocre physical quickness. Third, **being balanced and under control** is critical. Quickness without balance can be useless. Because defensive quickness involves the ability to start, stop, and change direction, you must also have control. Quickness under control, or quickness with balance, is what you need when playing defense.

PLAYING DEFENSE ON THE BALL

The most vital aspect of playing great defense is pressuring the dribbler. Pressuring the offensive point guard and best ball handler throughout the game keeps your opponent from focusing on running an offense.

Where on the court you will pick up the dribbler (full court, half-court, top of the circle, etc.) is determined by team strategy. When you are guarding an opponent with the ball, maintain position between the ball handler and the basket. Strive to give ground grudgingly. Whenever possible, force your opponent to pick up (stop) the dribble. You can then apply more pressure, with both hands up, against a shot or a pass. Four basic situations will determine how your team's defensive strategy establishes the position you take: turning the dribbler, forcing the dribbler to the sideline, funneling the dribbler to the middle, and forcing the dribbler to use the weak hand.

The basic idea in **turning the dribbler** is to dominate your opponent by applying maximum pressure on the ball. Work to establish defensive position a half body ahead in the direction the dribbler wants to go. This position is called **chest on the ball.** The objective is to prevent another dribble in the same direction and force the dribbler into a reverse dribble. With good anticipation, you may even draw a charge. If the dribbler tries a front change of direction, you should be able to steal the ball with a quick flick upward of your near hand. On the dribbler's reverse dribble, quickly change direction and again move for chest-on-the-ball position at least a half body ahead of the direction the dribbler wants to go. Continue forcing the dribbler to reverse turn.

The sideline can serve as a defensive aid. When **forced to the sideline,** the dribbler can pass in only one direction. Work for position a half body to the inside of the court, with your inside foot, the one closer to the middle, forward and your outside foot back. Force the dribbler to the sideline, then prevent a reverse dribble back to the middle of the court. By dribbling to the middle, the dribbler has more options to pass to either side or to attempt a high-percentage shot.

By taking a defensive position a half body to the outside of the court, you can **funnel the dribbler to the middle.** This strategy will move the dribbler toward your defensive teammate off the ball. In turn, your teammate may use one of several teaming tactics, including a switch, fake switch (hedge), trap, or steal. If your team has a shot blocker, you may benefit by funneling the dribbler in the direction of the shot blocker. The danger in funneling the dribbler to the middle is allowing that player to penetrate past you into the lane for a high-percentage shot or a pass to either side.

Few dribblers can drive with the weak hand as effectively as with the strong hand. By overplaying the strong hand, you **force your opponent to dribble with the weak hand.** Overplay the dribbler by taking a position a half body to the dribbler's strong-hand side, with your forward foot outside and your back foot aligned with the middle of the dribbler's body.

PLAYING DEFENSE OFF THE BALL

Positioning off the ball is an important part of team defense. To better understand team defensive positioning, think of how the court is divided from basket to basket into a strong side (also called ball side) and weak side (also called help side). The strong side refers to the ball side of the court, and the weak side refers to the side of the court away from the ball.

Playing good defense involves defending your opponent, the ball, and the basket. To accomplish this, you must move continually from one defensive responsibility to another. The phrase **help and recover** refers to being in good defensive position off the ball to help stop a penetrating pass or dribble by the player with the ball and then recovering to your own opponent.

When you are off the ball, you should take a position off your opponent and toward the ball, but able to see both. This is called the **ball–you–player principle.** You want to form an imaginary triangle between you, the ball, and your opponent.

The closer your opponent is to the ball, the closer you should be to your opponent. The farther the ball is from your opponent, the farther away you can play from your opponent and still give help to your teammate guarding the ball.

When you are off the ball on the strong side, you should work to deny a penetrating pass to a receiver on the wing inside the foul line extended (figure 10.1). To deny a pass to the ball-side wing, first take a ball–you–player position. Overplay your opponent by using a closed stance, lead foot and hand up in the passing lane. Keep the ball and your opponent in sight by keeping your head up and looking over the shoulder of your lead arm. Be ready to knock away a pass by having the palm of your lead hand facing out with your thumb down. Your back arm should be flexed and close to your body. Having your back hand touching your opponent can help you monitor movement. Be ready to move, keeping a wide base and flexed knees. React to your opponent's movements by using short, quick steps. As you move, keep your feet close to the floor and at least shoulder-width apart. Do not cross your feet or hop. Keep your head steady and over your waist, with your back straight to keep from leaning off balance. Be alert to knock away an outside pass to your opponent. On a backdoor pass, open to the ball on the pass and knock it away. Open to the ball by pivoting on your inside foot while dropping your lead foot back and toward the ball.

Figure 10.1 Defensive Positioning

STRONG-SIDE DENIAL	WEAK-SIDE HELP
1. Touching distance from opponent	1. Sagging off opponent
2. Closed stance	2. Open stance
3. Ball–you–player position	3. Ball–you–player position
4. Hand and foot up in passing lane; outside hand knocks ball away	4. Inside hand pointed at opponent, outside hand pointed at ball
5. Wide base with knees flexed	5. Wide base with knees flexed
6. Short, quick steps as feet move shoulder-width apart (do not cross feet)	6. Short, quick steps as feet move shoulder-width apart (do not cross feet)
7. Prepared to open to ball and knock it away on backdoor pass	7. Ready to help teammate on backdoor pass; yell to teammate, "You've got help!"

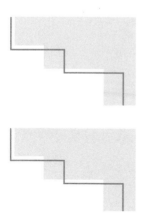

Misstep

You are unable to deny the pass after the wing fakes a step to the basket and cuts back for the ball.

Correction

Learn to ignore the wing's first step to the basket and understand that you will have defensive help from weak-side defenders on a backdoor pass.

Misstep

Defending on the weak side, you are too close to your opponent and not in position to give help on a drive or pass inside.

Correction

On the weak side, sag off your opponent and form an imaginary flat triangle between you, your opponent, and the ball. Be in an open stance to see both ball and opponent. Communicate to your teammate on the ball that you are in position to help by yelling "You've got help!"

When you are on the weak side, sag off your opponent and form an imaginary flat triangle between you, your opponent, and the ball. Be in an open stance to see both the ball and your opponent without turning your head. Point one hand at the ball and one hand at your opponent. Be ready to help on a drive or pass inside by the player with the ball. Communicate to your teammate on the ball that you are in position to help by yelling "You've got help!"

Defending Ball-Side Guard With Ball at Wing

When you defend the ball-side guard while the wing has the ball, you can choose from two options, depending on your team's defensive strategy. One option is to prevent ball reversal to the ball-side guard by overplaying the guard with a closed stance, lead foot and hand up in the passing lane. As shown in figure 10.2a, defensive player X1 takes a closed-stance position to prevent the ball reversal from the wing (3) to the ball-side guard (1).

The other option is getting into a help-and-recover position to help on a drive to the middle by the wing and to discourage a pass to the high post. As shown in figure 10.2b, defensive player X1 takes an open stance, sagging off the ball-side guard (1) to help teammate X3 on the drive to the middle by the wing (3). X1 then recovers on the pass to the ball-side guard.

Keep an open stance at least one step off an imaginary line between your opponent and the basket in a ball–you–player position. You want to form an imaginary flat triangle between you, your opponent, and the ball. Get your inside hand in the passing lane between the ball and the high post, and point your other hand at your opponent. Communicate to your teammate on the ball that you are in position to help by yelling "You've got help!" Be alert to prevent the ball-side guard from receiving a pass on a possible front or backdoor cut to the basket.

Defending Weak-Side Guard When Other Guard Has Ball

Be in an open stance at least one step off an imaginary line between your opponent and the basket in a ball–you–player position and in position to see both the ball and your opponent without turning your head. Point one hand at the ball and one hand at your opponent. Get in a help-and-recover position and communicate to your teammate on the ball that you are in position to help by yelling "You've got help!"

As shown in figure 10.3, defensive player X2 takes an open stance, sagging off the weak-side guard (2) to prevent the front cut by 2, give help on a drive to the middle by player 1, and recover on a pass to 2.

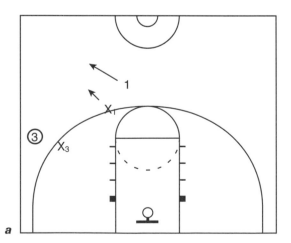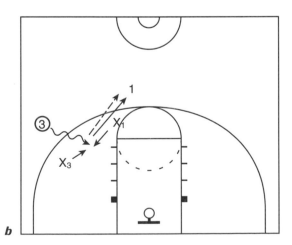

Figure 10.2 Defending the ball-side guard when the wing has the ball: *(a)* denial defensive position; *(b)* help-and-recover defensive position.

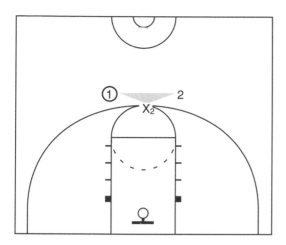

Figure 10.3   Defending the weak-side guard when the other guard has the ball.

Defending Weak-Side Wing When Guard Has Ball

Sag off your opponent in a ball–you–player position. Be in an open stance with at least one foot in the lane and able to see both the ball and your opponent without turning your head. Point one hand at the ball and one hand at your opponent. Communicate to your teammate on the ball that you are in position to help by yelling "You've got help!"

As shown in figure 10.4, defensive player X4 takes an open stance, sagging off the weak-side wing (4) to prevent 4's flash cut, give help on a drive to the middle or a pass inside by player 1, and recover on a pass to 4.

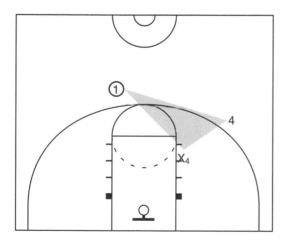

Figure 10.4   Defending the weak-side wing when the guard has the ball.

Defending Weak-Side Guard With Ball at Wing

Sag off your opponent in a ball–you–player position. Be in an open stance, one step to the weak side of the basket, and able to see both the ball and your opponent without turning your head. Point one hand at the ball and one hand at your opponent. Communicate to your teammate on the ball that you are in position to help by yelling "You've got help!" Be alert to prevent the weak-side guard from receiving a pass on a possible cut to the basket.

As shown in figure 10.5, defensive player X2 takes an open stance, sagging farther off the weak-side guard (2) to prevent 2's cut to the basket, give help on a drive to the middle by player 3, and recover on a pass to 2.

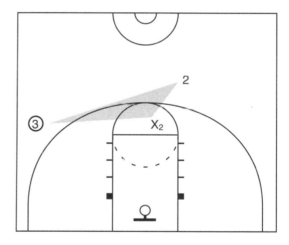

Figure 10.5   Defending the weak-side guard with the ball at the wing.

Defending Weak-Side Wing With Ball at Wing

Sag off your opponent in a ball–you–player position. Be in an open stance, one step to the weak side of the basket, and able to see both the ball and your opponent without turning your head. Point one hand at the ball and one hand at your opponent. Communicate to your teammate on the ball that you are in position to help by yelling "You've got help!" Be alert to prevent the weak-side wing from receiving a pass on a possible flash cut to the ball-side elbow or a cut to the low post.

As shown in figure 10.6, defensive player X4 takes an open stance, sagging farther off the weak-side wing (4) to prevent 4 from flashing to the ball-side elbow or cutting to the low post, give help on a drive to the baseline or backdoor cut by player 3, and recover on a pass to 4.

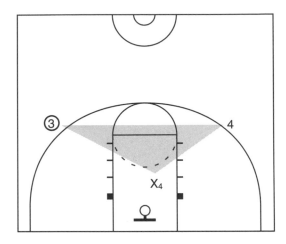

Figure 10.6 Defending the weak-side wing with the ball at the wing.

Defense off the Ball Drill 1. *Wing Denial*

A good defender is able to pressure and deny a penetrating pass to the ball-side wing. The wing denial drill provides practice at denying a pass inside the foul line extended. The drill requires three players, two on offense and one on defense. Offensive player 1 starts with the ball at the point position at the top of the circle. Offensive player 2 plays at the ball-side wing, starting at the foul line extended. You begin as the defensive player and take a denial defensive position on player 2.

To deny a pass to the ball-side wing, first take a ball–you–player position. Overplay your opponent by using a closed stance, with your lead foot and hand up in the passing lane. Keep the ball and your opponent in sight by keeping your head up and looking over the shoulder of your lead arm. Be ready to knock away a pass by having the palm of your lead hand out with your thumb down. Player 2, the ball-side wing, attempts to get open, moving within one step of the area above the foul line extended, lane line, baseline, and sideline. React to player 2's movements using short, quick steps, feet at least shoulder-width apart, staying alert to knock away an outside pass to your opponent. On a backdoor pass, open to the ball and knock the pass away by pivoting on your inside foot while dropping your lead foot back and toward the ball.

When the offensive wing receives the ball, the drill becomes a one-on-one drill. Continue the drill until the wing scores or you obtain possession via a rebound, steal, or interception. Go for 30 seconds before changing positions. You and your partner should play wing denial defense three times each.

Success Check

- Keep your head up to see the ball and your opponent.
- Read and react to the offensive player.
- Use short, quick steps.

Score Your Success

Give yourself 1 point each time you stop the wing from scoring. This is a competitive drill, so try to score more points than your opponents. Give yourself 5 points if you score more than your opponents.

Your score ___

Defense off the Ball Drill 2. *Weak-Side Help and Recover*

In this drill, you will practice opening up on the weak side, helping on a penetrating drive by the ball-side wing, and then, when the ball is passed out, recovering to the player you are guarding. The drill requires three players, two offensive players and one defender. Offensive player 1 starts with the ball at the foul line extended. Offensive player 2 starts as a weak-side wing at the foul line extended. You take a weak-side defensive position on player 2, the weak-side wing.

From the weak side, sag off your opponent in a ball–you–player position, forming an imaginary flat triangle between you, your opponent, and the ball. Be in an open stance, one step to the weak side of the basket. Position yourself to see both the ball and your opponent without turning your head. Point one hand at the ball and one hand at your opponent. Communicate to your imaginary teammate on the ball that you are in position to help by yelling "You've got help!"

Player 1 drives past an imaginary ball-side defensive wing on the baseline side toward the basket. Give help to this imaginary ball-side defensive wing by moving to the ball side of the basket to stop the drive or draw a charge. As you move, player 1 passes to player 2, the weak-side wing, who is flashing to the weak-side elbow. On the pass, recover quickly but under control to player 2. When player 2 receives the ball at the weak-side elbow, player 1 steps off the court, and the drill becomes a one-on-one contest between you and player 2.

Continue until the wing scores or you obtain possession via a rebound, steal, or interception. Change positions and continue the drill. Allow each player to play weak-side help-and-recover defense three times.

Success Check

- Use a ball–you–player position.
- Use verbal signals to let your imaginary teammate know you are available to help.
- Try to draw a charge when the offensive player with the ball drives to the basket.

Score Your Success

Give yourself 1 point each time you stop the weak-side wing from scoring. This is a competitive drill, so try to score more points than your opponents. Give yourself 5 points if you score more than your opponents.

Your score ___

DEFENDING THE LOW POST

Always attempt to keep your opponent from receiving a pass in good low-post position. Use a closed stance with your body in three-quarter defensive position between the ball and your opponent. When the ball is above the imaginary foul line extended, deny your low-post opponent from the topside. When the ball is below the imaginary foul line extended, deny your low-post opponent from the baseline side.

When a wing above the foul line extended passes the ball to a player in the corner below the foul line extended or in the reverse direction, from the corner to the wing, move quickly from one side of the low post to the other (figure 10.7). A denial defensive position can be maintained by

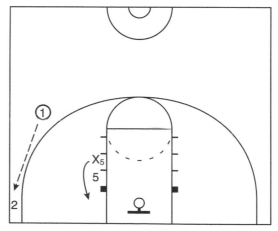

Figure 10.7 Low-post defensive positioning: Changing sides.

stepping in front of the low-post player as you change sides. Use quick footwork. Step through first with your inside foot, the one closer to the opponent, and then with your outside foot.

As shown in figure 10.7, as the ball is passed from wing player 1 to corner player 2, X5 quickly changes from topside to baseline side, stepping in front of low-post player 5.

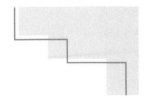

Misstep

When the ball is passed from wing to corner, or vice versa, you are unable to deny a pass to the low post.

Correction

As the ball is passed, change sides but maintain denial position by stepping in front of the low-post player with a quick two-step move.

Defending the Low Post Drill. *Low-Post Denial*

You should always attempt to deny your opponent from receiving a pass in good low-post position, and this drill gives you practice. The drill requires four players. You will start on defense and the other three will be on offense.

Offensive player 1 starts with the ball above the foul line extended on the ball side. Offensive player 2 takes a position below the foul line extended in the corner. Offensive player 3 takes a position in the low post above the box outside the lane. As the defensive player, take a position denying a pass to player 3 in the low post. Use a closed stance with your body in three-quarter defensive position between the ball and your opponent. Players 1 and 2 attempt to pass the ball inside to the low post while you attempt to deny a pass to the low post. Players 1 and 2 should pass the ball to each other, and player 3 should get good low-post position by sealing you off.

When the ball is above the imaginary foul line extended, deny the low post from the topside. When the ball is below the imaginary foul line extended, deny the low post from the baseline side. As player 1 above the foul line extended passes the ball to player 2 in the corner below the foul line extended, or as player 2 passes to player 1, move quickly from one side of the low post to the other. Maintain your

denial defensive position by stepping in front of the low-post player as you change sides.

Quick footwork is needed. Step through first with your inside foot and then with your outside foot. When player 3 receives the ball in the low post, the drill becomes a one-on-one drill until either the low post scores or you obtain possession via a rebound, steal, or interception. Allow each player to play low-post denial defense three times, then change sides.

Success Check

- Use a closed stance with your body in three-quarter defensive position between the ball and your opponent.
- Maintain correct denial defensive position.
- Use quick footwork.

Score Your Success

Give yourself 1 point each time you stop the low post from scoring. This is a competitive drill, so try to score more points than your opponents. Give yourself 5 points if you score more than your opponents.

Your score ___

DEFENDING THE CUTTER

When the opponent you are closely guarding on the perimeter passes the ball, you must move off your opponent in the direction of the pass. This is called *jump to the ball*. Jumping to the ball positions you to defend a give-and-go cut

by your opponent and allows you to give help on the ball.

You must move on the pass to establish ball–you–player position. If you wait for your opponent to cut before you move, you will get beat. The pass-and-cut is the most basic offensive play in basketball: It is as old as the game itself.

For playing defense off the ball, you should be in position to see both the ball and your opponent. To defend a cutter, position yourself off the cutter and toward the ball. Do not allow the cutter to move between you and the ball. Be in a strong, balanced stance, ready to withstand any contact that may occur as you prevent the cutter from going between you and the ball.

When the cutter approaches the lane area, be in position to bump the cutter (figure 10.8). Use a bump-and-release technique. Bump the cutter with the inside part of your body and release to a position between the cutter and the ball. If your opponent makes a backdoor cut to the basket, maintain a closed stance as you move with your opponent on the cut and then open to the ball as the pass is thrown. Use your lead hand to knock away a pass.

As shown in figure 10.8, as offensive player 1 passes to player 2, X1 quickly jumps to the ball

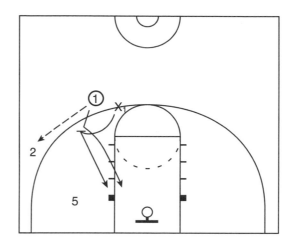

Figure 10.8 Defending the cutter.

and uses the bump-and-release technique, staying between the ball and player 1 on that player's cut. Deny the pass on a cut to the basket. Maintain a closed stance as you move with the opponent on the cut, then open to the ball as the pass is thrown.

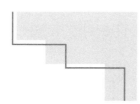

Misstep

On a cut, you allow the cutter to get between you and the ball.

Correction

Change to a closed stance and get your lead foot and hand into the passing lane. Force the cutter to go behind you.

DEFENDING THE FLASH CUT

A flash cut is a quick move by an opponent from the weak side toward the ball. Most offenses use a flash cut from the weak side into the high-post area. As a defender on the weak side, you should be in an open stance and in position to see both the ball and the opponent. When your opponent flashes to the high-post area, be alert to move and stop the flash (figure 10.9). Change to a closed stance with your lead foot and hand in the passing lane. Be in a strong, balanced stance, ready to withstand any contact that may take place as you stop the flash cut. Use your lead hand to knock away a pass.

If your opponent flashes high and then makes a backdoor cut to the basket, you must first get in a closed stance to deny the flash high. On the backdoor cut to the basket, maintain a closed

stance as you move with your opponent on the cut. Open to the ball as the pass is thrown.

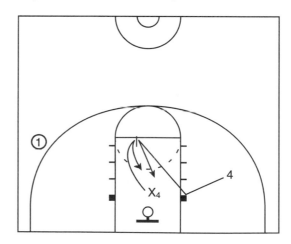

Figure 10.9 Defending the flash cut.

Misstep

Your opponent flashes high and then beats you on a backdoor cut to the basket.

Correction

First, get in a closed stance to deny the flash high. Maintain a closed stance as you move with your opponent on a backdoor cut, then open to the ball as the pass is thrown.

Defending the Flash Drill 1. *Deny the Flash and Deny the Backdoor Cut*

This drill gives you practice denying both a flash cut and a backdoor cut. The drill requires three players, two on offense and one on defense. Offensive player 1 starts with two balls at the foul line extended. Offensive player 2 is a weak-side wing, starting at the weak-side foul line extended. As the defensive player, take a weak-side defensive position on player 2. Use an open stance and point one hand at the ball and the other at your opponent. Communicate to your imaginary teammate on the ball that you are in position to help by yelling "You've got help!"

Player 2 starts the drill by cutting toward the basket for a few steps and then flashing to the ball-side elbow. React to stop the flash by changing to a closed stance, beating the weak-side wing to the ball-side elbow with your lead foot and hand up in the passing lane to deny a pass. Be strong and ready to withstand any contact that may take place as you stop player 2's flash. Use your lead hand to knock away a pass.

Player 1 attempts to pass the first ball to player 2 at the ball-side elbow. React to a pass on the

flash cut by deflecting the ball. Once you deny the flash, player 2 cuts backdoor to the basket. Player 1 then attempts to pass the second ball to player 2 cutting backdoor. React to a pass on the backdoor cut by opening up as the pass is thrown and then deflecting the ball. Change positions and continue the drill until each player has had three turns denying the flash cut and the backdoor cut.

Success Check

- Begin in an open stance, then react to the flash with a closed stance.
- Communicate verbally with your imaginary teammate on the ball.
- Be ready for contact as you stop the flash.

Score Your Success

Fewer than three denials = 0 points

Three or four denials = 1 point

Five or six denials = 5 points

Your score ___

Defending the Flash Drill 2. *Six Point*

This drill adds practice at stopping the drive, blocking out, rebounding, making an outlet pass, and converting from defense to offense. You will practice six points of defense: deny the wing; deny the low post; weak-side help position; deny the flash; stop the drive; and block out, rebound, outlet, and convert to offense.

The drill requires three players, one on defense and two on offense. Start by playing defense on player 2, who is the ball-side wing and starts at the foul line extended. Offensive player 1 starts with the ball at the point position at the top of the circle and gives commands.

The drill begins when player 1 calls out "Deny!" On this command, player 2 works to get open on the wing and you work to deny the pass.

Player 1 then yells "Low post!" and dribbles from above the foul line extended to below it while player 2 moves to get open in the low post on the ball side. Deny a pass to the low post by moving from the topside to the baseline side of the low post as the ball is dribbled from above the foul line extended to below it.

Player 1 then yells "Away!" On this command, player 2 moves away from the ball to the weak side. Move to a weak-side help-and-recover position only one step to the weak side of the basket. Be in an open stance, pointing one hand at the ball and one hand at your opponent, and say your key phrase to communicate to the imaginary teammate on the ball that you are in position to help.

Player 1 then calls out "Flash!" and player 2 cuts a few steps toward the basket before flashing to the ball-side elbow. React to stop the flash by closing your stance and beating player 2 to the ball-side elbow with your lead foot and hand up in the passing lane to deny a pass.

Player 1 next yells "Out!" and player 2 moves out to the top of the circle to receive a pass. Allow the pass to player 2, but then stop the one-on-one drive to the basket. On a shot, block out and go for the rebound. On a missed shot, rebound and make an outlet pass to player 1 on the wing. On a made shot, take the ball out of the net, run out of bounds, and make the outlet pass. Then run to the foul line for a return pass. Change positions and continue the drill, allowing each player to play defense.

Success Check

- Execute the correct defensive reaction to each of the offensive moves.
- On a shot, block out and be aggressive when going for the rebound.

Score Your Success

Give yourself 1 point for each correct defensive reaction to each of the six offensive moves.

Fewer than 4 correct reactions = 0 points

4 correct reactions = 1 point

5 correct reactions — 3 points

6 correct reactions = 5 points

Your score ___

DEFENDING AGAINST A SCREEN

To defend screens, you and your teammates must be able to communicate and help each other. The defender on the opponent who is setting the screen must alert the defender being screened by calling out the direction of the screen with the words *screen right* or *screen left*. The defender on the screener should also communicate how the screen will be defended.

Four players are directly involved in the screen, two on offense (the screener and cutter) and their two defenders. To aid our understanding of defending a screen, the cutter is always referred to as the first player. If the defender on the cutter goes over the screen, this is said to be going over or simply going second. If the defender on the cutter goes under the screen, this is said to be going under or third. If the defender on the cutter goes under both the screener and the screener's defender, this is said to be going fourth.

Four basic methods to defend a screen are show and trail the cutter's body, open and through, switch, and squeeze.

Show and trail cutter. When your opponent sets a screen on a teammate guarding a good shooter within shooting range, you should help your teammate stay with the cutter. Call out the screen and show by stepping out into the cutter's path (figure 10.10). This showing action will delay the cut or force the cutter to veer wide and allow your teammate time to follow the cutter (go second). When you show, keep a hand on the screener so you can stay with her if she releases early or slips to the basket. When you are the defensive player being screened, trail the cutter's body by getting directly behind it and following the cutter. It is more difficult to be screened when you are directly behind the cutter. Work to get over the screen by first getting a foot over the screen and then the remainder of your body.

As shown in figure 10.10, player 4 sets a screen for player 2. Defender X4 shows by stepping into player 2's path, giving teammate X2 time to trail the cutter's body (go second).

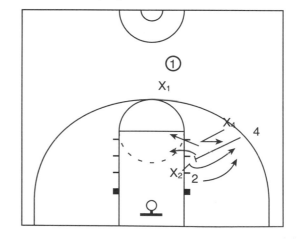

Figure 10.10 Show and trail cutter's body.

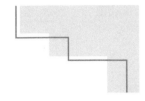

Misstep

Your teammate attempts to trail the cutter but gets beat on a quick cut.

Correction

Show by stepping out into the path of the cutter to delay the cut or force the cutter to veer wide, giving your teammate time to trail the cutter's body. When you are the defensive player being screened, get directly behind the cutter's body and follow the cutter. Work to get over the screen by getting a foot over the screen and then the remainder of your body.

Open and through. When your opponent sets a screen on a teammate guarding a quick driver or when outside your opponent's shooting range, you should help your teammate slide through the screen between you and the screener (go third). Call out the screen and yell "Open and through!" Drop back (open) to make room for your teammate to move between you and the screen to get to the cutter.

As shown in figure 10.11, player 4 sets a screen for player 2. Defender X4 drops back (opens), making room for teammate X2 to move under or slide through the screen (go third).

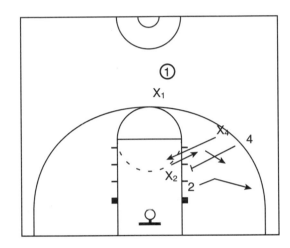

Figure 10.11 Open and through.

Misstep

Your teammate is not alert to being screened by your opponent.

Correction

As your opponent moves to set a screen on your teammate, call out the screen and its direction.

Switch. When you and your teammate are of equal size and defensive ability, you should switch opponents. If your size and defensive ability differ, switching should be the last option, as it allows the offense to take advantage of the mismatch. If you switch, first call out the screen by yelling "Switch!" As you switch, aggressively get into position to deny a pass to the cutter (switch and deny). The screener will roll to the basket or pop out for an outside shot. When you are the player being screened and you hear the key word *switch*, work to get defensive position on the ball side of the screener.

As shown in figure 10.12, player 4 sets a screen for player 2. Defender X4 switches and denies a pass to player 2. Defender X2 works to get defensive position on the ball side of screener 4, who is rolling to the basket.

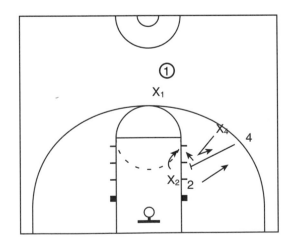

Figure 10.12 Switch.

Misstep

On a defensive switch, the screener gets open on a roll to the basket or a pop-out for an outside shot.

Correction

If you as the player being screened hear the key word *switch,* you must work to get defensive position on the ball side of the screener.

Squeeze. Occasionally, when the cutter is a good driver or likes to curl or cut inside and the screener is a good shooter and likes to pop out to shoot after screening, you should squeeze on the screener. This helps your teammate take a shortcut route under both you and the screener (go fourth). Call out the screen and yell "Squeeze!" Stay close to the screener, allowing room for your teammate to go under both of you to get to the cutter.

As shown in figure 10.13, player 4 sets a screen for player 2. Defender X4 squeezes on the screener, allowing room for teammate X2 to make a shortcut move under both screener 4 and defender X4 (go fourth).

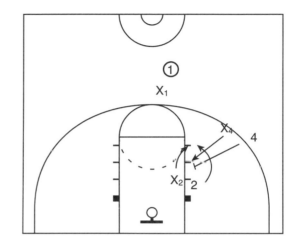

Figure 10.13 Squeeze.

Misstep

Your teammate attempts to go under but bumps into you.

Correction

Call out the screen and yell "Open!" or "Squeeze!" Drop back (open) to allow room for your teammate to move between you and the screener or squeeze so your teammate can shortcut under both you and the screener.

DEFENSIVE ROTATIONS

Defensive rotation means that when a team member leaves an assigned opponent to defend another player, teammates must rotate defensive positions to cover the player left open. Rotations may involve all five defenders. All defensive players must play as a team and communicate well. Communication is helped by using key words or phrases such as *switch, I've got the ball, I've got the post, I'm back,* and *I'm up.*

Imagine that your team traps the ball either away from the basket or in the low post. One of your teammates gets beat on a penetrating drive or a cut to an open area. When your team traps the ball, the defenders off the ball should rotate toward the ball to cover the immediate receivers

(figure 10.14). As they rotate, the defender farthest from the ball should split the distance and guard the two offensive players farthest from the ball. As shown in figure 10.14, defender X2 leaves player 2 to trap player 1. The weak-side defender (X4) rotates up to deny the pass to the weak-side guard (2). The farthest defender (X5) covers the two farthest offensive players (4 and 5).

When one of your teammates gets beat by a driver or backdoor cutter, your teammates should rotate defensive positions closer to the ball (figure 10.15). The nearest defender, either on the low post or weak-side wing, rotates to the player with the ball, the defender on the weak-side guard drops back to cover the basket,

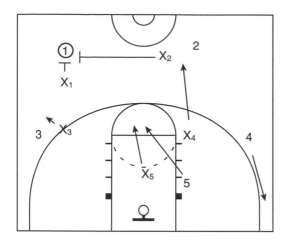

Figure 10.14 Rotating up on a guard-to-guard trap.

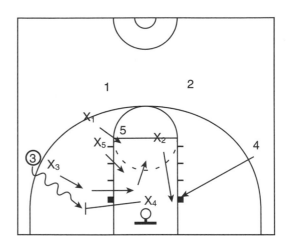

Figure 10.15 Rotating back to cover a baseline drive.

and the defenders on the high post and ball-side guard drop into the lane. As shown in figure 10.15, wing 3 beats defender X3 on a baseline drive. X4 rotates to help and switches to player 3. X2 rotates down to cover for teammate X4. X3 can trap with X4 or rotate to the weak side, looking to pick up first player 4, then player 2. X1 and X5 drop back into the lane.

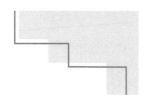

Misstep

When you leave an assigned opponent to defend another player, your teammates, unaware of what you are doing, fail to rotate defensive positions to cover the player you left open.

Correction

It is imperative to communicate to your teammates what you are doing. Reacting to any defensive situation, particularly one involving a defensive rotation, requires that all defensive players work as a team and communicate by using key phrases.

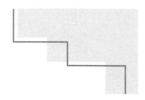

Misstep

You leave an assigned opponent near the basket to defend another player, but your teammates do not have time to rotate defensive positions to cover the player you left open, resulting in a pass to your opponent for an easy basket.

Correction

Use judgment and a defensive fake before leaving an opponent near the basket to pick up an open player. This will give your teammates time to rotate to the player you are leaving.

Defensive Rotation Drill 1. *Defensive Position Shell Drill*

This drill gives you practice in defensive positioning on the ball as well as defensive help-and-recover positioning for defending the ball-side and weak-side guard and forward. The drill requires eight players, four on offense and four on defense.

The four offensive players start with two guards at the top of the circle and two forwards at the wing positions. Each defender takes the correct defensive position. One of the offensive players is selected as the point guard or leader who will give commands. On the "In!" command, the guard passes the ball to the ball-side wing. On the "Out!" command, the ball is passed back out from the wing to the ball-side guard. On the "Over!" command, the ball is passed from guard to guard. Pass the ball around the perimeter (shell) in this drill for six passes: in, out, over, in, out, over. Check defensive positioning after each pass.

Each defender moves on each pass, adjusting defensive positioning. If the opponent you are guarding passes the ball, you must move off in the direction of the pass. The call for this move is "Jump to the ball!" By jumping to the ball, you get in position to defend a cut by your opponent and to give help on the ball.

Allow each defensive player to play for six passes at each of the four defensive positions. The defense then goes to offense and the offense goes to defense.

Success Check

- Defenders adjust on each pass.
- Jump to the ball if the player you are defending passes the ball.

Score Your Success

Each player earns 1 point for each correct change of defensive position on each pass, for a total of 24 points maximum.

Fewer than 10 points = 0 points

10 to 14 points = 1 point

15 to 19 points = 3 points

20 to 24 points = 5 points

Your score ___

Defensive Rotation Drill 2. Help and Recover Shell Drill

This drill is the same as the defensive position shell drill except that each offensive player with the ball is allowed one penetrating dribble. Defenders get practice in defensive help and recover. It is also a good offensive drill. Offensive players work on establishing triple-threat position and being able to penetrate and pass (draw-and-kick). Eight players form two teams of four players each, offense and defense.

The four offensive players start with two guards at the top of the circle and two forwards at the wing positions. Any offensive player with the ball is allowed one penetrating dribble. The defender nearest the ball moves to help stop penetration. Once the penetrating dribble is stopped, the penetrator passes the ball out to whichever player the helping defender left. After giving help to stop penetration, the defender recovers to his original opponent. The offensive player receiving the pass should be a triple threat to shoot, pass, or drive.

The offensive team gets 1 point each time it scores. If the defense commits a foul, the offense gets the ball and starts again. If an offensive player misses a shot and a teammate gets an offensive rebound, continue playing. The defense gets a point when it gets the ball on a steal or rebound or when it forces the offense into a violation. Play to 5 points, then switch roles.

Success Check

- On the dribble, move to stop penetration.
- After stopping the penetration, recover to your original assigned player.
- On offense, be a triple threat to shoot, pass, or drive.

Score Your Success

This is a competitive drill. As a team, try to score more points than your opponent, playing each game to 5 points. Win more games than your opponent. Give yourself 5 points if your team wins the most games.

Your score ___

Defensive Rotation Drill 3. *Defend the Cutter Shell Drill*

This drill is the same as the other shell drills except that you will allow cuts to the basket and unlimited dribbling. This drill provides offensive practice in making a front cut, backdoor cut, or flash cut. Start with two teams of four players each, offense and defense. The four offensive players are two guards at the top of the circle and two forwards at the wing positions.

Cutting will be allowed from only one position—the ball-side guard, weak-side guard, or weak-side wing. After cutting to the basket, the cutter moves to an open weak-side position. Each of the offensive players may rotate to the designated position for cutting, so you will have practice in defending a cut by the ball-side guard, weak-side guard, or weak-side wing.

To defend a cutter, be in position off the cutter and toward the ball. Do not allow the cutter to move between you and the ball. Be ready to withstand any contact that may occur as you prevent the cutter from going between you and the ball. If the cutter approaches the lane area, bump the cutter using the bump-and-release technique, staying between the cutter and the ball. If your opponent makes a backdoor cut to the basket, maintain a closed stance as you move on the ball side of the cutter, opening to the ball as the pass is thrown. Use your lead hand to knock away a pass.

The offensive team gets 1 point each time it scores. If the defense commits a foul, the offense gets the ball and starts again. If an offensive player misses a shot and a teammate gets an offensive rebound, continue playing. The defense gets 1 point when it gets the ball on a steal or rebound or when it forces the offense into a violation. Play to 5 points, then switch roles.

Success Check

- Do not allow the cutter to go between you and the ball.
- Be ready for contact.

Score Your Success

This is a competitive drill. As a team, try to score more points than your opponent, playing each game to 5 points. Win more games than your opponent. Give yourself 5 points if your team wins the most games.

Your score ___

Defensive Rotation Drill 4. *Shell Drill*

Start the drill with a baseline drive or backdoor cut by an offensive wing, giving you defensive practice in rotating positions. After allowing one of the defensive wings to get beat by a drive or backdoor cut, the drill becomes live. The offense attempts to score, and the defense tries to prevent a score by attacking the player with the ball and rotating defensive positions. The defender on the weak-side wing yells "Switch!" before attacking the player with the ball. The defender on the weak-side guard drops back to cover the weak-side wing, and the defender on the ball-side guard drops back into the lane and covers the weak-side guard. The wing who gets beat retreats to the basket, looking to recover to the originally guarded player. Seeing a good rotation, the wing will pick up the open player, the ball-side guard.

When defensive players rotate, they must all play as a team and communicate well, using key words or phrases such as *switch, I've got the ball, I've got the post, I'm back,* and *I'm up.* The offensive team gets 1 point each time it scores. If the defense commits a foul, the offense gets the ball and starts again. If an offensive player misses a shot and a teammate gets an offensive rebound, continue playing. The defense gets 1 point when it gets the ball on a steal or rebound or when it forces the offense into a violation. Play to 5 points, then switch roles.

Success Check

- On defense, communicate verbally with team-mates using the key words and phrases.
- React to the offense as a team.

ZONE DEFENSE

When you play zone defense, you are assigned to a designated area of the court, or zone, rather than to an individual opponent. Your zone position changes with each move of the ball. Zones may be adjusted from sagging inside to pressuring outside shots, overplaying passing lanes, and trapping the ball. Zone defenses are named according to the alignment of players from the top toward the basket and include the 3-2, 2-3, 2-1-2, 1-2-2, and 1-3-1 zones.

Each zone defense has strengths and weaknesses. The 3-2 and 1-2-2 zones are strong against outside shooting but are vulnerable inside and in the corners. The 2-1-2 and 2-3 zones are strong inside and in the corners but are susceptible on the top and wings. The 1-3-1 protects the high post and wing areas, but it can leave openings at the blocks and corners and is also susceptible to good offensive rebounding.

There are many good reasons for using a zone defense:

- It protects the inside against a team with good drivers and post-up players and poor outside shooters.
- It is more effective against screening and cutting.
- Defenders can be positioned in areas according to size and defensive skill. Taller players can be assigned to inside areas for shot blocking and rebounding, whereas smaller, quicker players can be assigned to outside areas for pressuring the ball and covering passing lanes.
- Players are in a better position to start the fast break.
- It is easier to learn and may overcome weaknesses in individual defensive fundamentals.
- It protects players who are in foul trouble.

- Changing to a zone may disrupt an opponent's rhythm.

Zone defenses also have some weaknesses:

- They are vulnerable to good outside shooting, especially three-point shooting, which can stretch the zone, creating openings inside.
- A fast break can beat the zone down court before it sets up, since it takes time for players to get in their assigned zones.
- Quick passing moves the ball quicker than zone defenders can shift.
- It is weak against penetration (draw-and-kick).
- The opposing team may stall more easily against a zone, causing you to change to individual defense if you are behind late in a game.
- Playing zone defense does not develop individual defensive skills.

3-2 Zone Defense

We will start with the 3-2 zone defense. The names of the defenders in a 3-2 zone, their starting alignments, and their responsibilities are as follows:

Ball at Top (figure 10.16)

P = Point, inside top of circle, cover area from elbow to elbow

W = Wing, inside foot on the elbow, cover area from elbow to foul line extended

D = Deep, straddle lane line above the box, cover area from inside foul line to corner

The responsibilities for the defenders change with each move of the ball. When the ball is on the wing (figure 10.17), the strong-side (ball-side)

215

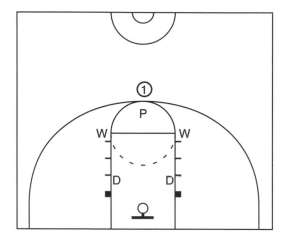

Figure 10.16 3-2 zone: Ball at top.

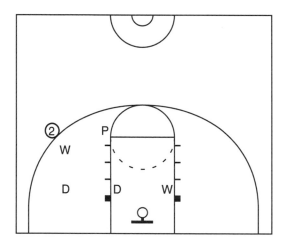

Figure 10.17 3-2 zone: Ball on wing.

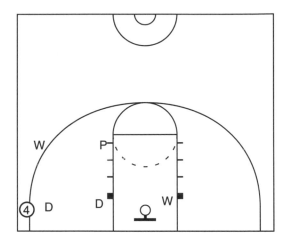

Figure 10.18 3-2 zone: Ball in corner.

wing, forcing a lob pass to the wing, and helps on a drive to the middle. The weak-side wing drops back to the weak-side box and is responsible for a weak-side rebound.

When the ball is at the high post (figure 10.19), the weak-side deep player yells "Up!" and defends the player with the ball. The strong-side deep player slides to the basket area, getting in position to cover a pass to the low post. The wing drops back to cover a pass to the baseline area and is responsible for a rebound in the box area. The point traps the high post.

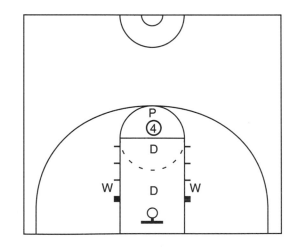

Figure 10.19 3-2 zone: Ball at high post.

wing defends the player with the ball. The point drops back to the strong-side elbow and places the hand closest to the basket in front of the high post. The strong-side deep player plays halfway between the low-post player and the corner player. The weak-side wing drops back to the level of the ball and directs the defense. The weak-side deep player slides to the middle and denies the pass to the low-post player with a hand in front of the player.

When the ball is in the corner (figure 10.18), the strong-side deep player defends the player with the ball. The weak-side deep player fronts and denies the pass to the low-post player. The point fronts and denies the pass to the high post and blocks out the high-post player on a shot. The strong-side wing plays the passing lane to the

When the ball is at the low post (figure 10.20), the weak-side deep player defends the low-post player with the ball. The strong-side deep player drops back and covers a pass to the baseline area. The strong-side wing drops to the level of the ball and covers the first pass out to the strong side. The

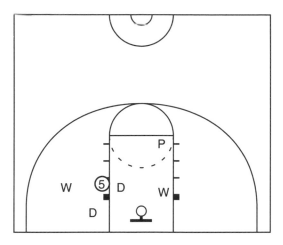

Figure 10.20 3-2 zone: Ball at low post.

weak-side wing drops back to the weak-side box and is responsible for any weak-side cutters. The point covers a pass to the opposite elbow area.

2-3 Zone Defense

The names of the defenders in a 2-3 zone, their starting alignments, and their responsibilities are as follows:

Ball at Top (figure 10.21)

G = Guard, one guard takes ball and the other drops to elbow, cover area from middle to wing

F = Forward, outside lane line above box, cover area from box to corner

C = Center, between basket and foul line, cover area inside lane

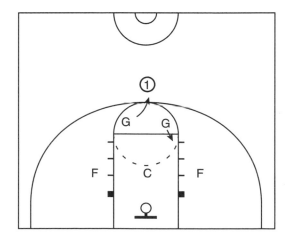

Figure 10.21 2-3 zone: Ball at top.

The responsibilities for the defenders change with each move of the ball. When the ball is on the wing (figure 10.22), the strong-side (ball-side) guard at the elbow pauses there before defending the wing player. The guard at the top drops back to the middle of the foul line. The strong-side forward uses a bump move (fakes at the wing until the strong-side guard gets to the wing), then drops back between the low-post player and the corner player. The center covers the strong-side low-post area. The weak-side forward slides to the middle of the lane and directs the defense.

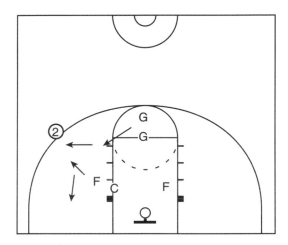

Figure 10.22 2-3 zone: Ball on wing, bump move.

When the ball is in the corner (figure 10.23), the strong-side forward defends the player with the ball. The center fronts and denies the pass to the low-post player. The weak-side forward covers the pass to the high post and blocks out the high-

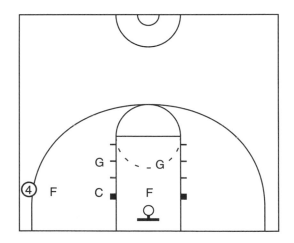

Figure 10.23 2-3 zone: Ball in corner.

post player on a shot. The strong-side guard drops back and helps on a pass to the low post. The weak-side guard moves inside the foul line and covers a diagonal pass out of the corner.

When the ball is at the high post (figure 10.24), the center defends the high-post player with the ball. The forwards cover the box area on their sides. The guards cover the elbow areas on their sides.

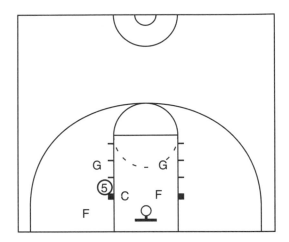

Figure 10.25   2-3 zone: Ball at low post.

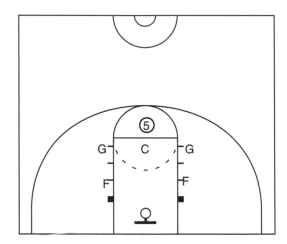

Figure 10.24   2-3 zone: Ball at high post.

When the ball is at the low post (figure 10.25), the center defends the low-post player with the ball. The strong-side forward drops back and covers a pass to the baseline area. The weak-side forward covers a pass to the middle of the lane

and is responsible for a weak-side rebound. The strong-side guard drops back to halfway between the low post and a pass out to the wing. The weak-side guard moves inside the foul line and covers a diagonal pass.

Match-Up Zone

Any of the zone defenses can be adjusted to a match-up zone. A match-up zone enables you to match up and defend an individual opponent in your zone area. If no one is in your area, drop back toward the basket and middle, looking for someone flashing into your area from behind. The match-up zone is particularly effective against an offense that does not use much movement.

COMBINATION DEFENSE

In a combination defense, one or two players are assigned to select individual opponents, for example, an outstanding shooter or ball handler, and the other players are deployed in zone areas. These are all special situation defenses, not primary defenses. Among the most common combination defenses are the box-and-one, diamond-and-one, and triangle-and-two.

In the box-and-one, one player is assigned to deny the ball to the opponent's best scorer,

shooter, or ball handler while the other four players set up in a 2-2 zone or box formation.

The diamond-and-one is similar to the box-and-one in that one player is assigned to deny the ball to the opponent's best scorer, shooter, or ball handler; however, the other four players are set up in a 1-2-1 zone or diamond alignment.

In the triangle-and-two, two players are assigned to individually defend two select opponents while three defenders are set up in a 1-2 zone or triangle inside the free throw line.

RATE YOUR SUCCESS

Working as a team on defense is vital if your team is to stop the opponent and regain control of the ball. Remember, only the team in possession of the ball can score. Thus, regaining possession from the offense is crucial to your own scoring success.

For this final step, look back at how you performed the drills. For each of the drills presented in this step, enter the points you earned, then add up your scores to rate your total success.

Defense off the Ball Drills

1. Wing Denial   ____ out of 5

2. Weak-Side Help and Recover ____ out of 5

Defending the Low Post Drill

1. Low-Post Denial   ____ out of 5

Defending the Flash Drill

1. Deny the Flash and Deny the Backdoor Cut ____ out of 5

2. Six Point Drill   ____ out of 5

Defensive Rotation Drills

1. Defensive Position Shell Drill ____ out of 5

2. Help and Recover Shell Drill ____ out of 5

3. Defend the Cutter Shell Drill ____ out of 5

4. Shell Drill   ____ out of 5

TOTAL   ____ *out of 45*

If you scored 35 or more points, congratulations! You have mastered the basics of this step. If you scored fewer than 35 points, you may want to spend more time on the fundamentals covered in this step. Practice the drills again to develop mastery of the techniques and increase your scores.

◨ About the Author

Hal Wissel is an assistant coach with the Memphis Grizzlies of the National Basketball Association. When he joined the Grizzlies in 2002, Wissel brought a wealth of NBA experience in coaching, scouting, and working in the front office. Wissel was an advance scout for the Dallas Mavericks (2000–2002) and served as an assistant coach/advance scout for the New Jersey Nets (1996–2000) and as director of player personnel for the Nets (1995–1996). Wissel also was a scout and special assignment coach with the Milwaukee Bucks (1990–1995) and an assistant coach and head scout with the Atlanta Hawks (1976–1977).

In addition to serving in the NBA, Wissel compiled more than 300 wins as a collegiate head coach at Springfield College, the University of North Carolina–Charlotte, Florida Southern, Fordham, Lafayette, and Trenton State. He led Florida Southern to four straight trips to the NCAA Division II Tournament and three straight trips to the Division II Final Four (1980, 1981, and 1982), winning the NCAA Division II Championship in 1981. In 1972, Wissel coached Fordham to the NIT Tournament. Wissel also coached the Dominican Republic National Team in 1975.

In 1972, Wissel founded Basketball World, Inc., a venture that conducts basketball camps and clinics and produces and distributes books and videos. Basketball World's highly successful Shoot It Better Mini Camps are conducted worldwide for players at all levels. Basketball World is now owned and operated by Wissel's son Paul.

Wissel received his bachelor's degree in physical education from Springfield College in 1960, his master's degree from Indiana University in 1961, and his doctorate in physical education from Springfield College in 1970. In addition to writing *Basketball: Steps to Success*, Wissel wrote *Becoming a Basketball Player: Individual Drills,* which has been made into five videos.

Wissel's honors include being named *Coach & Athlete* magazine's Eastern Coach of the Year in 1972; Sunshine State Conference Coach of the Year in 1979, 1980, 1981, and 1982; and Division II National Coach of the Year by the National Association of Basketball Coaches in 1980. Wissel has been inducted into the Florida Southern College Athletic Hall of Fame and the Sunshine State Conference Hall of Fame. In 1998, Wissel was named Sunshine State Conference Silver Anniversary Coach.

Wissel and his wife Trudy have five children—Steve, Scott, David, Paul, and Sharon—and a granddaughter Stephanie.